Frommer's®

P9-BYM-334

Bangkok
day BY day™

1st Edition

by Colin Hinshelwood

WILEY

Wiley Publishing Australia Pty Ltd

Contents

17 Favourite Moments   1

1 The Best Full-Day Tours   7
The Best in One Day   8
The Best in Two Days   18
The Best in Three Days   24

2 The Best Special-Interest Tours   29
Bangkok Food Safari   30
Buddhist Temples of Old Bangkok   34
Bangkok for Kids   40
Mind, Body & Soul   46

3 The Best Neighbourhood Tours   51
The Old City   52
Chao Phraya River   56
Chinatown   62

4 The Best Shopping   67
Shopping Best Bets   68
Bangkok Shopping A to Z   72

5 The Great Outdoors   81
Lumphini Park   82
Dusit Park   86

6 The Best Dining   89
Dining Best Bets   90
Bangkok Dining A to Z   94

7 The Best Nightlife 109
Nightlife Best Bets 110
Bangkok Nightlife A to Z 115

8 The Best Arts & Entertainment 123
Arts & Entertainment Best Bets 124
Arts & Entertainment A to Z 128

9 The Best Accommodation 133
Accommodation Best Bets 134
Bangkok Accommodation A to Z 138

10 The Best Day Trips & Excursions 147
Kanchanaburi 148
Khao Yai National Park 152
Pattaya 156
Ayutthaya 160

The Savvy Traveller 163
Before You Go 164
Getting There 166
Getting Around 167
Fast Facts 169
Local Customs, Traditions & Taboos 173
Useful Phrases & Menu Terms 174
Phone Numbers & Websites 177

Index 178

Published by:

John Wiley & Sons Australia, Ltd

42 McDougall Street, Milton Qld 4064
Office also in Melbourne

Copyright © 2009 John Wiley & Sons Australia, Ltd.

National Library of Australia Cataloguing-in-Publication Data:

Author:	Hinshelwood, Colin.
Title:	Bangkok day by day / Colin Hinshelwood.
ISBN:	978-1-7421-6854-8
Series:	Frommer's day by day city guide
Notes:	Includes index.
Subjects:	Bangkok (Thailand)—Guidebooks
Dewey Number:	915.93

Cartographer: Lohnes+Wright. Some map data provided by Lovell Johns.

Wiley also publishes its books in a variety of electronic formats. Some content that appears in print may not be available in electronic formats.

Printed in China by Printplus Limited

10 9 8 7 6 5 4 3 2 1

A Note from the Editorial Director

Organising your time. That's what this guide is all about.

Other guides give you long lists of things to see and do and then expect you to fit the pieces together. The Day by Day guides are different. These guides tell you the best of everything, and then they show you how to see it in the smartest, most time-efficient way. Our authors have designed detailed itineraries organised by time, neighbourhood or special interest. And each tour comes with a bulleted map that takes you from stop to stop.

Hoping to visit Bangkok's awe-inspiring temples and learn about Thai culture? Planning to jostle with the locals at the markets, or scream around Bangkok's backstreets in a tuktuk? Not only do we take you to the top attractions, hotels and restaurants, but we also help you access those special moments that locals get to experience—those 'finds' that turn tourists into travellers.

The Day by Days are also your top choice if you're looking for one complete guide for all your travel needs. The best hotels and restaurants for every budget, the greatest shopping value, the wildest nightlife—it's all here.

Why should you trust our judgment? Because our authors personally visit each place they write about. They're an independent lot who say what they think and would never include places they wouldn't recommend to their best friends. They're also open to suggestions from readers. If you'd like to contact them, please send your comments our way at feedback@frommers.com, and we'll pass them on.

Enjoy your Day by Day guide—the most helpful travel companion you can buy. And have the trip of a lifetime.

Warm regards,

Kelly Regan,
Editorial Director
Frommer's Travel Guides

About the Author

Colin Hinshelwood left his hometown of Glasgow, Scotland to travel the world when he was 18. He first arrived in Bangkok in 1987. After countless years in many foreign lands he returned to Thailand to settle in 2001. Working for CPA Media in northern Thailand, Colin, or 'Hinsh' as he is known, has written and contributed to several Asian tour guides. In between covering Burmese and Palestinian issues, he contributes regularly to magazines such as *Conde Nast Traveller* and *Travel & Leisure*.

Acknowledgements

First and foremost, my thanks go to Kannikar Kumtun, or 'Mui', who helped me to check and double-check the information in this book. She added a colourful Thai perspective to much of my commentary. Thanks also to my colleagues at CPA Media—Andrew Forbes, for passing on his encyclopaedic knowledge of Thai culture and history; and David Henley, for his thirst for adventure and for spending days with me down Bangkok backstreets mapping out the walking tours. Thanks must also go to the patient and professional staff at Wiley Australia, especially Brooke Lyons, for supporting me while I researched and wrote this guidebook.

An Additional Note

Please be advised that travel information is subject to change at any time— and this is especially true of prices. We therefore suggest that you write or call ahead for confirmation when making your travel plans. The author, editors and publisher cannot be held responsible for the experiences of readers while travelling. Your safety is important to us, however, so we encourage you to stay alert and be aware of your surroundings.

Star Ratings, Icons & Abbreviations

Every hotel, restaurant and attraction listing in this guide has been ranked for quality, value, service, amenities and special features using a **star-rating system**. Hotels, restaurants, attractions, shopping and nightlife are rated on a scale of zero stars (recommended) to three stars (exceptional). In addition to the star-rating system, we also use a **kids** icon to point out the best bets for families. Within each tour, we recommend cafes, bars or restaurants where you can take a break. Each of these stops appears in a shaded box marked with a coffee-cup-shaped bullet 🍵.

The following **abbreviations** are used for credit cards:

AE	American Express	DC	Diners Club
MC	MasterCard	V	Visa

Frommers.com

Now that you have this guidebook to help you plan a great trip, visit our website at **www.frommers.com** for additional travel information on more than 4000 destinations. We update features regularly to give you instant access to the most current trip-planning information available. At Frommers.com, you'll find scoops on the best airfares, accommodation rates and car rental bargains. You can even book your travel online through our reliable travel booking partners. Other popular features include:

- Online updates of our most popular guidebooks
- Vacation sweepstakes and contest giveaways
- Newsletters highlighting the hottest travel trends
- Podcasts, interactive maps and up-to-the-minute events listings
- Opinionated blog entries by Arthur Frommer himself
- Online travel message boards with featured travel discussions.

A Note on Prices

In the Take a Break and Best Bets sections of this book, we have used a system of dollar signs to show a range of costs for one night in a hotel (the price of a double-occupancy room) or the cost of a main meal at a restaurant. Use the following table to decipher the dollar signs:

Cost	Hotels	Restaurants
$	under 1500 baht	under 200 baht
$$	1500–3000 baht	200–500 baht
$$$	3000–6000 baht	500–1000 baht
$$$$	6000–10000 baht	1000–2000 baht
$$$$$	over 10000 baht	over 2000 baht

An Invitation to the Reader

In researching this book, we discovered many wonderful places—hotels, restaurants, shops and more. We're sure you'll find others. Please tell us about them, so we can share the information with your fellow travellers in upcoming editions. If you were disappointed with a recommendation, we'd love to know that, too. Please write to:

Frommer's Bangkok Day by Day, 1st Edition

John Wiley & Sons • 42 McDougall Street • Milton Qld Australia 4064

17 Favourite
Moments

17 Favourite Moments

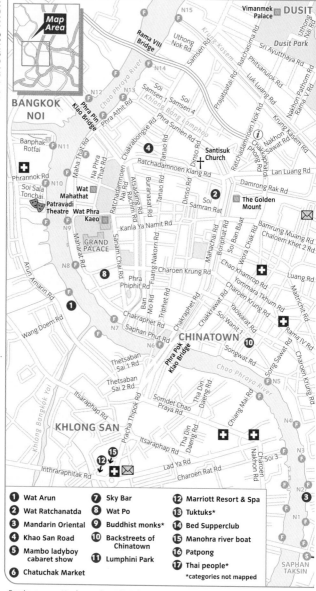

1 Wat Arun
2 Wat Ratchanatda
3 Mandarin Oriental
4 Khao San Road
5 Mambo ladyboy cabaret show
6 Chatuchak Market
7 Sky Bar
8 Wat Po
9 Buddhist monks*
10 Backstreets of Chinatown
11 Lumphini Park
12 Marriott Resort & Spa
13 Tuktuks*
14 Bed Supperclub
15 Manohra river boat
16 Patpong
17 Thai people*
*categories not mapped

Previous page: Monks go about their day at the Buddhist temple Wat Po.

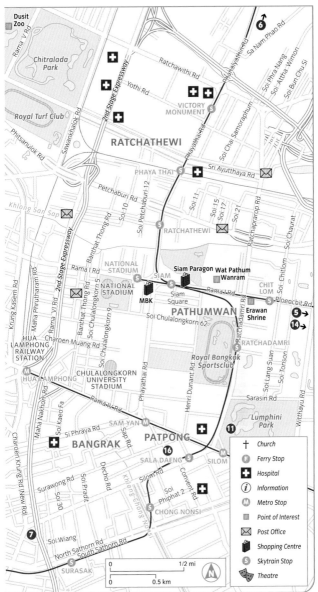

Dusit Zoo

Chitralada Park

Royal Turf Club

RATCHATHEWI

VICTORY MONUMENT

PHAYA THAI

RATCHATHEWI

NATIONAL STADIUM

NATIONAL STADIUM

MBK

Siam Square

Siam Paragon

Wat Pathum Wanram

PATHUMWAN

CHIT LOM

Erawan Shrine

RATCHADAMRI

HUA LAMPHONG RAILWAY STATION

HUA LAMPHONG

CHULALONGKORN UNIVERSITY STADIUM

Royal Bangkok Sportsclub

SAM YAN

Lumphini Park

BANGRAK

PATPONG

SALA DAENG

SILOM

CHONG NONSI

SURASAK

Rama V Rd · Rama I Rd · Yothi Rd · Ratchawithi Rd · Sa Nam Phao Rd · Soi Phra Nang · Soi Attha Wimon · Soi Bun Chu Si · Phitsanulok Rd · Sawankhalok Rd · 2nd Stage Expressway · Phayathai Rd · Sri Ayutthaya Rd · Soi Chai Samoraphum · Ratchaprarop Rd · Soi Chidlom · Soi Chaurat · Petchaburi Rd · Soi 10 · Soi Petchaburi 12 · Soi 11 · Soi 15 · Soi 17 · Soi 21 · Khlong San Sap · Banthat Thong Rd · Krung Kasem Rd · Maha Phrutharam Rd · Rama I Rd · Rama VI Rd · Banthat Thong Rd · Soi Chulalongkorn 5 · Soi Chulalongkorn 9 · Soi Chulalongkorn 62 · Charoen Muang Rd · Rama IV Rd · Henri Dunant Rd · Soi Lang Suan · Soi Tonlon · Witthayu Rd · Maha Nakhon Rd · Soi Kaeo Fa · Si Phraya Rd · Sap Rd · Sarasin Rd · Surawong Rd · Soi Pradit · Decho Rd · Silom Rd · Convent Rd · Soi Phiphat 2 · Khlong Chong Nonsi · Soi Wiang · North Sathorn Rd · South Sathorn Rd · Charoen Krung Rd (New Rd) · Soi 30

6
5→
14→
11
16
7

†	Church
F	Ferry Stop
+	Hospital
(i)	Information
M	Metro Stop
▪	Point of Interest
✉	Post Office
🛍	Shopping Centre
S	Skytrain Stop
🎭	Theatre

0 ___ 1/2 mi
0 ___ 0.5 km

Known in Thailand as the 'City of Angels', Bangkok has a rather devilish reputation. In recent years it has become one of the most popular destinations in the world. But what is it that this hot and crowded sprawling Asian city offers that great metropolises such as Paris, Rome, London and New York lack? Of course Bangkok has a deep culture, hundreds of sights to see, great restaurants and a pulsating nightlife, but there's something extra about Thailand's capital that makes people tingle. Even just the name 'Bangkok' conjures images of the exotic—a tropical paradise with an edgy reputation, perhaps a hint of danger and excitement. It's a city with a twist at every corner, a picture postcard of unexpected sights and superlative experiences. Everything you've heard about Bangkok is true . . . and there's more. For whatever Bangkok does, it does with passion. Here are some of my favourite Bangkok experiences.

❶ Gazing across the river at Wat Arun (the Temple of Dawn) as day is breaking. Watch the Buddhist monks in their bright saffron robes silently going about their morning chores. See the sun dancing on the millions of pieces of glass and ceramic on the stone walls of the temple, making it change colour and sparkle as if alive. *See p 15.*

❷ Feeling the mystic serenity of a Buddhist temple. My favourite is Wat Ratchanatda, where monks sweep leaves in the courtyard while others fetch water from a well or meditate in the temple. In a 24/7 city of more than 10 million people where the noise and heat are often exhausting, the sea of calm that washes over me as soon as I enter a temple never fails to impress. *See p 37.*

❸ Lounging around the Mandarin Oriental hotel on the lookout for celebrities. It is the most famous hotel in the world, after all! Perhaps if I wear a Panama hat and sip tea in the lobby someone will wonder if I'm a famous star or the reincarnation of Joseph Conrad, Oscar Wilde or W Somerset Maugham. Keep dreaming . . . *See p 57.*

❹ Listening to travellers' tales at a cafe on Khao San Road. Bangkok is a magnet for travellers visiting every corner of the world. Swap stories of journeys through the jungle, of bus rides from hell, of snakes and scorpions under mattresses, and the myriad other adventures that always happen when you are travelling in exotic lands. *See p 54.*

The gleaming spires of Wat Arun.

❺ Witnessing the incredulous looks on people's faces at Mambo ladyboy cabaret show. See the range of emotions as the audience struggles to believe that the beautiful girls in front of them are, in fact, beautiful boys. *See p 131.*

❻ Getting lost among the chaos at Chatuchak Market. It's easy to do for hours on end—without finding a postcard to send home to grandma. You'd better leave a trail of breadcrumbs as you wander the maze of shops and stalls at the biggest market in the world, because you'll never find your way out! Still, you're sure to find other treats—from parakeets to copper pots, from DVDs to Buddhist antiques, from silk scarves to moonshine snake whisky . . . but I've never seen any postcards. *See p 25.*

❼ Watching the sun set while sipping martinis at Sky Bar. The view from the 54th floor is spectacular, but no matter how many times I've met friends for cocktails at Sky Bar my heart still leaps into my throat when I look over the edge. I don't know any other city that would even allow a bar such as this to exist. *See p 117.*

❽ Getting a hot herbal massage at Wat Po, then falling asleep and awakening to find your body has turned to jelly. I'm not sure how I survived before I came to Bangkok and started the simple weekly ritual of getting all the tension and knots wrung from my body. Perhaps the most physically and mentally relaxing activity a person can do, massage is cheap, it's good for you and feels great. What more can you ask for? *See p 48.*

❾ Getting up at dawn to watch Buddhist monks collecting alms from local Bangkokians. Rich and poor

One of the many cheerful silk vendors at Chatuchak Market.

alike line the roadsides with freshly cooked pots of rice and curry to offer the monks in exchange for a prayer. The robed parade walking the streets single file and barefoot each morning is one of the most photogenic scenes in Asia.

❿ Taking in the aromas of food and spices down the backstreets of Chinatown. You'll find woks full of sizzling chillis, boiling pots of coconut soup, skewered fish barbecuing on grills and row upon row of cardamom and coriander, ginger and ginseng, colourful fruit and exotic herbs. *See p 62.*

⓫ Practicing Tai Chi with nimble octogenarians in Lumphini Park at dawn. I just join in at the back and follow the slow and controlled movements of the class as it flows to the rhythm of an old Chinese soundtrack. Various groups gather in the park every day for a one-hour session of this graceful martial art. Afterwards, they sit and chat and laugh and drink green tea. I'm sure this is the secret to living over 100. *See p 10.*

⓬ Lazing in the jacuzzi at the Marriott Resort & Spa on a sunny day. Sunbathing in Bangkok is usually a no-go: with the humidity, it's more like poaching yourself.

Spend a day luxuriating by the tropical pool and jacuzzi at the Marriott Resort & Spa.

The Marriott is just far enough from the city centre that the air is a bit fresher and a breeze comes off the river. With a day pass you can lie by the tropical pool and bask in the outdoor jacuzzi. *See p 143*.

🅱 **Screaming down the backstreets in a tuktuk, zigzagging through the traffic, mounting the kerbs and squeezing down alleys.** No trip to Bangkok is complete without a heart-stopping ride around the city's streets with a hysterical tuktuk driver (for more thrills, try a motorbike taxi!). *See p 168*.

🅱 **Dancing the night away at Bed Supperclub with Bangkok's 'beautiful people'.** Actually, I'm too old and frumpy to be in with the jet set, but even if I'm just lurking in the corner it's still great to hang out in this sexy, über-chic nightclub. *See p 121*.

🅱 **Wining and dining on a Manohra dinner cruise under the moonlight.** When romance beckons, an evening dinner on

a small cruise boat is the perfect option. It's intimate and exotic and the food is delicious. The Chao Phraya River is glorious at night, and what better way to see it than over a romantic dinner for two? *See p 102*.

🅱 **Haggling for souvenirs at Patpong.** Notorious Patpong comes alive at night in more ways than one. Stalls hug the pavements and spill over down the alleys. Vendors will lure you into a haggling match over little elephant statues, Buddha paintings and Samurai swords. *See p 17*.

🅱 **Smiling back at Thais— the friendliest people in the world.** Thailand is not known as the 'Land of Smiles' for nothing. A big beaming smile is as much part of a traditional greeting as a *wai*—the pressing of palms and little bow that Buddhists use to say 'hello'. Even if a Thai slips and falls and bangs his head, he will smile, maybe even laugh, and brush it off with the phrase '*mai pen rai*', meaning 'it doesn't matter'. ●

1

The Best
Full-Day Tours

The Best **in One Day**

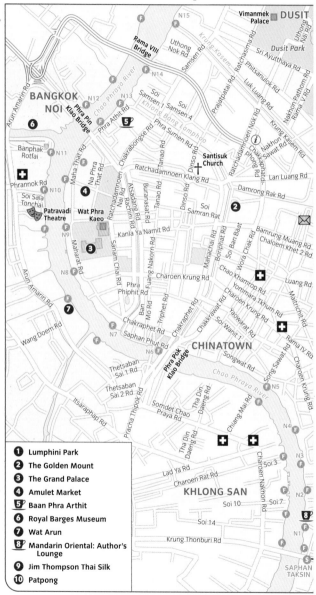

1. Lumphini Park
2. The Golden Mount
3. The Grand Palace
4. Amulet Market
5. Baan Phra Arthit
6. Royal Barges Museum
7. Wat Arun
8. Mandarin Oriental: Author's Lounge
9. Jim Thompson Thai Silk
10. Patpong

Previous page: A temple guardian stands sentry outside Wat Phra Kaeo.

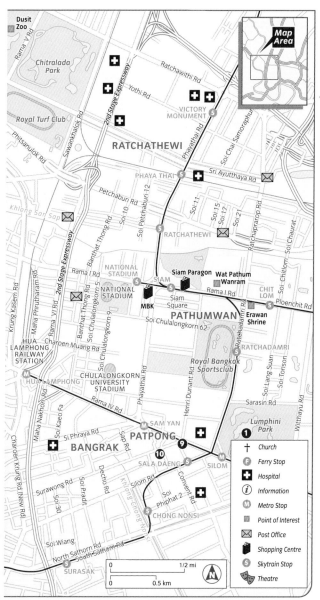

Map Area

Dusit Zoo

Rama V Rd

Chitralada Park

Royal Turf Club

Phitsanulok Rd

2nd Stage Expressway

Sawankhalok Rd

Ratchawithi Rd

Yothi Rd

VICTORY MONUMENT

RATCHATHEWI

Phaya Thai Rd

Soi Chai Samoraphum

PHAYA THAI

Sri Ayutthaya Rd

Petchaburi Rd

Soi Petchaburi 12

Soi 10

Soi 11

Soi 15

Soi 17

Soi 21

Ratchaprarop Rd

Soi Chaurat

Khlong San Sap

Banthat Thong Rd

RATCHATHEWI

Krung Kasem Rd

Maha Phrutharam Rd

Rama VI Rd

2nd Stage Expressway

NATIONAL STADIUM

Rama I Rd

SIAM

Siam Paragon

Wat Pathum Wanram

Rama I Rd

CHIT LOM

Ploenchit Rd

NATIONAL STADIUM

Banthat Thong Rd

Soi Chulalongkorn 5

MBK

Siam Square

PATHUMWAN

Erawan Shrine

Ratchadamri Rd

Charoen Muang Rd

Soi Chulalongkorn 9

Soi Chulalongkorn 62

RATCHADAMRI

HUA LAMPHONG RAILWAY STATION

HUALAMPHONG

CHULALONGKORN UNIVERSITY STADIUM

Phayathai Rd

Henri Dunant Rd

Royal Bangkok Sportsclub

Soi Lang Suan

Soi Tonson

Witthayu Rd

Rama IV Rd

Maha Nakhon Rd

Soi Kaeo Fa

SAM YAN

Sarasin Rd

Lumphini Park

❶

Charoen Krung Rd (New Rd)

Si Phraya Rd

Sap Rd

PATPONG

❾

BANGRAK

Surawong Rd

Soi Pradit

Decho Rd

SALA DAENG

❿

Silom Rd

SILOM

Convent Rd

Soi 30

Soi Wiang

Soi Phiphat 2

Khlong Chong Nonsi

CHONG NONSI

North Sathorn Rd

South Sathorn Rd

SURASAK

| | 0 | 1/2 mi |
| | 0 | 0.5 km |

N

Symbol	Legend
†	Church
Ⓕ	Ferry Stop
✚	Hospital
ⓘ	Information
Ⓜ	Metro Stop
▪	Point of Interest
✉	Post Office
👜	Shopping Centre
Ⓢ	Skytrain Stop
🎭	Theatre

*S*awatdee khrap! **Welcome to Bangkok! With just one day** to explore this mesmerising city, get up early and prepare for an exhilarating day full of eye-opening experiences. We're about to immerse ourselves in a one-day crash course in Thai and Buddhist culture. The one sight you can't miss is, of course, the Grand Palace, and I recommend you allow a whole morning to take it in. You won't regret it! Dress light but be sure to wear long sleeves and no shorts or short skirts or you will not be allowed inside the Grand Palace or Buddhist temples. Wear comfortable shoes for walking, too.

START: Silom or Sala Daeng metro stations.

A Kinnaree (half-woman, half-bird) statue in the grounds of the Grand Palace.

❶ ★★ Tai Chi at Lumphini Park. For those who can manage it, there's no better way to watch Bangkok wake up than by catching the locals at their early-morning exercises. From first light at dawn in Lumphini Park (see p 83, bullet **❷**), you can join in or watch people doing aerobics or karate, jogging, cycling and many other forms of sport. But the highlight for me is Tai Chi—especially popular around 6am. A crowd gathers and sways to the rhythm of an ancient chant for one hour. The gentle movement will invigorate your body and set you up for an energetic day.
🕐 *1 hr. Rama IV Rd (cnr Ratchadamri & Silom rds). Admission free. Daily 4am–8pm. Metro: Silom or Sala Daeng.*

Begin your day with meditation in lush Lumphini Park—in the middle of bustling Bangkok.

❷ ★★ The Golden Mount.

The hill was built from waste dredged from the canal in the 19th century, and the spire of the Golden Mount was for a long time the highest point in Bangkok at 78m. But don't worry, the walk isn't too strenuous. A stairway winds its way around the mount, passing small Buddhist shrines and gravestones along the way. There's even a small waterfall, and if it's a cool morning you may catch the scent of the frangipani that lines the path. You might even find a mystic fortune teller waiting for you at the top! A relic of the Buddha is said to be enshrined inside the *chedi*. While you catch your breath, you can take in the view of the Old City to the west. Behind you lies the temple of Wat Saket (see p 35, bullet ❶), which used to be the city crematorium. Best on a weekday as early as possible. ⏱ *1 hr. 344 Chakkraphatdiphong Rd (off Boriphat Rd).* ☎ *02 621 0576. Admission 10 baht. Daily 7.30am–5.30pm. No metro.*

❸ ★★★ The Grand Palace.

Built by King Rama I as the royal residence in the new capital in 1782, the Grand Palace and, in particular, its dazzling Buddhist temple, Wat Phra Kaeo, is Thailand's most revered and celebrated site. Nowhere else can you see Thai art, architecture and history brought together in such outstanding harmony. The royal family no longer lives here and the complex is essentially a tourist attraction nowadays, except on coronations and events of regal significance. It's best to think of Wat Phra Kaeo as a Buddhist complex within the royal complex (the Grand Palace). Thailand's holiest Buddhist site is a maze of glittering shrines and stupas, guarded by mythical creatures such as *nagas* (serpents),

Visit the Golden Mount for grand views over the Old City.

singhas (lions) and *garudas* (half-man, half-bird). Unlike other Buddhist temples, no monks live here. Go as early as you can to avoid tour groups (and the heat!). ⏱ *3 hr. Na Phra Lan Rd, Rattanakosin.* ☎ *02 623 5500. www.palaces.thai.net. Admission 250 baht. Daily 8.30am–3.30pm. No metro.*

The Grand Palace

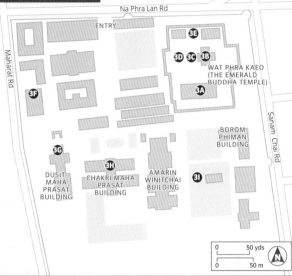

Na Phra Lan Rd

ENTRY

Maharat Rd

3E

3D **3C** **3B**

WAT PHRA KAEO
(THE EMERALD
BUDDHA TEMPLE)

3A

Sanam Chai Rd

BOROM
PHIMAN
BUILDING

3G

3H

DUSIT
MAHA
PRASAT
BUILDING

CHAKRI MAHA
PRASAT
BUILDING

AMARIN
WINITCHAI
BUILDING

3I

3F

0   50 yds
0   50 m

N

3A Emerald Buddha. The centrepiece of the temple is the Emerald Buddha, a 66cm-high statue, which is actually made of jade and believed to have come from Sri Lanka. It sits above a dazzling gold altar inside the *bot* (main temple). Remember to be quiet and respectful inside the *bot* and do not point your feet towards the Buddha. **3B Royal Pantheon.** Standing in the middle of the temple complex, the pantheon houses life-sized statues of the past kings of the current Chakri dynasty. **3C Phra Mondop.** Easily recognisable by its high spire, green mosaic and gold Buddha on the exterior is this *chedi* that acts as a repository for sacred Buddhist scriptures. **3D Phra Si Rattana Chedi.** This gold-tiled stupa was built by King Mongkut (played by

Yul Brynner in the movie *The King and I*). **3E kids Ramakien Gallery.** If you are familiar with the ancient Hindu epic *Ramayana*, then follow the intricate mural clockwise around the cloisters of the compound. The Thai version, *Ramakien*, is told in lively detail.

Hanuman, part of the Ramakien *murals.*

3F Wat Phra Kaeo Museum. There's a small cafe for much-needed respite next to the air-conditioned museum. The museum doesn't really feature much (robes of the Emerald Buddha and some white elephant bones), but it's usually a good resting spot. You can get soft drinks, coffee and snacks at the adjoining cafe. *Admission 50 baht.* **3G Dusit Throne Hall.** Built in 1784, this is a replica of a temple in the former capital, Ayutthaya. The tiers and awnings of this magnificent building are stepped up in layers and a golden spire reaches into the heavens as a triumphant testimony to Buddhist symmetry. Beautiful bonsai trees around the lawn in the foreground make this the most photogenic stop of your morning. Inside you'll find the original teak throne of King Rama I. **3H Chakri Maha Prasat.** Also known as the Chakri Throne Hall and designed by a British architect in a fusion of Thai and European neoclassical styles, this glitzy and lavish building acts as a reception hall for distinguished foreign guests and houses the ashes of former Chakri dynasty rulers. **3I Siwalai Gardens.** The king used these splendid manicured gardens in days of yore for entertaining his guests and ambassadors, as well as a recreation area for royal women and children. If you are tired from walking you'll appreciate the tranquility of this shaded area. King Rama IV's personal chapel is here, laid out in cool marble with blue-and-white glass mosaics.

A golden chedi (mound containing Buddhist relics) at Wat Phra Kaeo.

Watch the Dress Code!

You must wear long-sleeved shirts and trousers, and skirts and dresses must come below the knee—anyone entering the Grand Palace who is deemed inappropriately dressed will be asked to hire cotton shirts and trousers. It's also wise to carry a parasol and wear a hat and sunglasses to protect you from the bright, hot sun. Keep your ticket to get free entry to **Vimanmek Palace** (see p 22, bullet **7**). Once inside, you can hire an audio guide—or a real one—to explain the historical, religious and royal significance of each site. I recommend either option.

A Buddhist Nature

Visitors to the 'Land of Smiles' never fail to remark on the peaceful nature of the Thai people. After just a weekend in Bangkok, they come away with Thai expressions such as '*sabai-sabai*' (everything's good), '*jai yen-yen*' (keep cool) and '*mai pen rai*' (don't worry).

Some 94 per cent of Thai people are Buddhists and they will tell you that these expressions reflect a deeper spiritual concept—the practice of tolerance, humility and patience that is at the heart of Buddhism.

Followers of Buddha do not consider him a god. Instead, they believe in his ancient wisdom and seek to emulate his teachings. In many ways, Buddhism is more a philosophy than a religion. It teaches that we should follow a 'middle path'; that we should concentrate on the here and now; that we should forsake our cravings and instant pleasures; that by simply meditating we can achieve great knowledge; and that life and time are cyclic, and that all creatures are reincarnated according to their past actions, or karma.

The Buddha himself was Siddhartha Gautama, an Indian prince born in the 6th century BC. He gave up his luxuries for an ascetic life—much as Buddhist monks do nowadays. It is said he attained 'enlightenment' while meditating under a Bodhi tree and reached the state of nirvana.

Try to spot this detail on one of the historic exhibits at the Royal Barges Museum.

❹ ★★★ Amulet Market.

Running along the northern wall of Wat Mahathat, the shaded boulevard of Phra Chan Road is Bangkok's best-known area to buy Buddhist amulets and lucky charms. Vendors line the street with miniature Buddhas, astrological icons, pendants, ivory, gems and other assorted paraphernalia for the religious, the superstitious and the curious. Buyers study antique amulets through magnifying glasses while housewives haggle over marble pieces for their mantelpieces. There are even amulet magazines for devotees to scan. You too might like to buy a few souvenirs or an amulet to bring you health, wealth, protection from danger or even a new baby in the family! ⏲ *30 min. Phra Chan Rd. Daily 6am–8pm. No metro.*

Wat Arun silhouetted against the Bangkok sunset.

5 Baan Phra Arthit. Your feet will undoubtedly be feeling the pinch by now. Time to find a little air-conditioned diner with coffee, soft drinks, sandwiches, cakes and light meals. Located close to the river pier, this is a good choice before setting off on the next leg of your day trip. *102/1 Phra Arthit Rd, Banglamphu.* ☎ *02 280 7878. Daily 7am–8pm. $.*

6 Royal Barges Museum. If it's before 4pm, you still have time to visit Thailand's famous historical royal barges, which have been housed at this museum under the care of the Royal Thai Navy since 1932 when Thailand changed from an absolute monarchy to a constitutional one. The 50m-long boats have participated in royal ceremonies since the 18th century. They were damaged by bombing during WWII, but caught the eye of current monarch HM Bhumibol who lovingly restored them to their former glory. Like everything connected with the monarchy in Thailand, much pomp, pageantry and solemn respect is displayed. You can see the king's own barge, *Suppanahongse*, which is carved out of a single teak tree. Its bow is adorned with a golden swan. The best opportunity to see these majestic boats on the river (complete with trumpets and 30 oarsmen) is during the Royal Kathin Festival, which takes place every few years at auspicious times. 🕐 *30 min. West bank of Chao Phraya River (south of Phra Pinklao Bridge), Bang Phlat.* ☎ *02 424 0004. www.thailandmuseum.com. Admission adults 100 baht, kids 50 baht. Daily 9am–5pm. Ferry: express boat from Phra Arthit pier (N13) to Phra Pin Klao Bridge pier (N12), plus a 10-min walk.*

7 ★★★ Wat Arun. If it's just before sunset, catch the splendour of Wat Arun, the 'Temple of Dawn'. This Khmer-style stupa looks somewhat grey from a distance. However, once you get up close you'll see the walls of the temple are actually a mosaic of glass cuttings, Chinese porcelain and ceramic tiles. In the morning or sunset light, the pieces glisten and the temple sparkles, often appearing to be shades of orange or purple. The architectural design of Wat Arun is inspired by Hindu mythology. In the temple's niches you'll see the Hindu god Indra sitting astride Erawan, the three-headed elephant. And if you look closely you'll see there are tridents of Shiva on top of each spire. The temple itself has high vertical stairs, which can be daunting to climb. If you do manage to scale them, you will be rewarded with wonderful views of the Bangkok skyline across the river. 🕐 *45 min. Arun Amarin Rd, Thonburi.* ☎ *02 891 1149. www.watarun.org. Admission 50 baht. Daily 7am–6pm. Ferry: take a cross-river ferry from Tha Tien pier (N8) to Wat Arun pier.*

Start your own famous novel while you take high tea in the Author's Lounge at the renowned Mandarin Oriental.

8 ★★★ **The Mandarin Oriental: Author's Lounge.** For years the Oriental was acknowledged as 'The World's Greatest Hotel' and many, including myself, would argue that it has lost little of its timeless charm. Even if you are not staying at the Mandarin Oriental (see p 142) you will still want to take a look at it. Walk through the cool and tropical—but not ostentatious—lobby, past the boutiques and you'll come into a lounge with ceiling fans, French windows and a Kiplingesque air of British-Raj India. This is the Author's Lounge, where many of the greats, including Joseph Conrad, W Somerset Maugham and Noel Coward, penned their works. Soak up the atmosphere with coffee and cake or high tea and scones served on pristine china. ⏱ *45 min. 48 Oriental Ave, Bangrak.* ☎ *02 659 9000. www.mandarinoriental.com. Ferry: Oriental pier (N1). $$.*

9 ★★ **Jim Thompson Thai Silk.** You've taken in temples and Thai history all day; now it's time for some shopping. And what better way to remember Bangkok than with some fine silk products? For the best in quality silk shopping, visit the main retail outlet where you can buy clothes, curtains, pillowcases, scarves or just the fabrics themselves. The silks are irresistible and your friends will love you for buying them such a present. ⏱ *30 min. 9 Surawong Rd, Bangrak.* ☎ *02 632 81004. www. jimthompson.com. Daily 9am–9pm. Metro: Sala Daeng or Silom.*

Exquisite ceramic and silk goods at Jim Thompson Thai Silk.

There's plenty to see on the famous (and infamous) Patpong Road.

🔟 ★ **Patpong.** There's no getting away from the fact that Bangkok is synonymous with the sex industry. Sex tourism is undoubtedly a thriving business in this city and certain areas (Nana Plaza, Soi Cowboy and Patpong for starters) are lined with door-to-door go-go bars, sex shows, prostitution, massage services and the like. Despite the seedy nature of this underworld, many tourists can't resist having a peek at what goes on there. Patpong Road is probably the most tourist- and female-friendly area. The street has a night-time market selling souvenirs and kitsch, so female visitors should not feel particularly unsafe or unwanted. In fact, many couples and groups of gals like to visit the go-go bars.

King's Castle and King's Corner are two of the most reputable joints on Patpong Road, where female visitors and foreign couples are commonplace. You can sit quietly at the back and nurse a beer while entranced men ogle go-go dancers from around the stage. ***Warning***: In the street, touts will approach you and invite you to see their seedy shows, which involve nudity and sex acts. Even if they say it's free, you will have to pay a cover charge for these shows (perhaps 250 baht per head). However, there's a galaxy of open-air bars and cafes where you can soak up the atmosphere and watch the red-light district in action without getting involved. ⏱ *1 hr. Patpong Rd, Bangrak. Daily 7pm–2am. Metro: Sala Daeng.*

Royal Kathin Festival

The Kathin ceremony is a royal barge procession for the presentation of new robes to Buddhist monks. Thailand's traditional handmade wooden barges are world famous because of the artistic craftsmanship they embody. The royal barge procession on the Chao Phya River is exceptionally glittering and majestic. On the occasion, the royal barges will, in a stately procession, transport His Majesty the King from Vasukri Royal Pier along the Chao Phya River to Wat Arun where His Majesty will present saffron robes to the monastic community.

The Best **in Two Days**

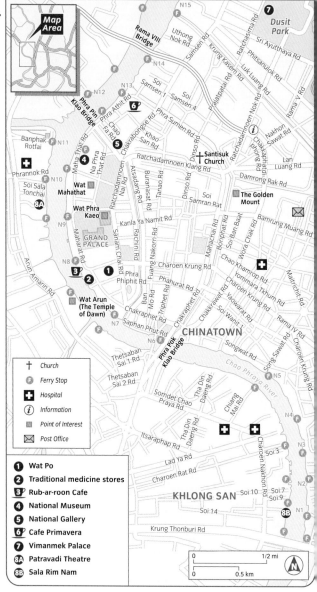

Map Area

N15

Rama VIII Bridge

Uthong Nok Rd

Krung Kasem Rd

Sri Ayutthaya Rd

Ratchasima Rd

Phitsanulok Rd

Luk Luang Rd

Rama V Rd

❼ Dusit Park

N14

Soi Samsen 1

Soi Samsen 4

Samsen Rd

Prachatipatai Rd

Ratchadamnoen Nok Rd

Nakhon Sawat Rd

ⓘ

N12

Phra Pin Klao Bridge

Phra Athit Rd

Phra Sumen Rd

Chao Fa Rd

N13

❻′

Khao San Rd

Chakrabongse Rd

Chakraphatdiphong Rd

Ratchadamnoen Klang Rd

✝ Santisuk Church

Lan Luang Rd

Banphak Rotfai

N11

Maha That Rd

❺

❹

Na Phra That Rd

Atsadang Rd

Buranasat Rd

Tanao Rd

Dinso Rd

Soi Samran Rat

Damrong Rak Rd

■ The Golden Mount

Phrannok Rd

➕

N10

Wat Mahathat ■

Ratchadamnoen Nai Rd

Bamrung Muang Rd

✉

Soi Sala Tonchai

❽ᴬ

Wat Phra Kaeo ■

Kanla Ya Namit Rd

Mahachai Rd

Boriphat Rd

Wora Chak Rd

N9

GRAND PALACE

Sanam Chai Rd

Rachini Rd

Fuang Nakorn Rd

Charoen Krung Rd

Chao Khamrop Rd

Yommara Tkhum Rd

Maitrichit Rd

N8

❸′

❷

❶

Mahdharat Rd

Phra Phiphit Rd

Phahurat Rd

Ban Mo Rd

Triphet Rd

Charoen Krung Rd

Yaowarat Rd

Soi Wanit 1

➕

Rama IV Rd

Arun Amarin Rd

Wat Arun (The Temple of Dawn)

N7

Saphan Phut Rd

Chakraphet Rd

Chakkrawat Rd

CHINATOWN

Song Sawat Rd

Charoen Krung Rd

N6

Phra Pok Klao Bridge

Songwat Rd

N5

Thetsaban Sai 1 Rd

Thetsaban Sai 2 Rd

Chao Phraya River

Somdet Chao Praya Rd

Tha Din Daeng Rd

Chiang Mai Rd

N4

Itsaraphap Rd

Tha Din Daeng Rd

Chiang Mai Rd

➕ ➕

Charoen Nakhon Rd

N3

Lad Ya Rd

Soi 3

N2

Charoen Rat Rd

KHLONG SAN

Soi 10

Soi 7

Soi 9

Soi 14

❽ᴮ

N1

Krung Thonburi Rd

Legend:

✝	Church
ⓕ	Ferry Stop
➕	Hospital
ⓘ	Information
■	Point of Interest
✉	Post Office

❶ Wat Po
❷ Traditional medicine stores
❸′ Rub-ar-roon Cafe
❹ National Museum
❺ National Gallery
❻′ Cafe Primavera
❼ Vimanmek Palace
❽ᴬ Patravadi Theatre
❽ᴮ Sala Rim Nam

0 — 1/2 mi
0 — 0.5 km

Ⓝ

On day two, we are going to delve a little deeper into Thai culture. Start the day by booking the evening's entertainment in advance (depending on availability you might want to swap nights two and three around—go to Thai boxing tonight instead and see the culture show tomorrow night). Whatever you choose, you're in for another great day out! If you would like to begin the day with a herbal Thai massage at Wat Po, have a very light breakfast. And remember about the dress code for Buddhist temples.

START: **Express boat to Tha Tien pier (N8).**

① ★★★ **Wat Po.** Bangkok's largest and oldest surviving temple is Wat Po. In many ways, this temple is more impressive than those of the Grand Palace—less colourful and dazzling, certainly, but more tranquil, more spiritual and

A Bodhi tree, said to have grown from Buddha's own, jostles for space with the golden chedi at Wat Po.

more captivating. It is here in Wat Po that you might discover your hidden Buddha. Dating as far back as the 16th century, the temple complex was favoured by several Siamese kings who maintained their residence next door at the Grand Palace. Known to Thais as Wat Phra Chetuphon, the site includes nearly 100 towering *chedi* and some 394 bronze Buddha images, mostly retrieved from the ancient ruins of Siam's previous capital, Ayutthaya, and the spiritual city of Sukhothai. Among the treasures in Wat Po is the famous Reclining Buddha, a 46m-long, gold-covered statue of the Buddha in repose, apparently passing into nirvana. The soles of the Buddha's feet are inlaid with intricate mother-of-pearl designs, while the walls of the room are lined with 108 collection bowls—believed to be the most auspicious number. Just outside the hall housing the Reclining Buddha is a Bodhi tree that is said to have grown from a cutting of the one in India under which the Buddha meditated. In the main pavilion you'll find the centrepiece is a bronze meditating Buddha. It is another item that was salvaged from the ruins of Ayutthaya. You can follow a mural carved into the outer base and inner doors of the pavilion that depicts scenes from the epic tale, *The Ramakien.* ⏱ *1½ hr. Sanam Chai Rd, Rattanakosin.* ☎ *02 225 5910. Ferry: Tha Tien pier (N8).*

Thai Massage

In between the main pavilion of Wat Po and the hall where the Buddha reclines is a traditional medicine centre (☎ 02 622 35501; daily 8.30am–6pm). This is one of the most popular attractions in Thailand as it is regarded as the home of Thai massage. The room contains plaques showing the body's acupressure points. The practitioners of this ancient art are said to be among the world's best, so if you have the time and can stand a little stretching and the sensation of hot stones bathed in herbs being ground into your muscles, then a Wat Po herbal massage is not to be missed.

❷ **Traditional medicine stores.** Fresh from your massage and spiritual journey around Wat Po, you should be feeling healthy, soulful and relaxed. Take a stroll along Maharat Road and take in the aromas of lemongrass, Kaffir lime, green tea, pickled snake and many other wild concoctions from the Chinese traditional medicine stores. Many of the pharmacists, or alchemists, can speak English and—whatever your ailment—will be ready to offer a herbal remedy. Of course, you may want to buy some ginseng roots, balms, essential oils or the like, but remember the import restrictions you may face when returning home. You might

want to check your government's website on customs regulations regarding bringing home raw foods, plants, drugs and medicines. *Maharat Rd. No credit cards. Ferry: Tha Tien pier (N8).*

❸ **Rub-ar-roon Cafe.** This teak house used to be a herbal dispensary. Now a pleasant cafe, it's a great spot to escape the heat either inside under the ceiling fans or on the footpath under a parasol, taking in the street atmosphere. It offers vegetarian and vegan dishes, as well as coffee, tea and fruit shakes. *310–312 Maharat Rd. ☎ 02 622 2312. Daily 8am–6pm. Ferry: Tha Tien pier (N8). $.*

Plaques in Wat Po showing the body's acupressure points.

Maharat Road offers some of Bangkok's best traditional medicine stores; visit this area to stock up on authentic herbal balms and oils.

4 ★★ **National Museum.**
Now that you have a taste for Thai culture, you shouldn't miss the Bangkok National Museum, which is host to perhaps the greatest collection of historical and archaeological artefacts, cultural art and Buddhist exhibits in South-East Asia. Two of the museum buildings—the Wang Na Palace and the Buddhaisawan Chapel—are architectural wonders in themselves, dating from the 18th century. Take, for instance, the black-and-gold motif lacquered doors to the palace or the murals in the chapel—stunning examples of Thai art. While historians will spend days in the museum, others can be inspired by just a quick inspection of some of the biggest attractions. Unfortunately, some parts of the museum have scant information about the exhibits in English, so you might be better off buying a guidebook. Most of the exhibits run in chronological order, from prehistoric earthenware and bronze items to early carvings, weapons and relics, to modern Buddhist art. Inside the chapel you'll find the *Phra Buddha Sihing*, a Buddha image shrouded in mystery. Some claim it comes from Sri Lanka, others that it was rescued from 13th-century Sukhothai, a religious centre in central Thailand. The image is paraded through the streets of the capital every April during the Songkran Festival. Another exhibit worth looking out for is that of the royal funeral chariots, which are made of gilded teak. ⏱ *1 hr. 1 Na Phra That Rd, Rattanakosin.* ☎ *02 224 1333. Admission 50 baht. Wed–Sun 9am–4pm. Ferry: Tha Phra Chan pier.*

The impressive exterior of the National Museum.

5 ★ **National Gallery.** Situated in a splendid colonial house that was once home to Thailand's Royal Mint, the National Gallery sits in notable contrast to the National Museum in that it is modern and displays contemporary art, featuring exhibitions from mainly local but also international artists. What is particularly pleasant about the gallery is the natural light, the cool breeze from the air-conditioning and the high ceilings, making this an ideal spot to rest and cool down.

A bed fit for a king in Vimanmek Palace.

🕐 *1 hr. 4 Chao Fa Rd, Banglamphu.* ☎ *02 282 2639. Wed–Sun 9am–4pm. Ferry: Phra Arthit pier (N13).*

6 ★ **Cafe Primavera.** You can't walk more than 10 paces without bumping into a noodle stall in this area. On nearby Khao San Road there are also the fast food joints we all recognise. But for a hearty lunch or just a coffee and a snack, Cafe Primavera gets my vote. It's a stone's throw from Phra Sumen Fort (see p 60, bullet **11**), and has great oven-baked pizzas, homemade ice-cream and lovely smiling staff. *56 Phra Sumen Rd, Banglamphu.* ☎ *02 281 4718. Daily 9am–11pm. Ferry: Phra Arthit pier (N13). $$.*

7 ★★★ **Vimanmek Palace.** Still got your ticket from the Grand Palace? Good! You get free entry. The centrepiece of the immaculate Dusit Park is this magnificent golden teak mansion, which was reassembled here in 1901 by royal order after being shipped over from the island of Ko Sichang. Amazingly, the entire three-storey structure was built using wooden pegs and no nails. It was the favourite retreat of King Chulalongkorn (1853–1910). The palace was the first building in Thailand to have electricity and an indoor toilet. Follow the teak corridors around 81 royal rooms, taking in the exhibits and furnishings and the distinctly 'Victorian' sense of interior design. Compulsory guided tours leave every 30 minutes; try to time your visit to catch free performances of Thai dance and martial arts in the lakeside pavilion at 10.30am and 2pm daily. Remember, this is a royal palace and dress codes apply. 🕐 *1 hr. Dusit Park.* ☎ *02 628 6300 9. Admission 100 baht. Daily 9.30am–3.15pm. No metro or ferry.*

This colonial-era building houses Bangkok's National Gallery.

are superb, so take your choice! **8A** **Patravadi Theatre** (see p 130) is an extravaganza of classical Thai and Asian epics, and **8B** **Sala Rim Nam** has awe-inspiring traditional Thai music and dance. *Patravadi Theatre: 69/1 Soi Wat Rakhang, Thonburi; ☎ 02 412 72878; www.patravaditheatre.com; ticket prices vary; Fri–Sat 7pm; no metro. Sala Rim Nam: private boat for guests leaves from Mandarin Oriental, 48 Oriental Ave, Bangrak; ☎ 02 659 9000; www.mandarinoriental.com; tickets from 2250 baht (w/ dinner); nightly 7.30pm; metro: Saphan Taksin.*

8 ★★★ **Thai culture show/dinner theatre.** I'll assume you've had a fulfilling day and have rested up at your hotel, booked your tickets and scrubbed up in your finery for tonight. No trip to Thailand is complete without an evening of fine dining with delicious Thai food and stage performances of traditional Thai dance, song, mime and drama. Both my suggested dinner theatre locations are on the west bank of the river, and both

A khon mask used in traditional Thai drama at the Patravadi Theatre.

King Chulalongkorn (1853–1910)

Thais still revere King Chulalongkorn, or Rama V. Photographs of him—easily recognisable by his flamboyant moustache—are on walls all over Bangkok. As a child he was tutored by Anna Leonowens, made famous in the movie *The King and I*. An admirer of British administration, King Chulalongkorn modernised the country, while avoiding the colonial desires of Britain and France. He is fondly remembered for introducing governmental and social reforms, and for abolishing slavery in Siam. King Chulalongkorn designed Dusit Park, which is the site of Vimanmek Palace (see p 87).

The Best in Three Days

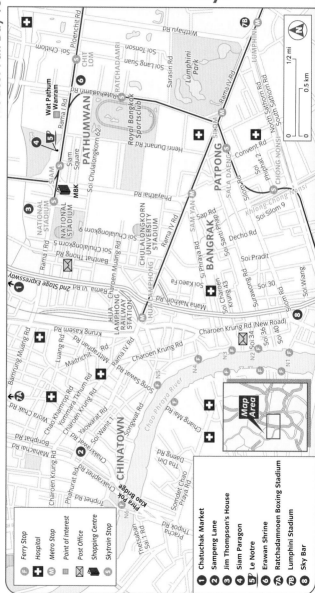

- **1** Chatuchak Market
- **2** Sampeng Lane
- **3** Jim Thompson's House
- **4** Siam Paragon
- **5** Le Notre
- **6** Erawan Shrine
- **7A** Ratchadamnoen Boxing Stadium
- **7B** Lumphini Stadium
- **8** Sky Bar

- **F** Ferry Stop
- **+** Hospital
- **M** Metro Stop
- **■** Point of Interest
- **⊠** Post Office
- **📖** Shopping Centre
- **S** Skytrain Stop

0   1/2 mi
0   0.5 km

Today we're going to avoid temples, do some shopping and rub shoulders with both ordinary Thai folks and high-society types. We're going to visit the former home of Bangkok's most famous foreigner and end the day with sunset cocktails at one of the most breathtaking locations you've ever seen. *Chok dee!* (Good luck!)

START: **If it's Saturday or Sunday we're going to Chatuchak Market, so take the metro to Mo Chit or Kampaeng Phet. If it is a weekday, get a taxi to Sampeng Lane in Chinatown.**

① kids ★★★ Chatuchak Market. Said to be the world's largest flea market; perhaps half a million people visit every weekend. Situated in the northern suburbs of the city and with no less than 15 000 stalls, it covers an area equivalent to five football fields. Chatuchak is a maze of merchandise with a cacophony of characters and an unexpected twist at every corner. You can find everything here—from clothes, plants and household goods to live snakes, exotic fish, Buddhist art, herbal medicine, CDs and hill-tribe handicrafts. Every possible type of Thai food is for sale—some of it still alive and twitching! If you have an eye for antiques, look around the stalls near the clock tower. Note that the Children's

Discovery Museum (see p 41, bullet ②), the Queen Sirikit Park and the Botanical Garden adjoin Chatuchak Market on its northern side, so there are alternatives for family members. ⏲ *2 hr. Phahonyothin Rd, Chatuchak. No credit cards. Sat & Sun 7am–6pm. Metro: Mo Chit or Kampaeng Phet.*

② ★★ Sampeng Lane. (Also known as Soi Wanit.) Not as good a shopping experience as Chatuchak by any means, but a great chance to experience the hustle 'n' bustle of a Thai market and see the strong work ethic of the local people. This is Chinatown, one of the original foundations of Bangkok. Sampeng Lane is a sheltered alleyway about

A colourful and fruity display at Chatuchak Market.

This Lopburi-style seated Buddha can be found in Jim Thompson's House.

1.5km long. Pedestrian traffic is slow and laboured and you'll have to squish and squeeze your way past shops and stalls selling sweets, dried fruit, cheap jewellery, gold and gems, clothes, toys, steaming dim sum and much more. It's a kaleidoscope of chaos and a feast for the senses. *Sampeng Lane. Daily 6am–9pm. No metro.*

3 ★ **Jim Thompson's House.**
American Jim Thompson was head of the OSS (forerunner to the CIA) in Thailand in 1945. He became enamored with Thailand and, in particular, silk. He founded the first Thai silk export company and was a celebrated socialite in Bangkok until his mysterious disappearance in Malaysia in 1967. His traditional Thai teak house has been preserved and now acts as a museum, housing his collection of antiques, artwork and elegant furniture. *6 Soi Kasemsan 2, Rama I Rd.* ☎ *02 216 7368. www.jimthompsonhouse.org. Admission 100 baht. Daily 9am–5pm. Metro: National Stadium.*

4 ★★ kids **Siam Paragon.**
Stomping ground of Bangkok's high society, this mega-luxurious shopping mall has something for everyone. First, there are outlets for Jimmy Choo, Hermès, Versace, Gucci and many other designers. There are Jim Thompson silk retailers, beauty parlours, IT, sports and book stores, and

Thai Silk

The art of weaving silk arrived in Thailand from China over 2000 years ago. Threads of silk are extracted from the cocoons of silkworms, which feed exclusively on mulberry leaves. The threads are reeled together into fibres by hand before being boiled and bleached to remove the natural yellow of silk yarn. The silk is then dyed before being hand-woven on a wooden loom. This labour-intensive system ensures each Thai silk product is unique. While a little more coarse than its shiny Chinese counterpart, Thai silk has a more subtle lustre and is an ideal material for making women's dresses and scarves and men's shirts, and is a luxurious fabric for furniture.

several boutiques on the fourth floor selling chic Thai crafts and furnishings. On the top floor you'll find an entertainment centre with cinemas and tenpin bowling. And, best of all, you can visit Siam Ocean World (see p 43, bullet **8**), a tunnelled aquarium with 3000 species of exotic fish and sea animals. *Cnr Rama I & Phayathai rds, Siam Square.* ☎ *02 690 1000. www.siamparagon.co.th. Daily 10am–10pm. Metro: Siam.*

Marketgoers skirt between the clothing stalls and fabric shops in Sampeng Lane.

5 **Le Notre.** A delightful French bakery with baguettes, croissants, cakes, ice-creams and coffee. It's situated in an air-conditioned food hall named 'Gourmet Paradise' alongside the requisite fast-food joints, a Chinese restaurant, a delicatessen and several Thai eateries, so you have plenty of choices. *Ground Floor, Siam Paragon, Siam Square. Daily 10am–8pm. Metro: Siam.* $.

6 ★★ **Erawan Shrine.** You've already seen your fair share of temples in Bangkok, but this strange little altar—sandwiched between shopping centres and towering hotels—is nonetheless quite magical. The shrine itself represents the four-headed Hindu god of creation, Brahma, and was erected in 1956 after a series of fatal mishaps befell the construction

of the original Erawan Hotel. Suddenly, all mishaps ceased, the hotel's business started booming and devotees began to flock in droves to the shrine in mystic reverence. As you approach the busy junction where the Erawan Shrine stands, you will smell the billows of incense and might hear music, as those whose wishes come true pay respect by hiring traditional dancers. For the non-Buddhist/ Hindu visitor, it's a colourful photo op, if not a mind-blowing sight with pin-striped businessmen praying for success, university students hoping for romance and housewives imploring the gods for winning lottery numbers. *Outside the Grand Hyatt Erawan Bangkok (see p 141), cnr Ratchadamri & Ploenchit rds, Pratunam. Daily 6am–10pm. Metro: Chit Lom or Ratchadamri.*

The intricate ceiling of Siam Paragon.

Lord Brahma watches over the faithful visiting the Erawan Shrine (p 27).

7 ★ **Thai boxing.** Thailand's national sport is *muay Thai*, a bloody contest of kickboxing, often fought by wiry little 50kg guys whose power and flexibility are remarkable. Thai boxing draws huge crowds who are as much part of the spectacle as the fighters.

Screaming, betting, drinking and jumping up and down in excitement are all par for the course. An evening usually involves eight bouts each with a maximum of five rounds, accompanied by traditional Thai music and some Sumo-esque rituals. Although you'll rarely see any serious injuries, some might find the sport too violent. There are two main stadiums in Bangkok: **7A Ratchadamnoen Boxing Stadium**, which is the national Thai boxing arena with championship bouts; and **7B Lumphini Stadium**, which is a bit smaller and certainly cheaper. *See p 132.*

8 ★★★ **Cocktails at Sky Bar.** Precariously situated like a diving board over a swimming pool on the 63rd floor of lebua Hotel is the Sky Bar. The spine-chilling views of the city below warrant at least enough time to enjoy a cocktail, a martini or a glass of wine to keep your knees from turning to jelly. *63rd floor, lebua at State Tower Hotel, 1055 Silom Rd, Bangrak.* ☎ *02 624 9555. www.thedomebkk.com. Daily 6pm–1am. Metro: Saphan Taksin.* ●

Night-time cocktails at Sky Bar, on top of the lebua Hotel, set high standards.

Bangkok Food Safari

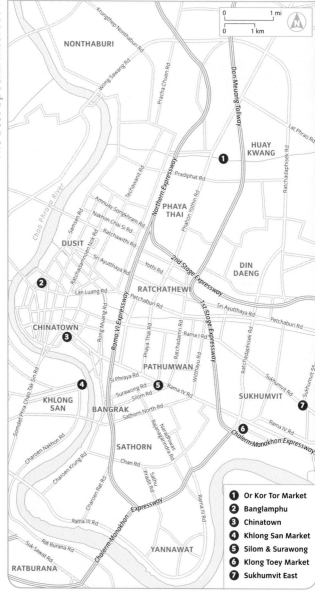

0   1 mi
0   1 km

NONTHABURI

HUAY KWANG

PHAYA THAI

DIN DAENG

DUSIT

RATCHATHEWI

CHINATOWN

PATHUMWAN

KHLONG SAN

BANGRAK

SUKHUMVIT

SATHORN

YANNAWAT

RATBURANA

1 Or Kor Tor Market
2 Banglamphu
3 Chinatown
4 Khlong San Market
5 Silom & Surawong
6 Klong Toey Market
7 Sukhumvit East

Previous page: The marble gleams at Wat Benchamabophit.

You can't walk more than 100m in Bangkok before you trip over a marketplace or a little stall on wheels offering fruit pancakes, fresh orange juice, grilled chicken, sticky rice, kebabs, coconut desserts or any one of a million dishes sizzling away in woks. Rather than concentrate on three hearty meals a day, Bangkokians tend to eat every few hours and, in between times, they love to snack. Whatever time of day, you'll see woks and stoves set up along the pavement and Thais of all classes sitting on little plastic stools at metal tables gratefully tucking in to whatever's on offer. There's a fantastic selection of lip-smacking street food available all over Bangkok—most dishes cost no more than 20 or 30 baht. Just let your nose do the walking. START: **Kampaeng Phet metro station.**

❶ Or Kor Tor Market. A cleaner, vacuum-packed, indoor version of the bustling Bangkok street kitchen, this is clearly a more up-market place to shop (and perhaps 25 to 50 per cent more expensive). Fruit, veg, meat, fish, sweets, condiments and spices are all available, but in a smell-free environment. *Directly outside Kampaeng Phet MRT, next to Chatuchak Market. Daily 6am–8pm. Metro: Kampaeng Phet.*

❷ Banglamphu. Backpackers love street food and the streets near Khao San Road are jam-packed with stalls selling *pat-thai* (fried noodles, vegetables and peanuts) for 30 baht, fresh orange juice and sugar cane juice (25 baht) and even deep-fried insects and scorpions. Pick up a nice dessert, such as coconut pudding in a banana-leaf cup, on Tani Road. *Khao San, Samsen & Tani rds. Daily 10am–1am. No metro or ferry.*

How many of this street vendor's delicacies are you game enough to try?

Papaya Salad *(Som-Tam)*

Aside from the ubiquitous noodle stalls, the most popular street food in Bangkok is arguably *som-tam*. Recognisable by her large wooden mortar and pestle, the *som-tam* vendor is an artist in her own right. She surrounds herself with a variety of ingredients in ceramic bowls and grinds them in the mortar one by one—cherry tomatoes, chillis, sugar, dried prawns, crab, peanuts, green beans, garlic, lemon juice, soy sauce, Chinese cabbage and the main ingredient, long shards of green papaya. Tell her how spicy you want it. I always ask for my *som-tam* without the salty prawns and crab, then eat it with a 10-baht portion of sticky rice and some fried chicken. The best 50-baht takeaway you can get!

Some som-tam *(papaya salad) with snake beans.*

❸ ★ **Chinatown.** A veritable festival of street food; just meander along Yaowarat Road in the evening and let the aromas lure you in. Bird's nest soup and shark fin soup are popular. Apart from the many seafood dishes, you should try 1000-year-old eggs, medicinal teas, boiled cockles, Thai porridge *(joak)*, Chinese cakes *(kanom piah)*, roasted chestnuts, fried banana and, my favourite, fried wonton. Chinatown hosts an annual vegetarian food festival in September/October. *Yaowarat, Charoen Krung & Chakkrawat rds. Daily 11am–11pm. Metro: Hua Lamphong.*

❹ **Khlong San Market.** Away from the baying hordes, this open-air market is just a short ferry ride across the Chao Phraya River. University students tend to come here for lunch. Half the market is dedicated to ladies' clothes and accessories, the other half to food—hot-off-the-wok chilli sensations, fruit such as apples, pears, rose-apples and pineapples, spicy salads and delicious hot fried doughnuts. Ask for *ho mok bla*— little fish curry cakes in banana-leaf cups—they're delicious. *Charoen Nathorn Rd, Thonburi. Daily 7am–10pm. Ferry: Klong San pier.*

❺ **Silom & Surawong.** Woks sizzle with chilli and garlic until the wee hours at this popular traveller hangout. I particularly recommend a dish of braised pork and rice

6 ★ **Klong Toey Market.** This crowded, pungent marketplace offers bowls of coconut soup, fried rice, *kwit-diao* (noodle soup) with prawns, fruit and spices—but visitors will be more intrigued by the array of live animals that are chopped up on the spot to provide meat, soup and tonics for locals. This is the final stop for many a snake, frog, eel, pig, chicken, duck and crab. Hold your breath! *Cnr Ratchadaphisek & Rama IV rds, Klong Toey. Daily 6am–midnight. Metro: Klong Toey or Queen Sirikit Convention Center.*

7 ★★ **Sukhumvit East.** On the north side of the Thong Lor MRT station, you'll see stalls selling a kaleidoscope of exotic fruit— rambutans, mangoes, durians, mangosteens, jackfruit and more. On the opposite side of the street, Soi 38 is one of Bangkok's hidden gems. Mobile stalls offer Chinese and Thai favourites, including dim sum, *khao mun gai* (chicken and rice), sticky rice and mango in coconut sauce (delicious!), pork satay and oyster omelettes. *Sukhumvit Rd sois 55 and 38. Daily noon–9pm. Metro: Thong Lor.*

You'll find a tongue-tingling array of spices for sale at Bangkok's markets.

(35 baht) from the English-speaking vendor who occupies a space on the lane next to Montien Hotel. *Surawong, Patpong & Silom rds. Daily 3pm–3am. Metro: Sala Daeng.*

Don't forget to try Thailand's most popular food, in any form: noodles!

Buddhist Temples
of Old Bangkok

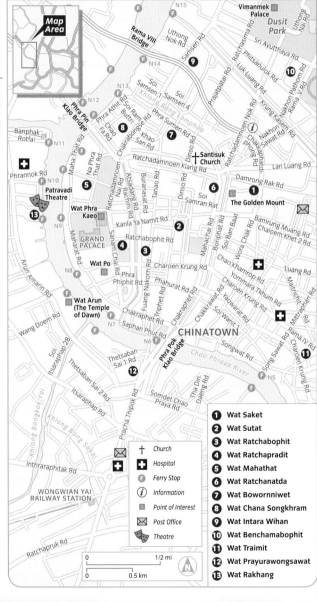

Church
Hospital
Ferry Stop
Information
Point of Interest
Post Office
Theatre

1 Wat Saket
2 Wat Sutat
3 Wat Ratchabophit
4 Wat Ratchapradit
5 Wat Mahathat
6 Wat Ratchanatda
7 Wat Bowornniwet
8 Wat Chana Songkhram
9 Wat Intara Wihan
10 Wat Benchamabophit
11 Wat Traimit
12 Wat Prayurawongsawat
13 Wat Rakhang

Virtually every neighbourhood in Thailand has its own
Buddhist temple where locals pray. Locals also subsidise
the temple and often help with repairs. In fact, you could say the
local temple is a spiritual community centre. The best place to see
a stunning variety of old temples and architectural styles is the
Old City in Bangkok. Please remember that these are holy places
and you must observe the dress code—no shorts, short skirts or
sleeveless shirts—and be respectful while you are in the compound.
These are also places to relax, gather thoughts, contemplate life
and meditate. Buddhist temples can be fascinating places, evoking
a deep sense of tranquility and awareness among visitors.

START: **Catch a taxi or a tuktuk to Wat Saket.**

❶ Wat Saket. Adjoining the 58m
Golden Mount (see p 11, bullet ❷),
this simple Buddhist temple tells
much of Bangkok's history. Built in
the late 18th century by King
Rama I just outside the new city
walls, Wat Saket served as the
capital's crematorium and,
over the next century, was the
pyre for some 60 000 plague
victims. The golden stupa
was added some years later,
built on rubble dredged from the
canal nearby. Later, King Rama V
reportedly placed relics (said to be
the Buddha's teeth) in the *chedi*.
Wat Saket hosts an annual fair
in November. *344 Chakkraphatdiphong Rd (between Boriphat
& Lan Luang rds), Phra Nakorn.
☎ 02 621 0576. Admission
10 baht. Daily 7.30am–5.30pm.
No metro or ferry.*

*Wat Saket and
the Golden
Mount.*

Soldiers guard Wat Ratchabophit.

2 Wat Sutat. Situated across from the Giant Swing (see p 54, bullet **3**) in the Old City, this temple is one of Bangkok's oldest. It is built in traditional Rattanakosin (Bangkok) style, with a high roof and pointed finials. On the east gable you'll see a representation of the god of the sun, while the west gable sports the god of the moon. *146 Bamrung Muang Rd, Phra Nakorn.* ☎ *02 222 6935. Admission 20 baht. Daily 8.30am–8pm. No metro or ferry.*

3 Wat Ratchabophit. If you have visited several Thai temples already, you will quickly notice

The famous 3m-high Golden Buddha at Wat Traimit (p 38).

the difference in style at Wat Ratchabophit. The main buildings are linked by a circular courtyard—probably a Chinese design. The exterior of the temple is glazed with handpainted tiles, which are definitely Thai, but then suddenly there rises a Gothic spire from one of the *chedis*. Architects might call it a cultural mishmash, but to me it's very appealing. *Fuang Nakorn Rd, Rattanakosin. Admission free. Daily 8am–5pm. Ferry: Tha Tien pier (N8).*

4 Wat Ratchapradit. Built by King Mongkut (Rama IV), who was played by Yul Brynner in the Hollywood epic *The King and I*, this temple has certain Khmer architectural features, including the faces on the side towers, reminiscent of those found at the Bayon in Cambodia. Its white walls are decorated in mother-of-pearl and marble tiles and it certainly glistens in the sunlight. Wat Ratchapradit also has some beautiful murals. Look out for a painting of King Mongkut studying an eclipse through a telescope. *Cnr of Rachini Rd & Saranrom Royal Park, Rattanakosin.* ☎ *02 223 8215. Admission free. Daily 9am–6pm. Ferry: Tha Tien pier (N8).*

5 Wat Mahathat. Originally built to house a relic of the Buddha, Wat Mahathat is nowadays the headquarters of Thailand's largest monastic order and Vipassana meditation centre. Classes in this meditation technique are held daily (see p 48, bullet **1**), often with English-language instruction. Fortune tellers often set up stalls inside the compound. Running along the northern wall outside the temple is the Amulet Market (see p 14, bullet **4**), where you can buy antique Buddha images and lucky charms. *Phra That Rd (near Sanam Luang), Rattanakosin. ☎ 02 222 8004. Admission free. Daily 8am–6pm. Ferry: Tha Phra Chan.*

6 Wat Ratchanatda. I find this Indian-style temple, with its 37 steel spires pointing to the sky, quite spectacular. It was built by King Rama III for his granddaughter in the 19th century. The large white temple is set in a compound with immaculate gardens and bonsai trees. You can easily find shade in one of the open-air *salas*. There's also a small Buddhist market in the

This Chinese-style statue can be found at Wat Bowornniwet.

compound where you can buy Hindu and Buddhist images and lucky charms. *Mahachai Rd, Phra Nakorn. ☎ 02 224 8807. Admission free. Daily 8am–4pm. No metro or ferry.*

7 Wat Bowornniwet. Founded in 1826, this temple also serves as a Buddhist university. At one time it was the traditional temple of members of the royal family when they entered monkhood. Nowadays you'll notice there are always foreign/western monks and many religious ceremonies are conducted in English. The temple contains murals depicting western life in the 19th century. In the compound you'll also find a pond full of giant turtles and catfish and a herbal medicine centre. *248 Phra Sumen Rd, Banglamphu. ☎ 02 281 2831. Admission free. Daily 5am–8pm. Ferry: Phra Arthit pier (N13).*

8 Wat Chana Songkhram. This Buddhist temple from the Ayutthaya period was presented to a group of ethnic Mon monks by King Rama I. Inside the *ubosot* (ordination hall) you'll find a statue

A golden Buddha holds court at Wat Benchamabophit (p 38).

of King Taksin the Great, and there's an interesting motif of the Hindu god Vishnu mounted on the bird Garuda. The temple monks are a happy bunch here and lay out market stalls to tempt tourists, no doubt due to the fact that the temple walkway provides a shortcut for foreign backpackers every day between Khao San Road and the river ferry pier. *Chakrabongse Rd, Banglamphu.* ☎ *02 281 8244. Daily 5am–8pm. Admission free. Ferry: Tha Phra Arthit pier (N13).*

❾ Wat Intara Wihan. Another temple of the Ayutthaya era, Wat Intara Wihan is famous for its 32m-high image of the Buddha

A mound covered in shrines at Wat Prayurawongsawat.

standing on a lotus leaf and holding an alms bowl, known as *Luangpor Toh*. This amazing statue took 60 years to build. It was commissioned by Rama IV in 1867, but not finished until the reign of Rama VII. The image was constructed of brick and stucco and decorated in glass mosaics and 24-carat gold. The temple draws crowds in early March when, for 10 days, it hosts a festival to honour Luangpor Toh. *114 Wisutkasat Rd, Bangkhunphrom.* ☎ *02 628 5550 2. Daily 6am–6pm. Admission free. Ferry: Tha Thewet pier (N15).*

❿ Wat Benchamabophit. (The Marble Temple.) I always feel like I'm in a theme park when I come here. Not because there's anything false or tacky about the Marble Temple—it's simply so picturesque I wonder if it's real. Commissioned by King Chulalongkorn in 1899, it is built of fine Italian white marble, which can be blinding on a sunny day. You can also find a large bodhi tree— representing the spot where the Buddha attained enlightenment— brought in from Bodgaya in India. *69 Rama V Rd, Dusit. Admission free. Daily 8am–5pm. No metro or ferry.*

⓫ Wat Traimit. Visitors both local and foreign flock here to see the outstanding 3m-high Golden Buddha image (see p 66, bullet ⓭). It is the largest solid-gold Buddha in the world, weighing some five tons, worth in the region of US$14 million, and is one of the country's greatest treasures. The image is over 700 years old, but it was not until 1957 that it was rediscovered. It had been encased in plaster—probably to hide it from Burmese invaders when it was smuggled out of Sukhothai. It was not until it was dropped by a crane while being moved that its golden majesty was uncovered. Within the compound, you can find some strange electronic

A statue of Prince Mahasurasinghanart, King Rama I's brother, at Wat Chana Songkhram.

fortune-telling machines, too, with prophesies in English, Thai and Chinese. *Cnr Mittaphap Thai-China & Yaowarat rds, Chinatown. ☎ 02 222 9019. Admission free. Daily 8am–5pm. Metro: Hua Lamphong.*

⑫ Wat Prayurawongsawat.

Built in the style of the old Thai capital, Ayutthaya, Wat Prayurawongsawat (or Wat Prayoon) has a towering white *chedi* that many people pass every day by river, but few take the time to visit. The temple has two curiosities. The first is a huge mound built in the centre of the compound that apparently represents the shape King Rama III witnessed when he watched a candle melting one night. Nowadays it is covered in shrines. The other interesting sight is the pond, or moat around the *chedi*, which is filled with turtles that feed on papaya. Strange, but true. *Thetsaban Sai 1, Thonburi. ☎ 02 465 0439. Admission free. Daily 8am–8pm. Ferry: Memorial Bridge pier (N6) & walk across the bridge.*

⑬ Wat Rakhang.

Built during the Ayutthaya period (1677–1767), Wat Rakhang was declared a royal temple by King Taksin when he established his capital at Thonburi. While the temple was being renovated in the late 18th century, a brass bell was unearthed. King Rama I found the bell so melodious he had it moved to Wat Phra Kaeo (see p 11, bullet ③) and five bells were given to Thonburi in exchange. 'Rakhang' means 'bells', and today a small belltower houses the five brass bells in the garden. I think the most interesting building is a small red house amongst the trees in the garden which used to be the home of King Rama I. Known as the *ho trai*, (the library), the teak house is now a scripture hall with artifacts from the reign of King Rama I, as well as his interred ashes and a mural depicting the Thai epic, *The Ramakien. 250 Arun Amorin Rd, Thonburi. ☎ 02 411 2039. Admission free. Daily 5am–9pm. Ferry: Tha Chang pier (N9).*

The famous Buddha statue at Wat Intara Wihan was 60 years in the making.

Bangkok for Kids

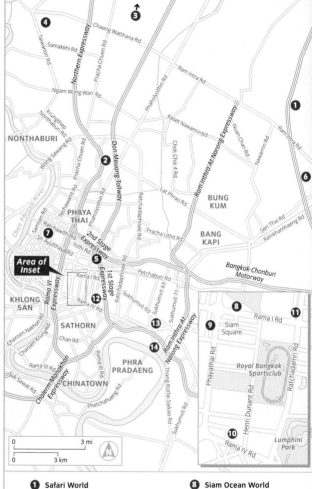

1 Safari World
2 Children's Discovery Museum
3 Dream World
4 Nonthaburi Equestrian
   Sports Club
5 Bangkok Dolls Museum
6 Siam Park City
7 Dusit Zoo

8 Siam Ocean World
9 Kim Bowl
10 Snake Farm
11 Bangkok TK Park
12 Joe Louis Puppet Theatre
13 Bangkok Planetarium
   & Science Museum
14 Combat Zone Paintball

Bangkok used to be a tough city with children—it's often hot and crowded, and most of the attractions involve walking around Buddhist temples and historical landmarks. However, in recent years Bangkok has exploded with family-friendly activities and now has some great zoos, safari parks, water parks, fun fairs and theme parks, most of which are in the suburbs and which operate all year round. Shopping malls usually provide some entertainment activities (see p 74) and there are seaside resorts within a few hours' drive that are safe for swimming (see p 157). **START: Catch a taxi or a tuktuk to Safari World.**

1 ★ Safari World. Very commercial in a theme-park kind of way, so kids love it! There's no end to the entertainment—jungle cruises, aquariums, dolphin shows, Hollywood cowboy movie shows, sea lion performances, crocodile wrestling and much more. A full day out for all the family. *99 Payaintra Rd, Samwatawantok, Klongsamwa.* ☎ *02 9144 1001 9. www.safariworld. com. Admission (for both Safari & Marine parks) 470 baht adults, 330 baht kids. Mon–Fri 9am–5pm, Sat & Sun 9am–6pm. No metro or ferry.*

2 ★★ Children's Discovery Museum. Fantastic for kids who love to touch everything! This is interactive education for youngsters—mostly aimed at the 5 to 10 age group—where skills are sharpened through practical experience. Kids can walk in Velcro feet, stand inside a giant bubble, test their reaction times with knobs

and levers, and generally learn how various things work in a fun way. There are paints and pencils, books, puppet shows and a toddlers' playground. The museum is located inside Queen Sirikit Park, which has pleasant botanical gardens, fountains and lotus ponds, and is very close to Chatuchak Market (see p 25, bullet **1**), so there should be enough variety to keep everyone happy for a day. *Queen Sirikit Park, Kamphaenphet Rd, Chatuchak.* ☎ *02 615 7333 or 02 272 4745. www.bkkchildrensmuseum.com. Tues–Fri 9am–5pm, Sat & Sun 10am–6pm. Admission 150 baht. Metro: Mo Chit or Chatuchak.*

A sea lion puts on a show at Safari World.

A brightly coloured doll at the Bangkok Dolls Museum.

❸ ★★ Dream World. Dream World is Bangkok's biggest theme park, with roller-coasters and fast rides, parades with cartoon characters and lots of teddy bears, train rides around models of the Great Wall of China and the Taj Mahal, water-park slides and a Hollywood action-movie film set. All in all, it's similar to Siam Park, but perhaps oriented towards younger children. Opening late 2009/early 2010 is a 4D action-adventure movie set. There are ice-cream parlours, restaurants and a host of booths around the park. It's situated outside the city; you should call ahead to organise packages, which include transfers from your hotel, lunch and all the rides in the price. Otherwise, a taxi is the best alternative. *62 Moo 1, Rangsit-Ongka Rak Rd, Km 7, Thanyaburi, Pathumthani. ☎ 02 533 1152. www.dreamworld-th.com. Admission 450 baht, kids under 90cm free; package with transfers 1000 baht. Mon–Fri 10am–5pm, Sat & Sun 10am–7pm. Bus: 538 from Victory Monument/Don Muang Bus Terminal.*

❹ Nonthaburi Equestrian Sports Club. Horse riding, either for accomplished riders or beginners, is available at Nonthaburi (see p 61, bullet ⓫), north of Bangkok. Children under five can ride ponies (700 baht per 30 minutes), while over-fives can have supervised rides for 2000 baht per hour. *25/843-5 Moo 6, Bangtalad, Pakkred, Nonthaburi. ☎ 02 962 2735 6. www.nonthaburihorses.com. Daily 8am–6pm. Ferry: express boat (1 hr) to Nonthaburi pier (N30), plus taxi.*

❺ Bangkok Dolls Museum. Founded in 1957, with some exquisite handcrafted pieces, this is a doll factory, a museum and a retail shop rolled into one. It also has a short history of dolls and some collectors' items. *85 Soi Ratchataphan, Ratchataphan Rd, Pratunam. ☎ 02 245 3008. Admission free. Tue–Sun 8am–5pm. Metro: Victory Monument, plus a 1km walk.*

❻ ★★★ Siam Park City. This is Bangkok's best and most over-the-top amusement centre and all-in-one theme park. What better way to cool down on a sweltering day than to get out of Bangkok and kick back at a water park? And when the kids finally get tired of sliding down the flumes, there's an amusement park, a botanical garden, an aviary, a zoo, a safari park and a *Jurassic Park* theme park to choose from. For me, though, it's the water park that is the highlight, despite the screaming and shouting of a thousand kids. Check the website first for the best deals. If you only want to visit the water park, prices are 200 baht (adults) and 100 baht (children), then you have a pay-per-ride system. For those who want to make a full day of it, you can buy combination tickets (350 to 1000 baht), which include most, if not all, attractions. *99 Seri Thai Rd, Kanna Yaow, Min Buri.*

☎ 02 919 7200 5. www.siamparkcity.com. Admission 400 baht adults, 300 baht kids. Daily 10am–6pm. No metro or ferry.

7 ★★ **Dusit Zoo.** Thailand's top zoo has more than 300 species of animals, including rhinos, elephants, hippos, tapirs, gibbons, lions, tigers, crocodiles and exotic birds. There are lots of lakes, which have pedalos and shaded places to sit and eat. It's very busy at weekends, so avoid it on Saturdays and Sundays if you can. Ratchawithi Rd (cnr Rama V Rd). ☎ 02 281 2000. Admission 100 baht adults, 50 baht kids. Daily 8am–6pm. Ferry: Tha Thewet pier (N15), plus a 1km walk.

8 ★ **Siam Ocean World.** Situated in the basement of the chic shopping mall Siam Paragon (see p 26, bullet **4**), this huge neon-lit aquarium is a surprise. Siam Ocean World is an easily accessible attraction that's very popular at weekends. Sharks, exotic fish, penguins, rays and otters abide down here. The show mainly entails feeding sessions, including shark feeding at 1pm and 4pm, but there's almost always something extra for young children, such as a 'magic mermaid' show. The only distasteful part for me is that foreigners have to pay two to three times the admission fee. Floor B1-B2, Siam Paragon, Siam Square, 991 Rama I Rd, Pathumwan. ☎ 02 687 2000. www.siamoceanworld.co.th. Admission foreigners 850 baht adults, 650 baht kids. Daily 9am–10pm. Metro: Siam.

9 ★ **Kim Bowl.** Almost every shopping mall has 10-pin bowling on its top floor alongside video game machines and karaoke booths. Kim Bowl is my favourite because it's always like a party—there's food and drink, flashing lights, loud pop music and 28 bowling lanes. Open 'til late and bags of fun! 7th floor, Mah Boon Krong Center, 444 Phayathai Rd, Pathumwan. ☎ 02 611 7171 4. Admission 70–90 baht. Metro: National Stadium.

A visit to the Ocean World aquarium in the basement of the Siam Paragon shopping mall will captivate young and old alike.

Get squeamishly close to snakes such as these Indian cobras, as well as giant pythons, at the snake farm.

⑩ Snake farm. Thailand has more snakes per square mile than any other country—they are a common sight outside the cities. And believe me, if you ever find a snake coiled up inside your toilet, you'll never sit down without thoroughly checking under the rim again! Known officially as the Queen Saovabha Memorial Institute, the snake farm was opened in 1923 by this queen as an arm of the Thai Red Cross. Why? Because the institute specialised in the production of antivenene. You can watch the snakes being 'milked' of venom and listen to a video explaining the institute's progress. That's where the education stops and the horror begins for the squeamish—after that, it's watching snakes being fed rats and other small animals, and a chance to get a photo with a giant python draped around your neck. *1871 Rama IV Rd, Lumphini. ☎ 02 252 0161. Admission 200 baht adults, 50 baht kids. Mon–Fri 8.30am–4.30pm, Sat & Sun 8.30am–1pm. Metro: Sala Daeng or Silom.*

⑪ Bangkok TK Park. A chance for your kids to get to know Thai children while you dredge the designer stores of CentralWorld mall (see p 74). 'TK' stands for 'Thailand

Knowledge', and the centre is half babysitting and half educational. There are lots of spatial awareness games for toddlers, books, paints and a play area for children. The activities mainly centre around computers, video games and

A Great Hornbill from the striking exotic bird collection at Dusit Zoo (p 43).

The Joe Louis Puppet Theatre brings cultural classics to life with these puppets.

new innovations, and it generally attracts 10 to 13 year olds. It's a smart, colourful, safe, supervised fun park for your children. *8th floor, CentralWorld, Siam Square, Rama I Rd, Pathumwan.* ☎ *02 257 4300. Admission 20 baht. Tues–Sun 10am–8pm. Metro: Siam or Chit Lom.*

⓬ ★ Joe Louis Puppet Theatre. This is not Punch 'n' Judy—it's more of a cultural performance. Every night you can see a re-enactment of the Hindu classic *Ramayana* featuring beautifully hand-carved puppets. *Suan Lum Night Bazaar, Rama IV Rd/ Wireless Rd.* ☎ *02 252 9683 4. www. thaipuppet.com. Admission 400 baht Thais, 900 baht foreigners. Daily 8pm. Metro: Lumphini.*

⓭ Bangkok Planetarium & Science Museum. Currently not very high-tech, but it has ambitions to become so. The planetarium offers visitors exhibits and shows in natural science, technology, the human body, astrology, astronomy and, of course, outer space. The centre is very popular with high school groups and certain times of the day are reserved for students. Check the website before you go. *928 Sukhumvit Rd (next to Ekkamai Bus Terminal).* ☎ *02 392 5951 5. www.bangkokplanetarium.com. Admission 50 baht. Tues–Sun 9.30am–4.30pm. Metro: Ekkamai.*

⓮ Combat Zone Paintball. For adventurous types aged seven and over, this is Bangkok's premier paintball field and it's easy to get to. Book in advance; it's busy on weekends. *117 Sukhumvit Rd Soi 62, Bangjar Prakanong.* ☎ *02 331 2863 or 089 771 3354. www.combatzone62.net. Admission 350 baht. Daily 9.30am–6pm. Metro: On Nut.*

Mind, Body & Soul

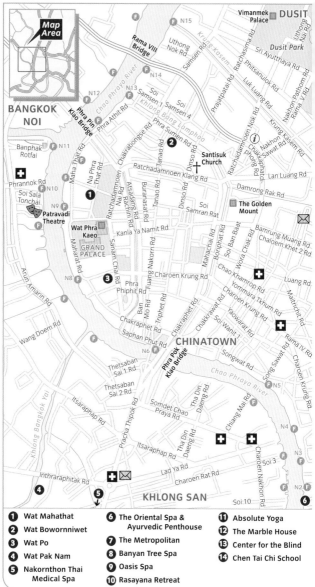

1. Wat Mahathat
2. Wat Bowornniwet
3. Wat Po
4. Wat Pak Nam
5. Nakornthon Thai Medical Spa
6. The Oriental Spa & Ayurvedic Penthouse
7. The Metropolitan
8. Banyan Tree Spa
9. Oasis Spa
10. Rasayana Retreat
11. Absolute Yoga
12. The Marble House
13. Center for the Blind
14. Chen Tai Chi School

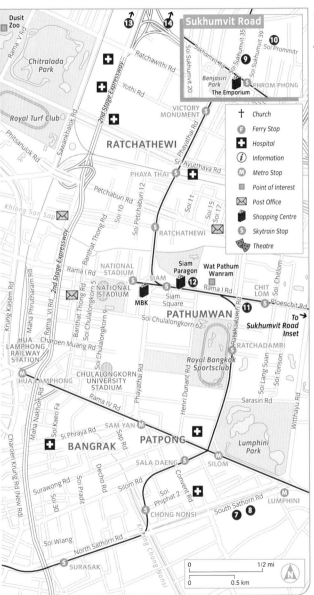

Sukhumvit Road

† Church
F Ferry Stop
✚ Hospital
ⓘ Information
Ⓜ Metro Stop
▪ Point of Interest
✉ Post Office
📚 Shopping Centre
Ⓢ Skytrain Stop
🎭 Theatre

0   1/2 mi
0   0.5 km

Thai culture is alive with holistic treatments and methods of relaxation for your mind, body and soul. Of course, Thai massage is famous all over the world and the country has enjoyed a boom in recent years in spas and resorts offering full-body cleansing and pampering so good you'll think you're melting. For those with physical ailments, you might feel the time has come to try alternative medicines such as Chinese remedies, herbal solutions or acupuncture. And for your troubled soul, where else would you turn to but a Thai meditation centre? START: **Tha Phra Chan ferry stop.**

❶ ★ Wat Mahathat. Vipassana Meditation involves sitting silently in the Buddha position and following your breath coming in through your nostrils, down to your stomach and then leaving the body. It is the main practice employed by Buddhist monks for cleansing the mind. As the centre of the Mahanikai school of Buddhism in Bangkok, this historical temple (see p 37, bullet **❺**) is a serious place to take group classes in meditation, which are taught by English-speaking monks. You can sleep at the temple in humble dormitories or go in every day. *Na Phra That Rd (near Sanam Luang), Rattanakosin. ☎ 02 222 6011. Courses free. Daily 7–10am, 1–4pm & 6–8.30pm. Ferry: Tha Phra Chan pier.*

❷ Wat Bowornniwet. Established as a Buddhist university in 1826, this temple allows visiting foreigners to meditate, but does not provide courses. Within the grounds there is a picturesque pond teeming with turtles and catfish, as well as a herbal medicine centre. *248 Phra Sumen Rd, Banglamphu. ☎ 02 281 2831. Admission free. Daily 5am–8pm. Ferry: Phra Arthit pier (N13).*

❸ ★★★ Wat Po. Thailand's most renowned centre of Thai massage has a well-earned reputation spanning a great many years. Many of the top masseurs and

masseuses in the country learn the craft at this massage school. Visitors to Wat Po can try a traditional Thai massage for 300 baht per hour, a foot massage for 250 baht per hour or (I recommend) an Ayurvedic massage with hot herbs ground into your body for 500 baht per hour. This will be one of the most therapeutic events of your life. *Sanam Chai Rd, Rattanakosin. ☎ 02 225 5910 (temple) or 02 221 2974 (massage school). www.watpomassage.com. Daily 8am–5pm. Ferry: Tha Tien pier (N8).*

❹ Wat Pak Nam. Perhaps it's better if you have practised meditation before or can speak some Thai, because you listen to Buddhist sermons in Thai language as you practice at this temple. The meditation technique taught here is recorded in an English book, *Samma Samadhi*, and involves high levels of concentration, which teachers say will allow you 'to develop penetrating insight'. Not for the casual passer-by. *Therdthai Rd, Phasi Charoen, Thonburi. ☎ 02 467 0811. www.watpaknam.org. Sermons: Mon–Fri 8am & 6pm; Sat & Sun 8am, 10am, 1pm & 6pm. No metro or ferry.*

The exterior of Wat Bowornniwet.

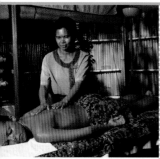

All your cares will be massaged away at one of Bangkok's many health spas.

5 Nakornthon Thai Medical Spa. As opposed to luxury and relaxation, this medical spa concentrates more on wellness and is popular with elderly visitors. Traditional acupressure massage and herbal scrubs are the norm and the friendly staff also like to recommend herbs/diets for your benefit. It's also much cheaper than hotel spas. *12th floor, Nakornthon Hospital, 49 Rama II Rd, Samaedum, Bangkhunthien.* ☎ *02 450 9912. www.nakornthonhospital.com. No metro or ferry.*

6 ★★ The Oriental Spa & Ayurvedic Penthouse. All the herbal oils, furnishings, techniques and even most of the staff come from India at this chic and refined resort spa. Employing the holistic Ayurvedic practice of massaging and treating the whole body at once, this place assures a genuinely regal experience. You will carry the scents of amber, myrrh, marjoram and nutmeg on your purified skin for weeks. *Mandarin Oriental Hotel, 48 Oriental Rd, Bangrak.* ☎ *02 659 9000, ext 7440. www.mandarinoriental.com. Daily 9am–8.30pm. Metro: Saphan Taksin.*

7 The Metropolitan. This is a stylish, minimalist hotel that prides itself on health and holism—and not only in its organic, low-calorie restaurants, Cy'an (p 97) and Glow (p 98). It also includes accessories and activities such as spas, yoga and meditation, to protect your body and soul. *27 South Sathorn Rd.* ☎ *02 625 3333. www.metropolitan.como.bz. 171 units. Doubles 10 850 baht. AE, DC, MC, V. Metro: Lumphini or Sala Daeng.*

8 Banyan Tree Spa. An exquisite spa with views over Bangkok's business district, the Banyan Tree offers scrubs, beauty treatments and a choice of Thai, Swedish or Balinese massage. The hotel (see p 138) also offers spa packages and in-room services for those who just can't get enough pampering. *21st floor, Banyan Tree Hotel, 21/100 South Sathorn Rd.* ☎ *02 679 1052 4. www.banyantreespa.com. Metro: Lumphini.*

9 ★ Oasis Spa. This award-winning spa is renowned for elegance, graceful service and the most soothing of treatments. Full- and half-day packages include oil massage, wrap, body scrub, facial and hydrotherapy. You're sure to leave glowing. *Sub-soi 4, 64 Soi 31 (Soi Sawadee), Sukhumvit Rd, Phrakanong.* ☎ *02 262 2122. www.chiangmaioasis.com. Metro: Phrom Phong.*

10 ★★ Rasayana Retreat. Check in for a full day's cleansing with detox, colonic irrigation, therapeutic massage, salt baths, saunas, acupuncture and even hypnotherapy. Very good value and highly recommended for those of us who eat, drink and smoke too much or are stressed, sedentary or suffer from insomnia. *57 Soi Prommitr, Sukhumvit Rd Soi 39, Wattana.* ☎ *02 662 4803 5. www.rasayanaretreat.com. Metro: Phrom Phong.*

⑪ Absolute Yoga. Visitors can join in a session at any of the six Absolute studios in the city. Be aware that many Thais are very flexible, so even what is deemed a 'beginners' class may be a high level. Daily classes in Bikram, Hatha, Pilates and more. *4th floor, Amarin Plaza (opp. Chit Lom BTS), Ploenchit Rd, Pathumwan.* ☎ *02 252 4400. www.absoluteyogabangkok.com. Daily 7am–9.15pm. Metro: Chit Lom.*

⑫ ★★ The Marble House. Many of my friends in Bangkok come here every week, because it is 'no-frills but exotic, professional but inexpensive'. A full-body massage—from toenails to the tips of your hair—costs just 250 baht per hour. Oil massage, foot reflexology and Ayurvedic massage cost a little more. Some of the masseuses might be half your height, but they're surprisingly strong and will stretch you into shape in no time. *410/6 Siam Square Soi 6 (opp. Novotel Hotel), Rama I Rd, Pathumwan.* ☎ *02 658 4124 5. Daily 9am–midnight. Metro: Siam.*

⑬ ★★ Center for the Blind. An excellent massage—and so much more. This is a half-day trip and a chance to get out of the city by river and meet blind people in a work environment—Thai massage being just one of their activities. In fact, traditionally in Thailand, many blind people become massage therapists—and darn good ones too. Many at the Center are old but strong as oxen and will really grind their thumbs and elbows into you. An experience you won't forget— ouch! *78/1 Moo 1, Thiwanon Rd, Pak Kret, Nonthaburi.* ☎ *02 583 7327. 120–160 baht for 1½ hr massage, 100 baht sauna (Sun only). Ferry: express boat to Nonthaburi (N30) or boat to Tha Pak Kret, plus a 10-min taxi ride.*

⑭ Chen Tai Chi School. Although you can join in this graceful martial art for free any morning at Lumphini Park (see p 10, bullet ①), it pays to learn the technique from professionals. English-language classes are available at Chen with special short-term courses for visitors. *Phahonyothin Soi 10, Phaya Thai.* ☎ *086 014 4050. www.chentaichithailand.com. Metro: Ari.* ●

The stylish Metropolitan (p 49) specialises in organic, low-calorie food and drink.

The Best Neighbourhood Tours

The Old City

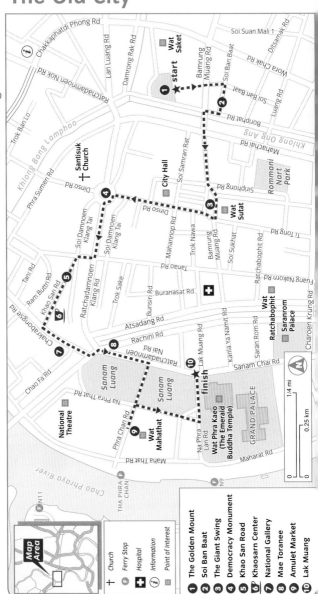

Previous page: The Golden Mount.

Bangkok's 'Old City' is in so many ways the heart of Thailand. It is the historical soul of Siam and home of the country's kings of yesteryear. The 'island' of Rattanakosin also hosts Thailand's national museum, art gallery and several government ministries. King Rama I established Phra Nakorn as the Thai capital in 1782 and founded his palace on the artificial island of Rattanakosin—bordered to the west by the Chao Phraya River and to the east by the Khlong Lord canal. This walk allows you to witness first-hand the sites that gave birth to Bangkok in the 18th century and the national treasures that all Thais hold dear.

START: **Taxi to the Golden Mount or canal boat to Phanfa and five-minute walk.**

---

❶ ★★★ The Golden Mount. This magnificent Buddhist temple is built on an artificial hill and is one of the only vantage points from which to enjoy a panoramic view of the Old City, because of a strict ban on high-rise buildings in the area. A gradual, spiraling climb of 320 stairs takes you past small graves, Buddhist shrines, a tidy forest with a waterfall and wild frangipani to the top. The original *chedi* collapsed long ago and the newer, larger golden dome you see today was commissioned by King Rama III, though it was not completed until the reign of King Rama V. In 1877 Rama V transferred a relic of the Buddha from the Grand Palace to Wat Saket, the temple just behind the Golden Mount. It was later enshrined in the pagoda at the top of the hill. Two decades later the British viceroy of India presented the Siamese king with more bones of the Buddha, which joined the original relic inside the Golden Mount. ⏱ *30 min; go weekdays as early as possible. 344 Chakkraphatdiphong Rd (off Boriphat Rd).* ☎ *02 621 0576. Admission 10 baht. Daily 7.30am–5.30pm. No metro or ferry.*

❷ ★★ Soi Ban Baat. Literally 'Monks Bowl Village Lane', this street is where the traditional artisans of *baat*—Buddhist monks' alms bowls—have lived for two centuries. You can watch the *baat*-smiths at work, hammering out metal bowls in their shops. Go at sunrise to see Buddhist monks collecting alms. ⏱ *30 min. Community headman's workshop: 71 Soi Ban Baat.* ☎ *02 221 4466. No metro or ferry.*

Soi Ban Baat is populated by baat*-smiths fashioning monks' alms bowls.*

The infamous remains of the Giant Swing; games that involved swinging off this structure were outlawed in the 1930s.

❸ The Giant Swing. In the 18th century, the giant swing that stood here was the focal point of a Brahmin festival, where volunteers would swing back and forth trying to snatch a bag of coins with their teeth. Competitors frequently fell and often died, and this pre-Olympic event was outlawed in the 1930s.

The Democracy Monument.

Now there's just a timber frame to remind us. *In front of Wat Sutat, Bamrung Muang Rd (see p 36, bullet ❷). No metro or ferry.*

❹ Democracy Monument. Designed by Italian sculptor Corrado Feroci and Thai architect Mew Aphaiwong in the 1930s, this monument became the rallying point for pro-democracy supporters in 1992 before the army suppressed the uprising and shot dead over 100 protesters. Some 250m west on this wide avenue is the October 14 Monument, which honours the victims of the 1973 mass uprising. *Ratchadamnoen Klang Rd. No metro or ferry.*

❺ ★★★ Khao San Road. In the '60s and '70s, western hippies and travellers came to Thailand curious to see its culture. Khao San Road became a backpackers' Mecca and, ironically, curious locals started coming to this street just to see the strange tourists and their culture of walking around barefoot and stoned, dressed in sarongs, bikinis and tie-dye vests. Every five yards or so, another hostel, diner, cafe or

bar blasts out music or videos—or both. It's like a scene from Dante's *Inferno*. Yet, Khao San Road's vibe is strangely infectious. It has that centre-of-the-world ambience and you get the sense that anything could happen. It's often seedy and illicit, but in recent years has become popular with hip young Thais for its effervescent nightlife and air of reckless abandon.
The 400m walk along Khao San usually takes at least an hour, as you have to walk a gauntlet of vendors, beggars, con artists, travel agents, hairdressers, tattoo artists, dentists, cobblers, jewellers and more. You can shop for cheap clothes, jewellery and CDs, sit at a cafe and people-watch or just have a drink and enjoy the Mardi Gras atmosphere. It's quiet in the mornings, becoming steadily busier and crazier as the day goes on.
🕐 *1 hr. Ferry: Phra Arthit pier (N13).*

6 Khaosarn Center. Ideally situated right in the middle of Khao San Road, this restaurant-bar-cafe has outdoor tables under parasols, or you can sit indoors under a fan. To be honest, the food's nothing special, but there's a full menu of Thai and Western dishes, hot and cold drinks, cocktails and ice-cream to choose from. This is essentially a people-watching stop. Get caught up in conversations with travellers who love to recount their tales to anyone who'll listen. *80–84 Khao San Rd.* ☎ *02 282 4366. Daily 24 hr. Ferry: Phra Arthit pier (N13).*

7 ★ National Gallery. Contemporary Thai art housed in an old colonial building. The tranquil ambience and air-conditioning offer blissful respite from the heat. *See p 22, bullet 5.*

8 Mae Toranee. Opposite the Royal Hotel is a small fountain dedicated to the Earth Goddess, whose statue sits inside the shrine washing her hair of evil spirits. *Opp Royal Hotel, Ratchadamnoen Ave. Ferry: Phra Arthit pier (N13).*

9 ★★★ Amulet Market. Throngs of religious devotees and the superstitious gather here to examine, discuss and haggle for Buddhist amulets and lucky charms. *See p 14, bullet 4.*

10 Lak Muang. Just to the east of the Grand Palace is the site of a wooden pillar erected by King Rama I in 1782 to mark the founding of Bangkok and to protect the city. The shrine has great spiritual significance and you will see devotees making offerings or even hiring classical dancers to perform. The pillar also marks the centre of the city, from which all mileages are taken. *Cnr Na Hap Phoei & Ratchadamnoen Nai rds. Admission free. Daily 6am–6pm. Ferry: Phra Arthit pier (N13).*

The golden pillar at Lak Muang marks the very centre of Bangkok.

Chao Phraya River

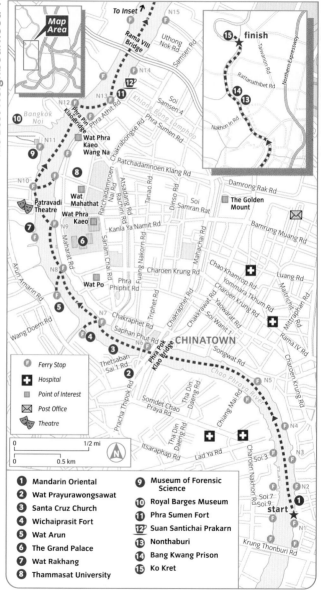

Map Area

To Inset ↑

Rama VIII Bridge

Bangkok Noi

CHINATOWN

Chao Phraya River

Legend:

🅕 Ferry Stop
➕ Hospital
◼ Point of Interest
✉ Post Office
🎭 Theatre

0   1/2 mi
0   0.5 km

1 Mandarin Oriental
2 Wat Prayurawongsawat
3 Santa Cruz Church
4 Wichaiprasit Fort
5 Wat Arun
6 The Grand Palace
7 Wat Rakhang
8 Thammasat University
9 Museum of Forensic Science
10 Royal Barges Museum
11 Phra Sumen Fort
12 Suan Santichai Prakarn
13 Nonthaburi
14 Bang Kwang Prison
15 Ko Kret

start ★

finish

What a great way to see Bangkok! Avoid the traffic and the heat and catch the cool breeze as you skip along the Chao Phraya River, which runs from north to south and flows into the Gulf of Thailand. Much of Bangkok's history and many interesting sights lie along its banks. There's also a fantastic express boat service (see p 168), which allows you to jump on and off whenever you like. You just pay between 15 and 30 baht for a ticket each time you jump on. Or, if you travel 'off peak' (after 9am or before 4pm), you can buy an unlimited boat pass for just 150 baht. **START: Metro to Saphan Taksin. Walk down to Sathorn ferry pier immediately below the metro station. You are on the east bank of the river and want express boats heading north. Buy a day pass or just pay as you go when you get on the boat. Note: Saphan Taksin is located immediately south (or just under) the bridge marked Krung Thonburi Road.**

① **Mandarin Oriental.** The first stop on the east bank is the world-famous Oriental Hotel. The colonial building is mostly shaded by palm trees, but you might catch a glimpse of the rich and famous dining on the hotel's riverfront terrace. On the opposite bank is the Royal Orchid Sheraton. Just after the Oriental, on your right, you pass the French and Portuguese embassies, the first foreign diplomatic residences in Thailand. As the river bends to the left you will see a six-storey Chinese pagoda. *See p 142.*

② ★ **Wat Prayurawongsawat.** As you pass under the first bridge, immediately on your left you'll see an impressive 60m-high white *chedi*. This temple has murals depicting the life of Buddha and its doors are decorated in mother-of-pearl. There's also a large pond where hundreds of turtles and fish swim. You can feed them—they like papaya! *See p 39, bullet* **⑫**.

③ ★ **Santa Cruz Church.** Just past the Memorial Bridge and opposite Pak Khlong flower market is the beige-and-pink Santa Cruz Church and convent with its octagonal dome on top. It was originally built in 1770 by Portuguese traders during the reign

The beige-and-pink Santa Cruz Church was originally built in 1770 by Portugese traders.

of King Taksin. The present church was constructed in 1910 and has a beautiful Italian-style ceiling. Church services are held on Sundays. ⏲ *30 min. 112 Thetsaban Sai I Rd, Thonburi.* ☎ *02 466 0347 or 02 472 0153 4. Daily 5.30–8.30am & 6–8pm. Ferry: Rajinee pier (N7).*

❹ Wichaiprasit Fort. This was built during the reign of Narai the Great (1656–1688) to protect the city from Burmese invaders. One hundred years later, after repulsing the Burmese, King Taksin built the Wang Derm Palace in the same compound when he chose Thonburi (the town west of the river) as his capital. Nowadays the Thai navy fires the cannon from the fort to celebrate special ceremonies. It is the naval banner you can see on the flagpole on top of the fort. Wang Derm Palace is open to the public, but the fort is not. ⏲ *30 min. 2 Royal Navy Headquarters, Phra Ratcha Wang Derm, Arun Amarin Rd,* *Thonburi.* ☎ *02 475 4117 or 02 466 9355. Admission 50 baht. Daily 8.30am–5pm. Ferry: Rajinee pier (N7).*

❺ ★★★ Wat Arun. On the west bank, just north of the tall Wat Kanlayanamit temple, is my favourite temple in Thailand—the Temple of Dawn, known in Thai as Wat Arun. This Hindu-inspired Khmer stupa becomes very photogenic both at sunrise and at sunset when the stonework changes to a mauve or orange hue. *See p 15, bullet* ❼.

❻ ★★★ The Grand Palace. Just north of Wat Arun is Bangkok's oldest temple, Wat Po (see p 19, bullet ❶), close to Tha Thien ferry pier (N8). The following pier on the east bank is Tha Chang (N9), meaning 'Elephant Pier', in reference to the days when flotillas of teak logs would be carried from the river to warehouses by the great tusked beasts. This is where to get off if you are visiting the Grand Palace.

An impressive line-up of golden Buddha figures at Wat Arun.

Travel Tip

You can get off the express boat and walk around ➋, ➌, ➍ and ➎ by changing at Rajinee Pier (N7) and taking a small cross-river boat to Wat Arun for just 3.5 baht. It's an interesting walk south from Wat Arun, taking you through modest backstreets. You will first pass Wat Kanlayanamit with its 15m-high Buddha. Then, take the waterfront boardwalk towards Santa Cruz Church. Hidden from view from the river, there's a small red Chinese temple called Wat Sanjaomaeguanim. Built in the 18th century, it shares Buddhist, Taoist and Confucianist influences. There are return boats to Rajinee from Wat Kanlayanamit Pier.

From the river you can get dazzling photographs of the golden spires, although much of the majesty is hidden behind a long white wall. On the west bank, you will see the imposing buildings of the Naval Harbour Department and the Quartermaster Department. *See p 11, bullet* ➌.

➐ **Wat Rakhang.** Sometimes called the Bell Temple for its collection of brass bells, this 18th-century *wat* houses an

The Grand Palace.

interesting teak library (where the ashes of King Rama I are interred) and murals depicting the Thai epic, *The Ramakien*. *See p 39, bullet* ⓭.

Ready for a Detour?

Running off to the west is Klong Bangkok Noi, the 'Small Bangkok Canal'. This canal can only be navigated as a separate tour by renting a longtail boat (approximately 800 baht per hour). It's a worthwhile trip. The canal winds its way in a 16km horseshoe around 'Small Bangkok' and comes out again at Nonthaburi (⓭). You'll pass several fine Thai houses, some squalid suburban homes on stilts and lots of temples. It's a wonderful opportunity to witness first-hand the real lifestyles of average Bangkokians. You can rent longboats at Phra Arthit pier (N13) and sometimes at Tha Chang pier (N9).

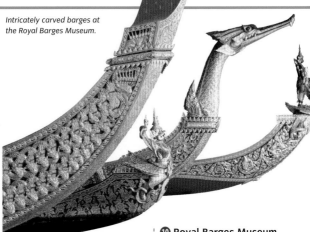

Intricately carved barges at the Royal Barges Museum.

❽ Thammasat University.
On the east bank of the river lies the historical area of Rattanakosin. There are several sights, but you need a separate day to take them in. If you were to jump off at Phra Chan pier, you could visit the National Gallery (see p 22, bullet ❺), the Bangkok National Museum (see p 21, bullet ❹), followed by Thammasat University, where many of the nation's elite were educated and which was the hub of political dissent in 1973 and 1976 when the army shot dead many students and protesters. *2 Prachan Rd. ☎ 02 613 3333. Ferry: Tha Phra Chan pier or change at Wang Lang pier (N10).*

❾ Museum of Forensic Science. It's definitely not my cup of tea, but if you have a fascination for the macabre you might want to spend an hour or two studying pathology via the remains of accident victims and exhibits of human parts kept in formaldehyde, including non-separated Siamese twins. Not for the squeamish. ⏱ *1 hr. Siriraj Hospital, Bangkok Noi. ☎ 02 419 7000. Admission free. Mon–Fri 8.30am–4.30pm. Ferry: Wang Lang pier (N10).*

❿ Royal Barges Museum.
A chance to see Thailand's famous historical royal barges. Used in royal ceremonies since the 18th century, the 50m-long royal longtail boats have been housed here under the care of the royal navy since 1932. *See p 15, bullet ❻.*

⓫ ★ Phra Sumen Fort. One of the two remaining forts still standing in Bangkok, Phra Sumen was built in 1783 by King Rama I to protect the Old City. From the river you can see the battlements and cannons and an observation tower. The fort was established at the confluence of the river and Banglamphu Canal, which carves an arc around the Old City, exiting further south at Memorial Bridge. With the river to the west, this canal effectively makes Rattanakosin an island. *Cnr Phra Arthit & Phra Sumeru rds. Daily 8am–8pm. Ferry: Phra Arthit pier (N13).*

⓬ Suan Santichai Prakarn.
This is a pleasant park to stretch your legs or relax and have a picnic. There are plenty of vendors around selling snacks and soft drinks. *Phra Arthit Rd. Ferry: Phra Arthit pier (N13). $.*

⓭ Nonthaburi. Next you go under the impressive Rama VIII Bridge (which looks like a giant golden harp lying on its side) and start heading north-east. You'll pass the Church of Holy Conception and St Francis Xavier Church, both further testaments to the prominent role of missionaries in 18th- and 19th-century Thailand. You'll notice that the river widens and becomes more industrial. You'll pass a jetty where old barges are moored, the Singha beer factory and the Bang Kwang Chinese temple just before you pull into Nonthaburi Pier. Now you have to decide whether to carry on to ⓮ and ⓯ or call it a day. You can get taxis back to town from Nonthaburi Pier or just take another express boat heading south. *Ferry: Nonthaburi Pier (N30).*

⓮ Bang Kwang Prison. The notorious 'Bangkok Hilton' hosts hundreds of foreign inmates, usually incarcerated for drug offences. Read Australian prisoner Warren Fellows's *The Damage Done* for a chilling insight into prison life here. It is not uncommon for tourists to visit their compatriots and take them some food, toiletries and magazines. *1 Nonthaburi Rd.* ☎ *02 525 0484. Mon–Fri 9.30–11.30am & 1.30–2:30pm. Ferry: Nonthaburi pier (N30).*

⓯ ★★★ Ko Kret. This enchanting little island on the river is home to hundreds of Mon—an ethnic group indigenous to the region. Some islanders grow lychees and durian in large orchards on the southern part of Ko Kret. Others are boatpeople. However, the most interesting and distinctive occupation of the Mon islanders is pottery-making. Perhaps 20 to 25 families maintain small factories where they sculpt red clay and fire earthenware in kilns, producing flower pots, mortars and larger water urns. The finished products have a red-black glaze; visitors are welcome to watch the potters and buy souvenirs. 🕑 *30 min. Ferry: Pakkret pier (N33).*

Get an impressive view of Wat Arun (p 58) from your ferry.

Chinatown

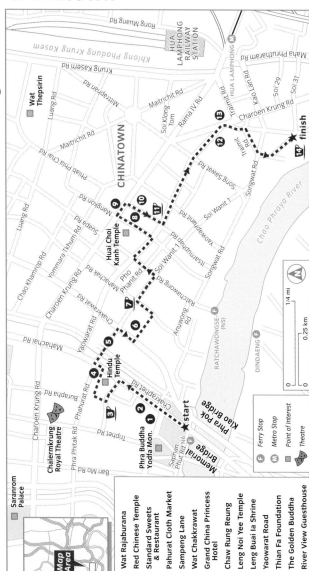

Rong Muang Rd

HUA LAMPHONG RAILWAY STATION

Khlong Phadung Krung Kasem

Maha Phruttharam Rd

Krung Kasem Rd

Maitrichit Rd

Mitrraphan Rd

Luang Rd

Wat Thepsirin

Trimit Rd

HUA LAMPHONG

Kao Lan Rd

Soi 29

Soi 31

Soi Khlong Tom

Rama IV Rd

Charoen Krung Rd

❸

Maitrichit Rd

Phlab Phla Chai Rd

CHINATOWN

❷

Trimit Rd

finish

❿

Song Swat Rd

Song Swat Rd

❾

Luang Rd

Mangkon Rd

Soi Eden

❽

❶⓪

❾

⓵

Huai Choi kanh Temple

Soi Wanit 1

Chao Khamrop Rd

Yommara Tkhum Rd

Charoen Krung Rd

Supa Rd

Mangkon Rd

Pho Phanit Rd

Soi Wanit 1

Tsarmphao Rd

Keowapharit Rd

Songwat Rd

Chakrawat Rd

Manachak Rd

❼

❻

Ratchawong Rd

Chao Phraya River

Mahachai Rd

Yaowarat Rd

❺

Hindu Temple

❹

Burapha Rd

Phahurat Rd

Chakraphet Rd

Aruwong Rd

RATCHAWONGSE (N5)

DINDAENG

¼ mi

0.25 km

Charoen Krung Rd

Chalermkrung Royal Theatre

Phra Phitak Rd

Triphet Rd

Phra Buddha Yodfa Mon.

❶

❷

❸

start

Chakraphet Rd

Phra Pok Kiao Bridge

Ban Mo Rd

Saphan Phut Rd N6

Memorial Bridge

Saranrom Palace

Map Area

Ⓕ Ferry Stop
Ⓜ Metro Stop
▪ Point of Interest
◢ Theatre

❶ Wat Rajaburana
❷ Red Chinese Temple
❸ Standard Sweets & Restaurant
❹ Pahurat Cloth Market
❺ Sampeng Lane
❻ Wat Chakkrawat
❼ Grand China Princess Hotel
❽ Chaw Rung Reung
❾ Leng Noi Yee Temple
❿ Leng Buai Ia Shrine
⓫ Yaowarat Road
⓬ Thian Fa Foundation
⓭ The Golden Buddha
⓮ River View Guesthouse

This three- to four-hour walk will take you on an adventure into the heart of Bangkok's Chinatown. It's where two great cultures, China and India, meet in harmony with an explosion of colours, smells and sights. Stroll through the bustling backstreets into the mystic temples and hidden shrines, and experience the lively banter of the marketplaces. Nothing here is polished for the tourist's benefit. I hope this walk will give you an insight into the real people of Bangkok, their rituals, idiosyncrasies and hard-working lifestyles. START: **Express boat to Memorial Bridge pier (Saphan Phut).**

Erawan, the Mount of Indra, at Wat Rajaburana.

1 Wat Rajaburana. This large, imposing Buddhist temple was built during the Ayutthaya period (1677–1767) by a Chinese merchant. I think it's a good introduction to temples, because the architectural style is typical of Bangkok Buddhist temples, with a high green roof accompanied by curved golden finials shaped like mythical *naga* serpents. On the east face under the awnings, you can see an intricate gilded facade guarded by three angels with a three-headed elephant known as Erawan, the Mount of Indra. 🕐 *15 min. Cnr Triphet & Chakkraphet rds. Daily 5am–8pm.*

2 Red Chinese Temple. You'll immediately notice the difference between a Thai temple and this typical Chinese shrine—*wat san chao*, as locals say. This temple represents the three main religions of China: Taoism, Buddhism and Confucianism. 🕐 *15 min. Chakkraphet Rd. Daily 6am–8pm.*

Chinese lanterns swing overhead at the Red Chinese Temple.

3 Standard Sweets & Restaurant.
Turn left 100m after the temple into a nice street lined with Indian shops selling spices, religious offerings, shawls and Indian foods. A simple diner sits next to another small red temple. It sells soft drinks, coffee, Indian masala tea and Indian sweets such as *gulab jaman*. *Soi Pahurat, 95/46–47 Chakkraphet Rd.* ☎ *086 708 1375. Daily 7am–7pm. $.*

4 ★ Pahurat Cloth Market.
Walk past the Sikh temple, Siri Guru Singh Sabha, and you find that you are in the middle of 'Little India'. Turn right and follow the narrow lane of vendors selling everything from satin saris and made-to-measure suits to Indian spices and Ayurvedic cures. 🕐 *15 min. Cnr Pahurat & Chakraphet rds. Daily 5am–9pm.*

5 ★★ Sampeng Lane.
(Also known as Soi Wanit.) The alleyway narrows and pedestrian traffic is slow and laboured as you squish and squeeze your way past shops and stalls that sell sweets, dried fruit, cheap jewellery, gold and gems, clothes, toys, steaming *dim sum* and much more. It's a kaleidoscope of chaos and a feast for the senses. 🕐 *30 min. Daily 6am–9pm.*

6 ★ kids Wat Chakkrawat.
Take a breather from the claustrophobic market and step into the compound of this simple temple. There's a fenced pond behind the temple with two huge crocodiles, plus a stuffed one in a glass case! 🕐 *15 min. Wanit Rd. Daily 5am–7pm.*

7 ★★ Grand China Princess Hotel.
After jostling your way through Sampeng Lane you surely deserve a break. Take the lift to the 25th floor of this hotel and you can sit in an air-conditioned restaurant that offers a magnificent 360-degree view of Bangkok. There are several hotels and rooftop restaurants higher than this, but the fact that you can see the Grand Palace and the Golden Mount from here makes this, in my opinion, the best view you can get of the city. The restaurant starts revolving at 6pm. The menu mainly offers Japanese, Chinese and seafood dishes. *215 Yaowarat Rd, Samphantawong.* ☎ *02 224 9977. Mon–Sat 11am–midnight, Sun 5pm–midnight. $$.*

8 Chaw Rung Reung.
On the right side of Mongkol Road you pass some open-front stores selling foods and spices. Look for one with large sacks of tea outside. There's green, jasmine, masala and many other authentic and aromatic teas. You can buy them by the half kilo. 🕐 *15 min. 609–611 Mongkol Rd.* ☎ *02 224 5240. Daily 8am–7pm.*

One of the residents of Wat Chakkrawat.

Leng Buai Ia Shrine, thought to be the oldest shrine in Thailand, is tucked away off Itsarnuphap Road.

⑨ ★★★ Leng Noi Yee Temple. Known in Thai as Wat Mangkol Kamalawat and in English as the Dragon Flower Temple, the magnificent Chinese Leng Noi Yee is the highest revered Mahayana Buddhist temple in Thailand. Built in 1871, the main shrine is guarded by gruesome giant 'guardians of the world' statues. Much praying to various shrines and icons goes on inside the temple, so be respectful. There are young boys—resident Chinese monks—who do chores. You'll see that they wear saffron-coloured pyjamas as opposed to robes. The temple is usually very busy with worshippers lighting lots of incense and candles and offering fruit, flowers and oil to the gods. One interesting thing to watch for is people buying what looks like Monopoly money, which is then burned as an offering on the basis that they can take the money with them into their next lives. This temple is especially popular at Chinese New Year (January to February). ⏲ *30 min. 423 Charoen Krung Rd. Daily 6am–6pm.*

⑩ Leng Buai Ia Shrine. With pungent whiffs of raw meat, fish, spices and roasted chestnuts at every turn, Itsarnuphap Road is a bustling alleyway straight out of a Hollywood set. Just 100m or so on the left, tucked quietly behind the marketplace, is a humble wee Chinese temple. This temple is thought to be the oldest shrine in Thailand, dating back to 1658. It is designed in Tae Chew style, which is Fujian, the origin of many of Bangkok's Chinese immigrants. ⏲ *15 min. Itsarnuphap Rd. Daily 7am–5pm.*

You'll find a multitude of teas for sale at Chaw Rung Reung.

Traditional Chinese clothing for sale on Yaowarat Road, Chinatown.

★ Yaowarat Road. There are several modest diners at the corner of Yaowarat and Plaengnarm roads serving bird's nest and shark's fin soup (although animal rights activists won't thank you). If you feel like a stop, why not just choose a steaming bowl of noodles? On the main street of Chinatown you are greeted by large signs in Chinese characters hanging over the street. As you cruise down the broad avenue, you'll pass gold retailers and Chinese medicine shops. *$.*

⑫ ★ Thian Fa Foundation. You are welcome to take a peek inside this Chinese medicine hospital, which was founded in 1902. The treatment centre, not surprisingly, has a shrine where patients pray for recovery. If you would like to say a prayer for good health—for yourself or for someone else—light an incense stick and a candle at the Kuan Si Yim shrine, where the four-faced Buddha sits. ⏱ *15 min. 606 Yaowarat Rd. ☎ 02 237 2190 4. Daily 7am–7pm.*

⑬ ★★ The Golden Buddha. The largest solid-gold Buddha image in the world is this 3m-high, 5.5 ton shimmering sculpture, which is housed in the 19th-century temple of Wat Traimit (see p 38, bullet ⑪) and is thought to date to the Sukhothai period (1238–1438). A new pavilion inside the compound, a *mondop*, recognisable by a towering golden spire, is due to be finished by the summer of 2009 and will thereafter house the enormous Buddha. ⏱ *15 min. Wat Traimit, cnr Mittaphap Thai-China & Yaowarat rds. Daily 8am–5pm.*

⑭ River View Guesthouse. From the Golden Buddha, it's just a 200m walk to the metro at Hua Lamphong Station. However, if you'd rather catch the express boat, turn right at what can only be called 'Greasy Mechanic Shops Junction' and head towards the river. River View Guesthouse is tricky to find, so ask locals. Head to the 8th-floor rooftop and put up your weary feet. Enjoy the view of the Chao Phraya River over a sandwich and coffee. *768 Soi Panurangsri, Songvad Rd. ☎ 02 234 5429. Daily 7am–10pm. $.* ●

Shopping **Best Bets**

Best **Antiques in an Antiquated House**
★★ House of Chao, *Decho Rd* (see p 72)

Best for **Buying an Engagement Ring in Secret**
Uthai's Gems, *28/7 Soi Ruam Rudi, Ploenchit Rd (see p 76)*

Best **Cameras**
★ Niks/Nava Import Export, *166 Silom Rd (see p 73)*

Best **Cheap Clothes That Will Last for Years**
★ Pratunam Market, *cnr Phetburi & Ratchaprarop rds (see p 78)*

Best **Designer Labels**
★★ Siam Paragon, *cnr Rama I & Phayathai rds, Siam Square (see p 74)*

Best **English Language Books**
★ Kinokuniya, *3rd floor, Emporium, Sukhumvit Soi 24 (see p 73)*

Most Likely Place to **Get Lost for a Day**
★★★ Chatuchak Market, *Phahonyothin Rd, Chatuchak (see p 77)*

Best **IT Supplies**
Pantip Plaza, *604/3 Petchaburi Rd, Pratunam (see p 75)*

Best **Made-to-Measure Suits for Men**
★★ Marco Tailors, *430/33 Soi 7, Siam Square (see p 79)*

Best for **Protection Against Evil Spirits**
Amulet Market, *Maharat Rd (see p 72)*

Best **Selection of Silk**
★★ Almeta, *20/3 Soi Prasarnmitr, Sukhumvit Soi 23 (see p 79)*

Best **Tie-Dye Shirts**
★ Khao San Road, *Banglamphu (see p 77)*

Best **Wedding Presents**
★★★ River City, *23 Trok Rongnamkhaeng, Bangrak (see p 79)*

Previous page: An array of colourful hats for sale at a Bangkok market.

Traditional silk dresses are a popular traveller purchase.

Sukhumvit Road Shopping

Almeta **4**

Asia Books **1**

Elite Used Books **5**

Emporium Shopping Centre **7**

Kai **9**

Kinokuniya **8**

L'Arcadia **3**

Robinson **2**

Villa Market **6**

Central Bangkok Shopping

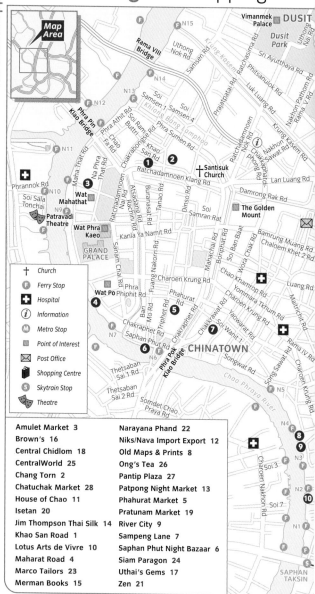

Map Area

Legend:

✝	Church
🄵	Ferry Stop
➕	Hospital
ⓘ	Information
Ⓜ	Metro Stop
▪	Point of Interest
✉	Post Office
🏬	Shopping Centre
Ⓢ	Skytrain Stop
🎭	Theatre

Amulet Market 3
Brown's 16
Central Chidlom 18
CentralWorld 25
Chang Torn 2
Chatuchak Market 28
House of Chao 11
Isetan 20
Jim Thompson Thai Silk 14
Khao San Road 1
Lotus Arts de Vivre 10
Maharat Road 4
Marco Tailors 23
Merman Books 15

Narayana Phand 22
Niks/Nava Import Export 12
Old Maps & Prints 8
Ong's Tea 26
Pantip Plaza 27
Patpong Night Market 13
Phahurat Market 5
Pratunam Market 19
River City 9
Sampeng Lane 7
Saphan Phut Night Bazaar 6
Siam Paragon 24
Uthai's Gems 17
Zen 21

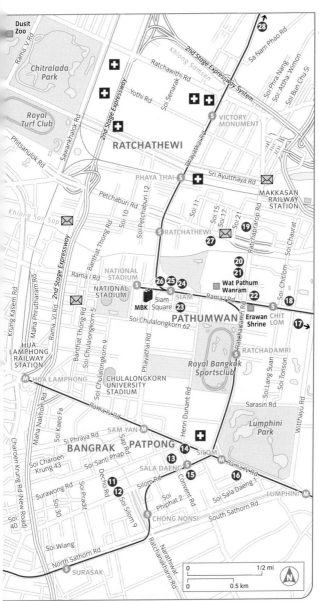

The Best Shopping

Bangkok Shopping A to Z

Amulets

Amulet Market RATTANAKOSIN
Even if you're not interested in buying a little Buddha to hang around your neck, this street market is an interesting circus of superstition and magic as Thais consult astrologers to see which Buddhist amulets to wear to ward off ghosts, diseases, debt and motorbike accidents. *Maharat Rd (north of the Grand Palace). No credit cards. No metro or ferry. Map p 70.*

Antiques

★★ House of Chao SILOM I love this three-storey colonial house. I just want to live here with all the antiques—from the chandeliers to the beds to the clocks and artwork. *Decho Rd.* ☎ *02 635 7188. AE, MC, V. Metro: Chong Nonsi or Sam Yan. Map p 70.*

★ L'Arcadia SUKHUMVIT For the discerning antique explorer, this is where you can sift through Khmer, Burmese and Thai pieces, including religious icons and wooden artefacts. *12/2 Soi Sukhumvit 23.* ☎ *02 259 9595. www.larcadia. net. AE, MC, V. Metro: Asok or Sukhumvit. Map p 69.*

Books

Asia Books SUKHUMVIT
This bookstore has a large selection of novels, travel guides and international newspapers. *221 Sukhumvit Rd (between Soi 19 & Soi 21).* ☎ *02 252 7277. www. asiabooks.com. AE, DC, MC, V. Metro: Asok or Sukhumvit. Map p 69.*

Elite Used Books SUKHUMVIT
Elite Used Books sells thousands of second-hand books in various languages at reasonable prices. *593–595 Sukhumvit Rd (between Soi 33 & Soi 35).* ☎ *02 258 0221. No credit cards. Metro: Phrom Phong. Map p 69.*

Some wares for sale at the Amulet Market.

★ **Kinokuniya** SUKHUMVIT This is my favourite store for browsing. You can find almost everything here: all the latest releases, maps, guides and books on Thailand. There's also a branch at the Isetan Centre. *3rd floor, Emporium, Soi Sukhumvit 24. ☎ 02 664 8554. www.kinokuniya.com. AE, MC, MC, V. Metro: Phrom Phong. Map p 69.*

★ **Merman Books** BANGRAK This store specialises in rare books, journals and anything you desire relating to Thailand and its culture. *4th floor, Silom complex, Silom Rd. ☎ 02 231 3300. AE, DC, MC, V. Metro: Sala Daeng or Silom. Map p 70.*

Antique Buddha statues are a popular souvenir, but you'll need to pay a visit to the Department of Fine Arts before you take one home.

Cameras

★ **Niks/Nava Import Export** BANGRAK This is the best place in the city for cameras, equipment and accessories, both digital and manual. A repair service is also available. *166 Silom Rd. ☎ 02 235 2929. www.niksthailand. com. AE, DC, MC, V. Metro: Chong Nongsi. Map p 70.*

Department Stores & Shopping Centres

kids **Central Chidlom** PATHUMWAN Seven air-conditioned storeys of cosmetics, international fashion and clothing stores, as well as children's toys, electronics, supermarkets, restaurants and much more. *1027 Ploenchit Rd. ☎ 02 655 7777. www.central. co.th. AE, DC, MC, V. Metro: Chit Lom. Map p 70.*

Taking Antiques Home

The people of Thailand are understandably sensitive about antique Buddhist statues and art leaving the country. Certificates must be ob-tained from the Department of Fine Arts for authentic Buddha images (over 200 years old) that you plan to export. However, this law is essentially applied to antique Buddhas that may have been taken from temples rather than amulets and objets d'art you might find in a market.

CentralWorld shopping mall is the place to see and be seen.

★ kids CentralWorld
PATHUMWAN The latest hip place for young socialites to shop is also the largest shopping mall in South-East Asia. It includes designer stores, 50 restaurants, 21 cinemas, a bowling alley and a kids' entertainment zone. *Siam Square, Rama I Rd.* ☎ *02 635 1111. www.centralworld.co.th. AE, DC, MC, V. Metro: Siam. Map p 70.*

Emporium Shopping Centre
SUKHUMVIT A mid-range assortment of fashion stores, souvenirs, Thai handicrafts, silk stores and food centres. *622 Sukhumvit Rd, Soi 24.* ☎ *02 269 1000. www.emporiumthailand.com. AE, DC, MC, V. Metro: Phrom Phong. Map p 69.*

Isetan PATHUMWAN This
Japanese-owned mall features an up-market selection of men's and women's clothes stores. *4/1–2 Ratchadamri Rd.* ☎ *02 255 9898 9. AE, DC, MC, V. Metro: Chit Lom. Map p 70.*

Robinson SUKHUMVIT Rather
than designer gear, Robinson pulls in shoppers for its reliable local brands and cheaper prices. There are also outlets on Silom Road, Ratchadaphisek Road and Seacon Square. *259 Sukhumvit Rd (between Soi 17 & Soi 19).* ☎ *02 651 1533. AE, DC, MC, V. Metro: Asok or Sukhumvit. Map p 69.*

★★ kids Siam Paragon
PATHUMWAN The trendiest place to be seen is this luxurious mega-complex. It features über-chic fashion stores, perfumeries, Starbucks, gourmet cafes and more. Note that there are cinemas and kids' entertainment on the top floor and Siam Ocean World is downstairs—great for those who are unwilling to shop for hours. *Cnr Rama I & Phayathai rds.* ☎ *02 690 1000. AE, DC, MC, V. Metro: Siam. Map p 70.*

The entrance to Siam Paragon, Bangkok's lavish mega-mall.

A traditional
tea in a traditional cup.

Zen PATHUMWAM Specialising in women's stores, this is where you'll find local and international labels at cheaper prices. *World Trade Centre, 4/1–2 Ratchadamri Rd.* ☎ *02 255 9669. AE, DC, MC, V. Metro: Chit Lom. Map p 70.*

Electronics

Pantip Plaza PATHUMWAN Not where I would personally hang out at weekends, but if you love electronics and computers this will be heaven. There are hundreds of vendors and bargains with on-the-spot servicing and upgrading. *604/3 Petchaburi Rd, Pratunam.* ☎ *02 251 9008. Most stores accept MC & V, but some are cash only. Metro: Ratchathewi or Chit Lom. Map p 70.*

Fashion

Brown's LUMPHINI Hallelujah! A full range of 'outsize' clothing for women who find Thai sizes too petite. Brown's also has an outlet

at Emporium. *1st floor, U Chia-Liang Building, Rama IV Rd, opp. Lumphini Park.* ☎ *02 632 4424. AE, DC, MC, V. Metro: Silom or Sala Daeng. Map p 70.*

Kai SUKHUMVIT Leading fashion designer Chatri Teng-Ha creates provocative and bold attire for ladies. Kai specialises in delicate fabrics such as cotton, linen and chiffon in subtle shades. *1st floor, Emporium, Sukhumvit Rd, Soi 24.* ☎ *02 664 8000 ext. 1533. AE, DC, MC, V. Metro: Phrom Phong. Map p 69.*

Food & Drink

Ong's Tea PATHUMWAN Take a break at Ong's and sample some of his majestic tea leaves from China, Japan and, of course, Thailand. Ceramic tea ceremony sets are available. *4th floor, Siam Discovery Centre, Rama I Rd.* ☎ *02 658 0445. AE, MC, V. Metro: Siam. Map p 70.*

This traditional Thai handicraft, known as Benjarong ware, is porcelain painted with enamel and gold. The name 'Benjarong' means 'five colours'.

★★ Villa Market
SUKHUMVIT This delicatessen is my—and many other expats'—favourite retreat in Bangkok when in desperate need of cheeses, olives, wines, salami, tortillas, Vegemite and other imported goodies from afar. There are several outlets of this place around town. *595 Sukhumvit Rd, Soi 33. ☎ 02 662 1000. www.villamarket.com. AE, DC, MC, V. Metro: Phrom Phong. Map p 69.*

Handicrafts
★ Narayana Phand PRATUNAM
I always buy souvenirs here before heading home. You can find an eclectic variety of good-quality handicrafts and artefacts, perfect to take home to friends and family. *7th floor, President Tower (Inter-Continental Hotel), 973 Ploenchit Rd. ☎ 02 656 0398 9 or02 656 0400. www.naraiphand.com. AE, DC, MC, V. Metro: Chit Lom. Map p 70.*

Jewellery & Gems
Uthai's Gems PLOENCHIT
Due to the dark nature of this business, I am loath to recommend tourists to the seedy world of gemstones. However, Uthai appears to be the most honest broker in Bangkok, and can custom design jewellery for you with rubies, sapphires and emeralds. *28/7 Soi Ruam Rudi, Ploenchit Rd. ☎ 02 253 8582. AE, MC, V. Metro: Ploenchit. Map p 70.*

Maps
★ Old Maps & Prints
BANGRAK I love this little cubbyhole; it stocks some great old maps of Thailand and Asia, navigational charts and engravings. Heaven for map lovers! *4th floor, River City Complex, Si Phaya Pier, Yotha Rd. ☎ 02 237 0077 8. AE, MC, V. Metro: Saphan Taksin. Map p 70.*

VAT Refunds

As a tourist, you can get 7 per cent of the cost of your purchases refunded at customs when you are leaving Thailand. But you have to jump through a few hurdles: the refund only applies at shops that have 'VAT refund for tourists' signs; each purchase must cost more than 2000 baht and the total must be more than 5000 baht; and you must present your passport and fill in a VAT refund form with the sales assistant.

Markets

★★★ Chatuchak Market

CHATUCHAK Perhaps half a million people visit this market every weekend. With 15 000 stalls you can expect to find everything—from clothes, plants and household goods to live snakes, Buddhist antiques, herbal medicines, CDs and hill-tribe handicrafts. *Phahonyothin Rd. No credit cards. Metro: Kampaeng Phet. Map p 70.*

★ Khao San Road

BANGLAMPHU It's hippy heaven on Bangkok's backpacker boulevard. Tie-dye T-shirts, floppy hats, baggy pants, second-hand books, cheap jewellery, CDs, fake student cards and some of the best wee souvenirs you can buy for less than 100 baht. *Khao San Rd. No credit cards. No metro. Map p 70.*

★★ Patpong Night Market

SILOM Competing with go-go bars and seedy shows on Thailand's most famous street are countless stalls of Thai souvenirs and counterfeit goods, especially watches and designer labels. This is the place to get haggling. *Patpong Rd. No credit cards. Metro: Silom or Sala Daeng. Map p 70.*

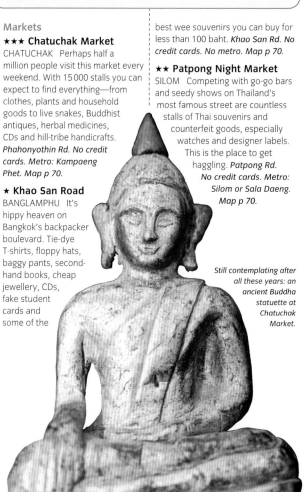

Still contemplating after all these years: an ancient Buddha statuette at Chatuchak Market.

Bargaining

Haggling is fun! It's an acceptable part of Thai culture, so don't take it as an affront. Smile and be playful. My personal tip is not to start haggling until you are sure you want to buy something, otherwise the canny market vendors will simply throw an inflated price at you to get a reaction. 'What?' you scream. '500 baht just for this?' 'Okay', mellows the salesperson. 'So, how much do you want to pay?' And next thing you know you are haggling for an Akha hill-tribe hat that you will never wear. Remember: you can bargain at any outdoor market or Chatuchak, but not in department stores.

You'll find both modern and traditional souvenirs at Bangkok's markets.

★ **Phahurat Market** PHAHURAT Little India meets Chinatown at this colourful market. Silks, textiles and saris are for sale, as well as Indian spices. *Cnr Phahurat & Thiphet rds. No credit cards. Map p 70.*

★ **Pratunam Market** PRATUNAM This is the place to get cheap clothes, whether it be fake designer gear or sturdy local garments. *Cnr Phetburi & Ratchaprarop rds. No credit cards. Metro: Chit Lom. Map p 70.*

Sampeng Lane CHINATOWN This narrow alley is everything you would expect of a Chinese backstreet—bustling, loud and dirty. However, you might find a gemstone or a herbal concoction that you cannot resist. *Soi Wanit 1, Ratchawong Rd. No credit cards. Metro: Hua Lamphong. Map p 70.*

Saphan Phut Night Bazaar CHINATOWN Located on either side of the Memorial Bridge on the Chao Phraya River, this 24-hour down-to-earth market offers late-night snacks, cheap clothes and other discounted goods. *Saphan Phut Rd. No credit cards. No metro. Map p 70.*

The lotus flower is an important symbol for Buddhists, representing purity of the mind and body.

A selection of the enormous array of silken goods will make great souvenirs: small and light enough to squeeze into your suitcase.

Menswear

★★ Chang Torn BANGLAMPHU
There are a lot of Indian tailors around Banglamphu offering great deals on suits (with free ties and shirts included). However, you must be very careful—many of the stores are fronts for sweatshops and the quality is poor. Chang Torn is experienced, unassuming and reliable. Prices are higher than at many other tailors, but it's well worth it. *95 Tanao Rd.* ☎ *02 282 9390. MC, V. No metro. Map p 70.*

★★ Marco Tailors SIAM SQUARE
The best in made-to-measure men's cotton suits, especially for conservative styles. Note that you will need two weeks and two fittings. *430/33 Soi 7, Siam Square.* ☎ *02 251 7633. AE. Metro: Siam. Map p 70.*

Objets d'Art

★★ Lotus Arts de Vivre
BANGRAK You will be dazzled by the exquisite and intricately designed jewellery and home decor at this high-end boutique. There is also a branch at Four Seasons Hotel on Ratchadamri Road. *Mandarin Oriental Hotel, 48 Oriental Ave.* ☎ *02 236 0400. www. lotusartsdevivre.com. AE, DC, MC, V. Metro: Saphan Taksin. Map p 70.*

★★★ River City BANGRAK
This is a high-end complex, managed by the Mandarin Oriental, that offers objets d'art, antiques and handicrafts to treasure. *23 Trok Rongnamkhaeng, Si Phaya Pier, Yotha Rd.* ☎ *02 237 0077. AE, MC, V. Metro: Saphan Taksin. Map p 70.*

Silk

★★ Almeta SUKHUMVIT The creator of 'à la carte' silk shopping, Almeta offers a choice of some 50 000 colours and weaves in the finest Thai and Chinese silk for gorgeous made-to-measure gowns, kimonos and suits. *20/3 Soi Prasarnmitr, Soi Sukhumvit 23.* ☎ *02 204 1413. www.almeta. com. AE, DC, MC, V. Metro: Asok or Sukhumvit. Map p 69.*

★★ Jim Thompson Thai Silk
BANGRAK You still can't beat Jim Thompson's after all these years. It's a wonderland of lustrous colours and fabrics. Everybody in your life deserves a silken gift from JT's. *9 Surawong Rd.* ☎ *02 632 8100 4. www.jimthompson.com. AE, DC, MC, V. Metro: Sala Daeng or Silom. Map p 70.*

Traditional Medicines
Maharat Road

RATTANAKOSIN A series of small, dark Chinese stores line the street and entice passers-by with jars of exotic creatures and the aromatic scents of magical herbs and spices. *Running along the river, west of Wat Po, near Tha Tien pier. No credit cards. No metro. Map p 70.* ●

You might not be able to read the label, but these herbal remedies should cure any ailments.

The Conscientious Shopper

Many visitors to the Land of Smiles worry how much blood, sweat and tears go into the making of the cut-price clothes and handicrafts they buy. Some believe Bangkok's suburbs to be dark slums where tiny orphans toil in sweatshops night and day. In fact, such a Dickensian scenario is rarely reported in Thailand nowadays, but there's no 100 per cent guarantee. The copyright laws are unenforced, so you will come across counterfeit DVDs, sunglasses, designer handbags and much more at marketplaces. That is not to say they're poor quality—many of the fake items are excellent and will last years—but of course if it's cut-price and bootlegged it's made by lowly paid factory workers. Tailors that offer made-to-measure suits will often send the measurements to factories to make them. Many factory workers are Burmese migrants, but few are children.

If you want to guarantee that your purchases help the people who make the products, look out for OTOP or Royal Project signs. OTOP—One *Tambon* (village), One Product—is a system of encouraging rural villages to undertake community projects producing handicrafts, furniture, woodcrafts, lacquerware, ceramics, candles, etc. Profits from sales return to the respective villages. Royal Projects mainly centre on agriculture. Hill-tribe villages in northern Thailand have been pushed to abandon opium production in favor of growing coffee, strawberries, and other organic fruit and vegetables. These cooperative projects are sanctioned by the Thai royal family.

Lumphini Park

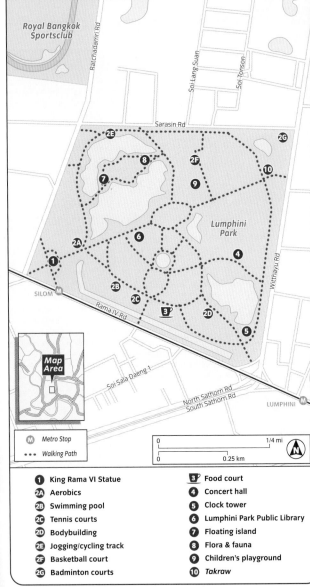

1	King Rama VI Statue	**3**	Food court
2A	Aerobics	**4**	Concert hall
2B	Swimming pool	**5**	Clock tower
2C	Tennis courts	**6**	Lumphini Park Public Library
2D	Bodybuilding	**7**	Floating island
2E	Jogging/cycling track	**8**	Flora & fauna
2F	Basketball court	**9**	Children's playground
2G	Badminton courts	**10**	*Takraw*

Previous page: An abundance of colourful flora such as this can be found in Bangkok's delightful gardens.

An oasis of greenery in the heart of Bangkok's business and shopping districts, Lumphini Park is where hundreds of Bangkokians seek refuge every day. It's a hive of activity with Tai Chi, aerobics, bodybuilding and jogging all going on first thing in the morning. In the evening, office workers shed their ties and don shorts to play *takraw*—a Thai version of foot-tennis with a rattan ball—while children fly kites and young lovers stroll hand-in-hand around the lake enjoying ice-cream. This charming park, often referred to as the 'Lungs of Bangkok', is open every day from 4am to 9pm. START: **Metro to Silom.**

❶ King Rama VI Statue.

King Rama VI, or King Vajiravudh, presented Lumphini Park (which is named after the Nepalese village where the Buddha was born) to the people of the city in 1925. A statue of the king stands outside the south-western entrance to the park, near the junction of Ratchadamri and Rama IV roads. 🕐 *5 min. Metro: Silom.*

❷ Sports.

Feel free to join in group **2A aerobics**, usually held every day at 6am and 6pm. Sessions are free, but you should drop some coins in a collection box. There's a **2B swimming pool** (daily 7am–7.30pm), which costs just 40 baht for a year's membership. Unfortunately, foreigners are

obliged to produce their passports and a medical certificate to gain a membership. There are four all-weather **2C tennis courts** (daily 7am–8pm; 35 baht per hour), however, you have to bring your own racquet. There's a small outdoor **2D bodybuilding** zone with free weights, which costs just 25 baht for an hour. An asphalt **2E jogging/cycling track** winds its way for about 3 to 4km around the park. Behind the children's playground you'll find a **2F basketball court**. In the northeastern corner of the park, you'll find **2G badminton courts**, which are free to the public. Again, you must bring your own equipment. 🕐 *1½ hr.*

Open-air health classes are a daily happening at Lumphini Park.

3 Food court. The only place in the park that sells food is this small plaza. There's a selection of about 10 stalls selling noodles, rice dishes, sweets and snacks. You can also buy soft drinks and beer.

4 Concert hall. There are free concerts at 5pm every Sunday from February to April at this outdoor amphitheatre. The Bangkok Symphony Orchestra even makes an appearance a couple of times a year. There's also an indoor hall for concerts in front of the tennis courts, which is used during the rainy season. 🕐 *1 hr.*

5 Clock tower. This Chinese-style structure was built for the 1925 trade fair. It is situated at the south-western corner of the park (near Lumphini metro station). You can rent paddle boats or rowing boats here (80 baht per hour) and buy food for feeding the fish. 🕐 *5 min.*

Rent one of these playful paddle boats and take a tour around the lake at Lumphini Park.

Lumphini Park is endowed with native plants from all over Thailand, including this palm tree.

6 Lumphini Park Public Library. This was the first public library in Thailand. It has 30 000 books and has opened audio and visual exhibits and services to the public. 🕐 *15 min.*

7 Floating island. So called because it is artificial, this shaded area is ideal for picnics, sunbathing or finding some cool shade. There's a small botanical garden and usually lots of elderly Thai-Chinese chatting away, cooking lunch, playing chess or practicing martial arts. 🕐 *30 min.*

8 Flora & fauna. King Rama VI arranged for examples of native plants from all regions of the country to be planted here as an educational exercise. Many trees and shrubs are marked with the names. Birdwatchers will be pleased to know that migrating birds head for the forests and ponds in Lumphini Park every year. You might see or hear oriental magpie robins, coppersmith barbets, pied fantails, mynas, bulbuls, doves, flycatchers and warblers around the lakes. 🕐 *30 min.*

A small shrine in Lumphini Park.

9 Children's playground. This is a safe, enclosed area for young children and toddlers with rides, slides and climbing frames. ⏱ *30 min.*

10 Takraw. Near the north-eastern corner of the park you can find teenagers playing football, basketball and, most interestingly, the Thai national sport of *takraw*. It's like volleyball with no hands, usually played between two teams of three players each. They use a hard rattan ball and you will be amazed by the flexibility and agility of many players as they overhead-kick the ball and still land on their feet. ⏱ *30 min.*

Bangkok's 'Green Lung'

Lumphini Park truly is one of the few outdoor places in Bangkok where it is possible to (almost) escape the noise and traffic of the city.

You can rent a rowboat to paddle around the lake, or simply find a spot to yourself and relax before the heat of the day kicks in. On Saturday and Sunday evenings you can enjoy some cool jazz music in the park before heading to more nightlife at Patpong.

Dusit Park

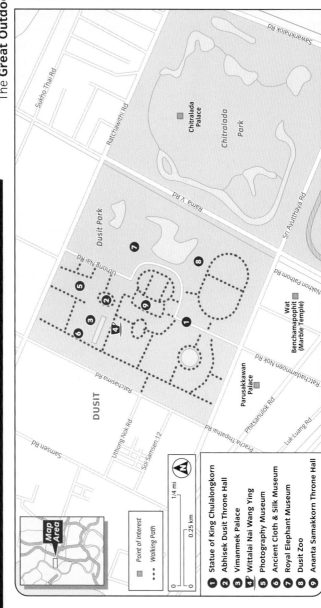

1 Statue of King Chulalongkorn
2 Abhisek Dusit Throne Hall
3 Vimanmek Palace
4 Wittalai Nai Wang Ying
5 Photography Museum
6 Ancient Cloth & Silk Museum
7 Royal Elephant Museum
8 Dusit Zoo
9 Ananta Samakkorn Throne Hall

Point of Interest
Walking Path

Map Area

0   1/4 mi
0   0.25 km

In my opinion, Dusit Park is Bangkok's most underrated attraction. The gardens are delightful, the architecture sublime. Inspired by his travels to Europe, King Chulalongkorn (also known as King Rama V; 1868–1910) designed Dusit Park and ordered that manicured gardens and stately homes be built within its grounds. He then moved his entire family there from the Grand Palace. Today, the Thai king lives at Chitralada Palace, next to Dusit Park. Visitors have to pay 100 baht (50 baht for kids) to enter the park, which includes admission to the stately attractions within. However, if you're canny, you'll visit the Grand Palace first, keep the ticket and use it to get free admission to Dusit Park and its sights. Please note that if you wish to visit Vimanmek Palace, you have to wear long sleeves and no shorts or skirts above the knees. START: **Express boat to Tha Thewet pier. Walk/taxi to junction of Ratchadamnoen Road and Sri Ayutthaya Road.**

The Abhisek Dusit Throne Hall in Dusit Park.

❶ Statue of King Chulalongkorn. You will see the dashing mustachioed portrait of King Chulalongkorn—perhaps the most fondly remembered of Thailand's kings—adorning the walls of half the houses in Thailand. He was a great moderniser and had a penchant for all things European. He abolished slavery, introduced a cabinet-style government and skillfully avoided French and British colonialism. He died in 1910 aged 57, having fathered at least 77 children to four queens and numerous concubines. This memorial of King Rama V on horseback overlooks the entrance to the park. ⏱ *5 min.*

❷ ★ Abhisek Dusit Throne Hall. The red-tile Moroccan villa just across a canal from the Vimanmek Palace used to host state functions for foreign ambassadors during the early part of the 20th century. It was restored and reopened by the current king and queen in 1993 and now houses arts and crafts produced in Thailand under a royal foundation. ⏱ *30 min. Admission 50 baht. Daily 9am–4pm.*

❸ ★★★ Vimanmek Palace. Resembling a Victorian mansion, this beautiful three-storey golden teak mansion was built using wooden pegs instead of nails. Compulsory guided tours leave every 30 minutes; try to time your visit to catch free performances of Thai dance and martial arts in the lakeside pavilion at 10.30am and 2pm daily. ⏱ *1 hr. See p 22, bullet* ❼.

4 Wittalai Nai Wang Ying. Of the two canteens in the park, this one at the Women's College is the better option, with tasty Thai dishes, drinks, desserts and cakes. *1st floor, Administration Building (behind Tourist Information).* ☎ *02 628 6300, ext 5185. Daily 10.30am–3.30pm. $.*

❺ Photography Museum. Most of the photographs here were taken by the current king, Bhumibhol, who is an avid photographer. Many of the pictures are of the royal family. ⏱ *30 min. Daily 9.30am–3.15pm.*

❻ Ancient Cloth & Silk Museum. If you have time, take a quick stroll around this charming French-style building and see different silks and textiles from around Thailand, and the robes of kings Rama IV and V. ⏱ *15 min. Daily 9.30am–3.15pm.*

❼ Royal Elephant Museum. Formerly a stable for three 'albino' elephants, this small exhibition tells the tales and superstitions regarding elephants in Thailand, especially white elephants, which are considered holy and must be presented to the king. ⏱ *30 min. Daily 9.30am–3.15pm.*

❽ ★★ kids Dusit Zoo. Just east of Dusit Park, with an entrance to the north, is Thailand's premier zoo. Over 300 species of animal dwell here. Avoid visiting on weekends— it gets crowded. ⏱ *2 hr. See p 43, bullet* ❼.

❾ ★ Ananta Samakkorn Throne Hall. This exquisite marble hall was built in Italian Renaissance style by the king in 1907 to receive foreign dignitaries. Check out the frescoes on the domed ceiling depicting the succession of Thai kings. ⏱ *15 min. Daily 8.30am–4.30pm.* ●

Sun bears are most commonly found in the rainforests of South-East Asia, but you can also see these silky-sleek animals at the Dusit Zoo.

Dining **Best Bets**

Best **Anniversary Present**
★★★ The Manohra $$$$ *Bangkok Marriott Resort & Spa, 257 Charoen Nakorn Rd (p 102)*

Most **Authentic Chinatown Experience**
★ Hua Seng Hong $$$ *371–373 Yaowarat Rd (p 98)*

Best **Chinese**
★★ The Chinese Restaurant $$$ *Grand Hyatt Erawan Hotel, 494 Ratchadamri Rd (p 96)*

Best **Classic Indian**
★ Rang Mahal $$$$ *Rembrandt Hotel, 19 Soi 18, Sukhumvit Rd (p 104)*

Best Place to **Dine Like a Siamese King**
★ Benjarong $$$$ *Dusit Thani Hotel, 946 Rama IV Rd (p 95)*

Best **Fast Food Escape**
Oh My Cod! $$ *95D Rambuttri Village Inn, Soi Rambuttri, Chakrapong Rd (p 103)*

Most **Futuristic Dining Scenario**
★★ Bed Supperclub $$$$ *26 Soi 11, Sukhumvit Rd (p 94)*

Best **Homemade Italian Meal**
★★★ La Piola $$$ *31/4 Soi 11, Sukhumvit Rd (p 100)*

Best **Japanese**
★★★ Koi $$$ *26 Soi 20, Sukhumvit Rd (p 99)*

Best **Meal for $1**
Kuaytiaw Reua Tha Siam $ *Siam Square Soi 3, Rama I Rd (p 99)*

Best **Meal for $30**
★★★ Eat Me $$$ *Soi Phiphat 2 (p 97)*

Best **'Once-in-a-Lifetime' Dinner for Two**
★★★ Le Normandie $$$$$ *Mandarin Oriental Hotel, 48 Oriental Rd (p 101)*

Most **Romantic Dinner**
★ Deck by the River $$$ *Arun Residence, 36–38 Soi Pratoo Nok Yooung, Maharaj Rd (p 97)*

Best **Steak**
New York Steakhouse $$$$ *JW Marriott Hotel, 4 Soi 2, Sukhumvit Rd (p 103)*

Best **Traditional Thai Dinner for Two**
★ Thiptara $$$$ *Peninsula Hotel, 333 Charoen Nakorn Rd (p 108)*

Best **Views of Bangkok by Night**
★★ Sirocco $$$$$ *The Dome at State Tower, 1055 Silom Rd (p 106)*

Previous page: The popular meal of satay.

Thai desserts make a delicious end to any meal.

Sukhumvit Road Dining

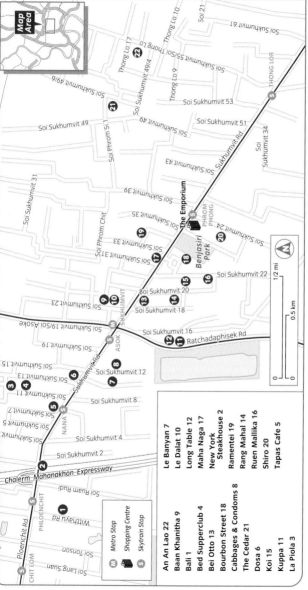

An An Lao 22
Baan Khanitha 9
Bali 1
Bed Supperclub 4
Bei Otto 13
Bourbon Street 18
Cabbages & Condoms 8
The Cedar 21
Dosa 6
Koi 15
Kuppa 11
La Piola 3

Le Banyan 7
Le Dalat 10
Long Table 12
Maha Naga 17
New York
Steakhouse 2
Ramentei 19
Rang Mahal 14
Ruen Mallika 16
Shiro 20
Tapas Cafe 5

Metro Stop
Shopping Centre
Skytrain Stop

The Best Dining

Central Bangkok Dining

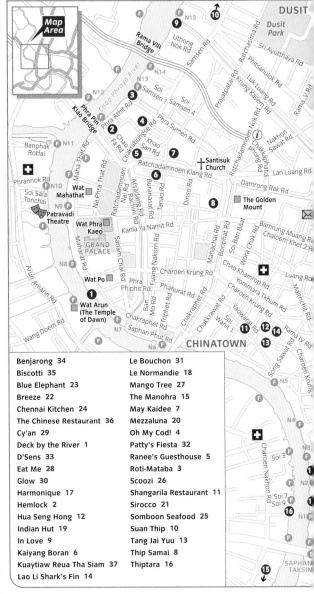

Benjarong 34	Le Bouchon 31
Biscotti 35	Le Normandie 18
Blue Elephant 23	Mango Tree 27
Breeze 22	The Manohra 15
Chennai Kitchen 24	May Kaidee 7
The Chinese Restaurant 36	Mezzaluna 20
Cy'an 29	Oh My Cod! 4
D'Sens 33	Patty's Fiesta 32
Deck by the River 1	Ranee's Guesthouse 5
Eat Me 28	Roti-Mataba 3
Glow 30	Scoozi 26
Harmonique 17	Shangarila Restaurant 11
Hemlock 2	Sirocco 21
Hua Seng Hong 12	Somboon Seafood 25
Indian Hut 19	Suan Thip 10
In Love 9	Tang Jai Yuu 13
Kaiyang Boran 6	Thip Samai 8
Kuaytiaw Reua Tha Siam 37	Thiptara 16
Lao Li Shark's Fin 14	

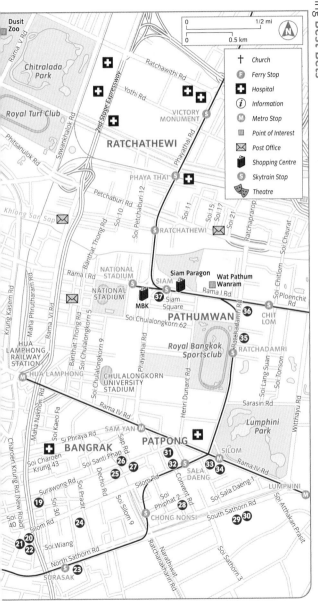

Dusit Zoo

Chitralada Park

Royal Turf Club

Phitsanulok Rd

Rama V Rd

2nd Stage Expressway

Sawankhalok Rd

Ratchawithi Rd

Yothi Rd

Ratchaprarop Rd

VICTORY MONUMENT

RATCHATHEWI

Phayathai Rd

PHAYA THAI

Petchaburi Rd

Soi Petchaburi 12

Soi 10

Soi 11

Soi 15
Soi 17

Soi 21

Khlong San Sap

RATCHATHEWI

Banthat Thong Rd

Rama I Rd

NATIONAL STADIUM

NATIONAL STADIUM

Siam Paragon

Wat Pathum Wanram

SIAM

Rama I Rd

MBK

37 Siam Square

Soi Chaurat

Soi Chitlom

Ploenchit Rd

CHIT LOM

36

Krung Kasem Rd

Maha Phrutharam Rd

Maha Phrutharam Rd

Rama VI Rd

Banthat Thong Rd

Soi Chulalongkorn 5

Soi Chulalongkorn 9

Phayathai Rd

PATHUMWAN

Soi Chulalongkorn 62

Royal Bangkok Sportsclub

Ratchadamri Rd

35

RATCHADAMRI

HUA LAMPHONG RAILWAY STATION

HUA LAMPHONG

CHULALONGKORN UNIVERSITY STADIUM

Rama IV Rd

Henri Dunant Rd

Soi Lang Suan

Soi Torson

Sarasin Rd

Lumphini Park

Withayu Rd

Maha Nakhon Rd

Soi Kaeo Fa

Si Phraya Rd

SAM YAN

San Rd

PATPONG

SILOM

Sarasin Rd

Rama IV Rd

LUMPHINI

Charoen Krung Rd (New Road)

Soi Charoen Krung 43

BANGRAK

Soi Santi Phap

Decho Rd

Surawong Rd

Soi Pradit

26

27

25

Silom Rd

Soi Silom 9

31

32

SALA DAENG

33 34

Convent Rd

SALA DAENG

Soi Sala Daeng 1

Soi 30

Soi 40

19

24

Soi Phiphat 2

28

CHONG NONSI

South Sathorn Rd

29 30

LUMPHINI

Soi Atthakan Prasit

21

20

22

Soi Wiang

Silom Rd

North Sathorn Rd

23

SURASAK

Ratchadamri Rd

Narathiwat Rd

Soi Sathorn 3

Legend:

† Church
F Ferry Stop
✚ Hospital
ⓘ Information
Ⓜ Metro Stop
◾ Point of Interest
✉ Post Office
📖 Shopping Centre
Ⓢ Skytrain Stop
🎭 Theatre

0   1/2 mi
0   0.5 km

Bangkok Dining A to Z

★★ An An Lao KLONG TOEY *CHINESE* Ever heard of Betong chicken? (Neither had I.) The recipe comes from a Chinese town in southern Thailand—the savoury chicken is served cold and complemented with watercress. You know this place must be good when you see Chinese people queuing up to come in. *331/1–3 Soi Thong Lo (Soi 55), Sukhumvit Rd. ☎ 02 392 6447. Meals 350 baht. AE, MC, V. Lunch & dinner daily. Metro: Thong Lo. Map p 91.*

★★ Baan Khanitha SUKHUMVIT *THAI* As good an introduction to traditional Thai cuisine as you can get. Signature dishes include prawns in tamarind sauce, soft-shell crab curry, pomelo salad and roast duck and grape red curry. There's another location at 69 South Sathorn Road that is equally good. *36/1 Soi 23, Sukhumvit Rd. ☎ 02 258 4128. Meals 700–900 baht. AE, MC, V. Lunch & dinner daily. Metro: Ploen Chit. Map p 91.*

Bali PATHUMWAN *INDONESIAN* To my knowledge this is the sole Indonesian restaurant in Bangkok and it has quickly developed a grateful following. Fruity favourites such as the jackfruit curry and *gado-gado* (vegetables in a peanut satay sauce) make for a distinctly different Asian option. *15/3 Soi Ruamdee. ☎ 02 250 0711. Meals 500 baht. AE, MC, V. Lunch & dinner Mon–Sat. Metro: Ploen Chit. Map p 91.*

Delicious dim sum can be found at many Bangkok restaurants.

★★ Bed Supperclub SUKHUMVIT *INTERNATIONAL* Ready for midnight fusion cuisine served as breakfast-in-bed inside a white spaceship full of supermodels? What can I say—it's young, trendy and overpriced, but infectiously glamorous. Reserve in advance or no chance. *26 Soi 11, Sukhumvit Rd. ☎ 02 651 3537. Meals 1000–1500 baht. AE, DC, MC, V. Dinner Fri & Sat, served promptly at 8.30pm. Metro: Nana. Map p 91.*

★ Bei Otto SUKHUMVIT *GERMAN* Solid portions of pork knuckle, sauerkraut, liver sausage, potato salad and frothy white beer make this is a favourite for those craving a rice-free meal. Otto's also has a good delicatessen and bakery attached. *1 Soi 20, Sukhumvit Rd, Klong Toey. ☎ 02 262 0892. Meals 800–1000 baht. AE, MC, V. Lunch & dinner daily. Metro: Sukhumvit or Asok. Map p 91.*

These dumplings are among some of the imaginative and dignified offerings at the Blue Elephant.

★ **Benjarong** BANGRAK *ROYAL THAI* You should feel like royalty when you dine here—the service is exemplary, and the decor is refined under the subtle glow of chandeliers. The recipes here were, at one time, served only to the Thai royal family. *Dusit Thani Hotel, 946 Rama IV Rd, cnr Silom Rd, Lumphini.* ☎ *02 236 0450. Meals 1000 baht. AE, DC, MC, V. Lunch & dinner daily. Metro: Silom or Sala Daeng. Map p 92.*

Biscotti PATHUMWAN *ITALIAN* This is Italian with elegance, from the polished wooden floors to the open-view kitchen to the delicate little antipasti offerings such as tuna tartare, duck-liver terrine and roasted scallops. *The Four Seasons Hotel, 155 Ratchadamri Rd.* ☎ *02 251 6127. Meals 1000 baht. AE, DC, MC, V. Lunch & dinner daily. Metro: Ratchadamri. Map p 92.*

Blue Elephant SATHORN *ROYAL THAI* A very dignified colonial-style enterprise, which has even exported this cuisine (originally created only for the Thai royal family) to branches in Europe and the Middle East. The menu includes a selection of delicate culinary delights from around Thailand. *233 South Sathorn Rd.* ☎ *02 673 9353. Set menus 1300–1450 baht. AE, DC, MC, V. Lunch & dinner daily. Metro: Surasak. Map p 92.*

Bourbon Street SUKHUMVIT *AMERICAN* This is as much a social club as a restaurant and has a faithful following for its Tex-Mex dishes, barbecued ribs and New Orleans/ Creole-style crayfish, gumbo and jambalaya. *29/4–6 Soi 22, Washington Square, Sukhumvit Rd, Klong Toey.* ☎ *02 259 0328 9. Meals 500–800 baht. AE, DC, MC, V. Breakfast, lunch & dinner daily. Metro: Phrom Phong. Map p 91.*

Breeze BANGRAK *SEAFOOD* You enter via a neon-lit glass walkway 51 storeys above the city. If that doesn't take your breath away, the prices certainly will. Breeze is unashamedly ostentatious, but the wasabi prawns and poached lobster are melt-in-the-mouth delicious and the desserts are to die for. *lebua at State Tower, 1055 Silom Rd, cnr Charoen Krung Rd.* ☎ *02 624 9555. Meals 3000–5000 baht. AE, DC, MC, V. Lunch & dinner daily. Metro: Saphan Taksin. Map p 92.*

When you visit The Cedar you can enjoy the best Middle Eastern cuisine in Bangkok while appreciating the Bedouin-style interior.

Cabbages & Condoms

SUKHUMVIT *THAI* You might dine at this curious franchise just to check out the 'safe sex' theme that is exhibited. Nonetheless, the meals are certainly fresh and wholesome—the green curry, chicken wrapped in pandan leaves and coconut soup are all delicious. *10 Soi 12, Sukhumvit Rd.* ☎ *02 229 4611. Meals 400 baht. AE, DC, MC, V. Lunch & dinner daily. Metro: Asoke or Sukhumvit. Map p 91.*

★★ **The Cedar** SUKHUMVIT *LEBANESE* The best Middle Eastern restaurant in the city, The Cedar has been around for some 30 years. The restaurant's interior is designed like a large Bedouin tent—quite funky. The menu offers solid Lebanese favourites such as falafel, humus, kebabs and racks of lamb, but also has some Greek dishes—dolmades, feta and moussaka. *6/1 Soi 49/9, Sukhumvit Rd, Klong Toey.* ☎ *02 714 7206. Meals 600–800 baht. AE, DC, MC, V.*

Lunch & dinner daily. Metro: Phrom Phong. Map p 91.

Chennai Kitchen BANGRAK *INDIAN* If you've never been to India before, this is as authentic as it gets. Not the creamy kormas you get back home, this is natural spiced southern Indian fare, which can be served on a banana leaf and scooped up with handfuls of roti and naan. And it's near the Hindu temple. *10 Pan Rd, Silom.* ☎ *02 234 1266. Meals 100 baht. No credit cards. Lunch daily. Metro: Chong Nonsi or Surasak. Map p 92.*

★★ **The Chinese Restaurant** PATHUMWAN *CHINESE* Despite the unimaginative name, there is plenty of imagination about this restaurant's Cantonese cuisine, modern decor and classy setting. I recommend the baked lobster and chicken marinated in Chinese wine. *Grand Hyatt Erawan Hotel, 494 Ratchadamri Rd.* ☎ *02 254 1234. Meals 1000 baht. Lunch & dinner daily. Metro: Chit Lom. Map p 92.*

★ **Cy'an** SATHORN *INTERNATIONAL*
Aussie chef Daniel Moran thinks
up the rich, dainty nouveau cuisine
for both Cy'an and Glow in the
Metropolitan Hotel. The crayfish
and lobster are from Australia, the
scallops and salmon from Scotland,
the wine French and the ambience
designer chic. *Metropolitan Hotel,
27 South Sathorn Rd, Silom.*
☎ *02 625 3333. Meals 2000–3000
baht. AE, DC, MC, V. Breakfast, lunch
& dinner daily. Metro: Silom or Sala
Daeng. Map p 92.*

★ **Deck by the River**
RATTANAKOSIN *THAI/
INTERNATIONAL* With fresh, healthy
Thai fare and a few western dishes,
the Deck offers intimate dining on
an open-air wooden terrace. Go
at sunset to gaze at the changing
hues of the Temple of Dawn. *Arun
Residence, 36–38 Soi Pratoo Nok
Yooung, Maharaj Rd.* ☎ *02 221
9158. Meals 800–1400 baht. AE, MC,
V. Lunch & dinner daily. No metro.
Map p 92.*

★ **Dosa** SUKHUMVIT *INDIAN/
VEGETARIAN* A small air-
conditioned diner that caters to
aficionados of Indian cuisine (and
vegans) with authentic dishes from
around the country. I recommend
the *paneer tikka*, the *bhindi do
piazza* and, of course, the *Punjabi*

*Eat Me restaurant
provides modern
Australian cuisine for
homesick visitors.*

dosa. 153/7 Soi 11/1, Sukhumvit Rd.
☎ *02 651 1700. Meals 300 baht. AE,
MC, V. Lunch & dinner daily. Metro:
Nana. Map p 91.*

★★★ **D'Sens** BANGRAK *FRENCH*
Designed by three-star Michelin
chefs and regularly hosting visiting
Michelin chefs, this is an exquisite
restaurant with great views over
Lumphini Park and the city. I
recommend the blue lobster terrine,
the roasted duck breast and the
chocolate soufflé. *22nd floor, Dusit
Thani Hotel, 946 Rama IV Rd, cnr
Silom Rd, Lumphini.* ☎ *02 200 9000.
Meals 2000–2500 baht. AE, DC, MC,
V. Lunch Mon–Fri, dinner Mon–Sat.
Metro: Silom or Sala Daeng.
Map p 92.*

★★★ **Eat Me** BANGRAK *MODERN
AUSTRALIAN* Dare I call this 'haute
cuisine for the budget diner'? I guess
so. Personally, I love it. If you can
live without chandeliers and silver
service, and concentrate on the
delicious Modern Australian–cum-
Mediterranean cuisine, you're in
for a treat—it's excellent value for
money. Try the mouthwatering rack
of lamb. *Soi Phiphat 2 (off Convent
Rd), Silom.* ☎ *02 238 0931. Meals
600–800 baht. MC, V. Dinner daily.
Metro: Sala Daeng or Silom.
Map p 92.*

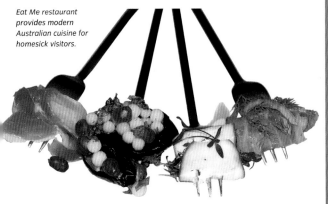

★ **Glow** SATHORN *HEALTH CUISINE* Fine dining with a holistic kick—chef Daniel Moran rustles up low-calorie, healthy haute cuisine. Try the fennel salad with lip-smacking Japanese dressing and the Australian trout. *Metropolitan Hotel, 27 South Sathorn Rd, Silom.* ☎ *02 625 3333. Meals 2000–3000 baht. AE, DC, MC, V. Breakfast, lunch & dinner daily. Metro: Silom or Sala Daeng. Map p 92.*

Harmonique BANGRAK *THAI* Mouthwatering seafood by the riverfront. Unfortunately it's not well known and quite hard to find. Look for the big banyan tree by an old colonial mansion. Harmonique is in the courtyard. Try the fish *tom yum*—so good it'll make you cry! *22 Soi 34 (Soi Wat Muang Kae), Charoen Krung Rd.* ☎ *02 237 8175. Meals 600–800 baht. AE, MC, V. Lunch & dinner Mon–Sat. Metro: Saphan Taksin. Map p 92.*

Hemlock BANGLAMPHU *THAI* Don't be put off by the modest shopfront exterior—this place is well known for its wholesome traditional

fare, incorporating recipes from across Thailand that include plenty of herbs and spices. *56 Phra Arthit Rd.* ☎ *02 282 7507. Meals 400–600 baht. Dinner daily. MC, V. No metro. Map p 92.*

★ **Hua Seng Hong** CHINATOWN *CHINESE* This busy diner is what I imagine the backstreets of Hong Kong to have been like in the 1930s, with sizzling woks, skinned geese hanging from the ceiling and the entire food production on display. I highly recommend the roast duck, *dim sum* and bird's nest soup. *371–373 Yaowarat Rd.* ☎ *02 222 0635. Meals 500–600 baht. MC, V. Lunch & dinner daily. Metro: Hua Lamphong. Map p 92.*

Indian Hut BANGRAK *INDIAN* Plenty of vegetarian choices, Punjabi and Goan specialties and hot vindaloo to choose from. Wine is available. *311/2–5 Surawong Rd, Silom.* ☎ *02 635 7876. Meals 600–700 baht. AE, DC, MC, V. Lunch & dinner daily. Metro: Surasak. Map p 92.*

Glow offers food that is both good for your body and satisfying for your taste buds.

Challenge your stomach: deep-fried insects can be found at many street food stalls in Bangkok.

★★ In Love DUSIT *SEAFOOD*
Refurbished in a chic minimalist design, In Love is an inexpensive option for soft-shell crab, king prawns, grilled fish and spicy sauces, and commands a stunning view over the river. *Tha Thewet pier, Krung Kasem, Thewet.* ☎ *02 281 2900. Meals 500–700 baht. AE, MC, V. Lunch & dinner daily. No metro. Map p 92.*

Kaiyang Boran BANGLAMPHU
ISAAN You must try north-eastern Thai (Isaan) food at least once! The sticky rice, chillis, papaya salad, fermented fish and eye-watering sauces make for a distinctly unique Thai experience. *474–476 Tanao Rd.* ☎ *02 622 2349. Meals 200–300 baht. No credit cards. Lunch & dinner daily. No metro. Map p 92.*

★★★ Koi SUKHUMVIT *JAPANESE*
As an aficionado of Japanese cuisine, it is with some gravitas that I pronounce Koi the number-one Japanese restaurant in town. It's chic, romantic and thoroughly sensual. Apart from the sushi and (melt-in-your-mouth) sashimi, most dishes are done with an exquisite international touch. *26 Soi 20, Sukhumvit Rd.* ☎ *02 258 1590. Meals 1600–2000 baht. AE, MC, V. Dinner daily. Metro: Sukhumvit or Asok. Map p 91.*

Kuaytiaw Reua Tha Siam SIAM
SQUARE *THAI Kuay tiaw* (Thai noodle soup) is quick, cheap and tasty, so if you are unsure about eating from street stalls here is a clean diner with fresh vegetables where you can slurp up Thailand's most popular dish. *Siam Square Soi 3, Rama I Rd.* ☎ *02 252 8353. Meals 40 baht. No credit cards. Breakfast, lunch & dinner daily. Metro: Siam. Map p 92.*

Anyone for Cricket?

At many marketplaces or along Sukhumvit and Khao San roads you may well encounter vendors offering deep-fried grasshoppers, grubs, scorpions and beetles. In north-eastern Thailand they are considered a good source of protein—and they don't taste that bad. If you want to take the plunge, I recommend the deep-fried beetles—they're just like crunchy, crispy chicken wings.

Kuppa SUKHUMVIT *THAI/ INTERNATIONAL* There's a bit of everything here with Thai, Chinese, Italian and French cuisines competing to sate your appetite. Kuppa is popular at lunchtime, perhaps because of the strong aromatic coffee that the hostess, Robin, grinds up. *39 Soi 16, Sukhumvit Rd, Klong Toey.* ☎ *02 663 0450. Meals 600–1000 baht. AE, MC, V. Lunch & dinner Tues–Sun. Metro: Sukhumvit or Asok. Map p 91.*

★ **Lao Li Shark's Fin** CHINATOWN *CHINESE* Garishly decorated, this busy diner nevertheless offers great traditional Chinese fare. I recommend any of the goat's meat specials with pan-fried mixed vegetables. Or how about sea cucumber? *457–461 Yaowarat Rd, cnr Padung Dao Rd.* ☎ *02 223 0325. Meals 500 baht. MC, V. Lunch & dinner daily. Metro: Hua Lamphong. Map p 92.*

★★★ **La Piola** SUKHUMVIT *ITALIAN* My favourite Italian restaurant in the world! *Mamma Mia!* You cannot get more homely and authentic than this—even if you were in Tuscany. You have the choice of three set menus, everything lovingly prepared fresh and savoury by 'mamma'. Go quickly before everyone discovers it! *31/4 Soi 11, Sukhumvit Rd.* ☎ *02 250 7270. Set meals 900–1200 baht. AE, MC, V. Lunch Mon–Sat, dinner daily. Metro: Nana. Map p 91.*

★ **Le Banyan** SUKHUMVIT *FRENCH* Sophisticated and traditional, this is a good choice for dining alfresco by candlelight in a lush garden on a cool evening. Unfortunately, the service is somewhat effusive, but connoisseurs of fine French cuisine won't be disappointed. *59 Soi 8, Sukhumvit Rd.* ☎ *02 253 5556. Meals 2000–3000 baht. AE, DC, MC, V. Dinner Mon–Sat. Metro: Nana. Map p 91.*

Le Bouchon PATPONG *FRENCH* This cozy wee bistro is curiously located in the heart of the red-light area, but manages to offer a romantic ambience. I recommend gorging on the starters—goat's cheese, pâté, frog's legs, niçoise salad and much more. *37/17 Patpong Soi 2, Silom.* ☎ *02 234 9109. Meals 800–900 baht. AE, DC, MC, V. Lunch & dinner daily. Metro: Sala Daeng or Silom. Map p 92.*

Kuppa, on Sukhumvit Road, serves up cuisine from around the world.

Le Dalat SUKHUMVIT *VIETNAMESE*
This old Thai house is decorated
with Vietnamese and Chinese
antiques and has a charming air. I
recommend *bi guon* (pork spring
rolls), *naem nuang* (wrapped
meatballs with mango) and Hanoi-
style fish. *14 Soi 23, Sukhumvit Rd.*
☎ *02 661 7967. Meals 500–
700 baht. AE, DC, MC, V. Lunch &
dinner daily. Metro: Sukhumvit or
Asok. Map p 91.*

★★★ **Le Normandie** BANGRAK
FRENCH Gracing the top floor of
what is arguably the greatest hotel
in the world, this dazzling restaurant
is the epitome of fine dining. The
superb menu is frequently updated
by visiting Michelin chefs. Jackets
are required for gents in the
evening. The excellent buffet lunch
is just 1050 baht. *Mandarin Oriental
hotel, 48 Oriental Rd.* ☎ *02 659
9000. Meals 2500–5000 baht. Lunch
Mon–Sat, dinner daily. AE, DC, MC,
V. Metro: Saphan Taksin. Map p 92.*

*For fantastic French food, visit
Le Normandie at the Mandarin Oriental.*

Long Table. SUKHUMVIT
INTERNATIONAL I haven't dined
here yet, but since it opened in
mid-2008 Long Table has been
recommended to me independently
by three culinary experts in
Bangkok. It's reputed to be chic,
sophisticated and expensive,
specialising in Thai fusion and

Thai Dining Etiquette

Thai people have very high standards of hygiene and politeness.
A few rules of thumb:
• When sharing several dishes in the centre of the table, remember that once you put your fork or spoon in your mouth you
  can no longer use it to help yourself from the common bowls.
  Each dish should have its own ladle.
• Chopsticks are used in Chinese restaurants or to eat noodles;
  plain rice is eaten with a spoon; only sticky rice is eaten with
  your hand.
• If you invite others to dinner, it will probably be assumed that
  you are paying. In a small group, the most 'senior' person nor-
  mally picks up the tab.
• Tipping is not obligatory.

The Manohra dining cruise boats, which are converted rice barges, offer excellent food with an ever-changing background.

contemporary fine dining. It's high on my 'to do' list. *25th floor, the Column Residence, Sukhumvit Soi 16.* ☎ *02 302 2557 9. Meals 1500–2000 baht. AE, DC, MC, V. Lunch daily. Metro: Asok. Map p 91.*

Maha Naga SUKHUMVIT *FUSION* East meets west in the kitchen of this elegant Thai pavilion. A quiet, gentle ambience offset by fountains, and Thai-western concoctions such as pork chops in spicy papaya salad and grilled fillet in a spicy mint sauce make for a romantic evening. *2 Soi 29, Sukhumvit Rd, Klong Toey.* ☎ *02 662 3060. Meals 1000–1200 baht. AE, DC, MC, V. Lunch & dinner daily. Metro: Phrom Phong. Map p 91.*

★★ **Mango Tree** BANGRAK *THAI* An excellent choice if you are in Bangkok for just one evening, because the food is rich and spicy (I recommend the duck dishes and *tom yum* soup) and the ambience

is classical Siamese with traditional music and charming service. *37 Soi Tantawan (opp. Tawana Ramada Hotel).* ☎ *02 236 2820. Meals 750–850 baht. AE, DC, MC, V. Lunch & dinner daily. Metro: Sala Daeng. Map p 92.*

★★★ **kids** **The Manohra** CHAO PHRAYA *THAI* One night in Bangkok? Why not wine and dine by candlelight and moonlight on a converted rice barge cruising on the Chao Phraya River? And an excellent dinner it is, too. (It also does lunches, but it's just too hot!). The barge picks up diners at Taksin pier and the Marriott; call to reserve. *Bangkok Marriott Resort & Spa, 257 Charoen Nakorn Rd, Thonburi.* ☎ *02 476 0022. Set menu 1990 baht (not including wine/drinks). AE, DC, MC, V. Cruises leave the Marriott at 7pm & Taksin pier at 7.30pm daily. Metro: Saphan Taksin. Map p 92.*

★ **May Kaidee** BANGLAMPHU *VEGETARIAN* Although tucked down an alley, everyone knows smiling May and her excellent vegetarian/vegan diner with lots of coconut curries and sour soups to choose from. May offers a Thai vegetarian cooking school for foreigners. There's also a branch at 33 Samsen Road. *Behind Burger King, Tanao Rd.* ☎ *086 398 4808. Meals 100 baht. No credit cards. Breakfast, lunch & dinner daily. No metro. Map p 92.*

★ **Mezzaluna** BANGRAK *ITALIAN* While most Italian restaurants aspire to be homely, Mezzaluna focuses squarely on elegance and sophistication. Its high ceilings allow for panoramic views across Bangkok, but unlike its brothers in the State Tower, Breeze and Sirocco, this is fine dining indoors, so you don't get quite the same feeling of vertigo. Divine seafood dishes and caviar are on offer. *State Tower, 1055 Silom Rd, cnr Charoen Krung Rd.* ☎ *02 624 9555. Meals 2000–2500 baht. AE, DC, MC, V. Metro: Saphan Taksin. Map p 92.*

New York Steakhouse SUKHUMVIT *AMERICAN* If you are homesick for a thick, juicy steak, barbeque pork ribs or other comfort foods, this is a dream come true. Mind you, it's not fast food here— it's rather posh, in fact! *2nd floor, JW Marriott Hotel, 4 Soi 2, Sukhumvit Rd.* ☎ *02 656 7700. Meals 1500 baht. AE, DC, MC, V. Dinner daily. Metro: Nana. Map p 91.*

Oh My Cod! BANGLAMPHU *FISH AND CHIPS* Thailand is a culinary delight, yet you might inexplicably find yourself craving good old fish and chips or sausage, beans and fried bread. Well, your prayers are answered at Oh My Cod! *95D Rambuttri Village Inn, Soi Rambuttri, Chakrapong Rd.* ☎ *02 282 6553. Meals 350–450 baht. Breakfast, lunch & dinner daily. No metro. Map p 92.*

You're sure to feel welcome from the moment you set foot inside vegetarian/vegan restaurant May Kaidee.

★ kids Patty's Fiesta

PATPONG *MEXICAN* For me, Mexican should never be a fine-dining experience, but more of a slapstick colourful cantina with a mariachi band, margaritas, sizzling fajitas and a carnival ambience. And that's Patty's! It's in Patpong, too, so expect *muchisimo* revelry. *109–111 Patpong Soi 1 (cnr Silom Rd), Bangrak. ☎ 02 632 7898. Meals 800–900 baht. AE, DC, MC, V. Lunch & dinner daily. Metro: Sala Daeng. Map p 92.*

Ramentei SUKHUMVIT

JAPANESE Fans of *ramen* (Japanese meat-based noodle soups) will flock to this bustling diner, which is understandably popular with Japanese expats at lunchtime. *593/23–24 Soi 33/1, Sukhumvit Rd. ☎ 02 662 0050. Meals 200 baht. No credit cards. Lunch & dinner daily. Metro: Phrom Phong. Map p 91.*

Ranee's Guesthouse

BANGLAMPHU *VEGETARIAN* A backpacker's favourite. I often head to Ranee's not only for the shaded courtyard and the healthy Thai vegetarian dishes, but also for the freshly baked breads and cakes. *77 Trok Mayom, behind Chakrapong Rd. ☎ 02 282 4072. Meals 300 baht. No credit cards. Breakfast, lunch & dinner daily. No metro. Map p 92.*

★ Rang Mahal SUKHUMVIT

INDIAN Fine dining and Indian cuisine are not often found together in Thailand, but this rooftop restaurant is elegant and chic, and offers a sumptuous selection of culinary delights from every corner of India. Try the tender grilled lamb marinated in rum, herbs and spices. *Top floor, Rembrandt Hotel, 19 Soi 18, Sukhumvit Rd. ☎ 02 261 7100. Meals 1000 baht. AE, MC, V. Lunch & dinner daily. Metro: Sukhumvit or Asok. Map p 91.*

You'll find sweets in all shapes, sizes and colours in Bangkok.

Every detail has been attended to at Ruen Mallika, a converted teak house where beautifully presented food is served by charming wait staff.

★ **Roti-Mataba** BANG–
LAMPHU *MUSLIM* A popular backpacker haunt offering halal meat, Thai massaman curry and stuffed Indian pancakes. *136 Phra Arthit Rd. ☎ 02 282 2119. Meals 250–350 baht. No credit cards. Breakfast, lunch & dinner Tues–Sun. No metro. Map p 92.*

kids Ruen Mallika SUKHUMVIT *THAI* An old Siamese teak house converted into a pleasant tourist-friendly restaurant serving the full range of traditional Thai favourites, beautifully presented by charming wait staff. *Soi Sedhi, 89 Soi 22, Sukhumvit Rd, Klong Toey. ☎ 02 663 3211. Meals 800–900 baht. AE, DC, MC, V. Lunch & dinner daily. Metro: Asoke or Sukhumvit. Map p 91.*

Scoozi BANGRAK *ITALIAN*
If you're on the lookout for pizzas, Scoozi has three outlets in Bangkok (also at Khao San Road and Sukhumvit Soi 55), all serving thin-crust pizzas baked in wood-fired ovens, as well as good lobster bisque, parma ham and Argentinean steaks. *174 Surawong Rd, Silom. ☎ 02 234 6999. Meals 800–900 baht. AE, DC, MC, V. Lunch & dinner daily. Metro: Chong Nonsi. Map p 92.*

Shangarila Restaurant
CHINATOWN *CANTONESE*
A banquet-sized eating hall for banquet-sized portions of steaming *dim sum* and fried Cantonese specialties. *306 Yaowarat Rd. ☎ 02 224 5933. Meals 500 baht. MC, V. Lunch & dinner daily. No metro. Map p 92.*

The ornate plaque for the Scoozi restaurants.

Shiro SUKHUMVIT *JAPANESE*
You'll get good value at this modest Japanese diner, which has a small sushi bar and tables for dining. Delicate sashimi, good sushi platters, fried fish and warm soups make for an especially great lunch. *21 Soi 24, Sukhumvit Rd, Klong Toey.* ☎ *02 258 7016. Meals 500–600 baht. AE, MC, V. Lunch & dinner daily. Metro: Phrom Phong. Map p 91.*

★★ Sirocco BANGRAK
INTERNATIONAL Of the State Tower's trinity of high-end restaurants (Sirocco, Breeze and Mezzaluna), I would say Sirocco is the best. It's majestically situated on the edge of a glass tower high above the city, but still manages to offer the relaxing ambience of a live jazz venue. Exquisite entrees such as guinea chicken stuffed with foie gras and truffles should remind you this is a once-in-a-lifetime experience. *The Dome at State Tower, 1055 Silom Rd, cnr Charoen Krung Rd.* ☎ *02 624 9555. Meals 2000–3000 baht. AE, DC, MC, V. Lunch & dinner daily. Metro: Saphan Taksin. Map p 92.*

★ Somboon Seafood
BANGRAK *SEAFOOD* I would call this a seafood warehouse, with masses of tables overflowing with lobster shells and beer bottles, dozens of wait staff crisscrossing the floor and an aquarium of live crabs, prawns, fish and crustaceans for you to peruse. Do not miss the curry-paste crab! Branches also at Ratchadaphisek Road, Sukhumvit Soi 103 and Samyan. *169/7–11 Surawong Rd (cnr Ratchanakharin Rd), Silom.* ☎ *02 233 3104. Meals 600–1000 baht. No credit cards. Dinner daily. Metro: Chong Nonsi. Map p 92.*

★★ Suan Thip. NONTHABURI
THAI I was once out in Nonthaburi and found this wonderful restaurant, serving excellent traditional Thai food set in a lush garden on the river. Try the massaman chicken curry. *Changwattana Pak Kret 3 Rd (Soi Wat Koo), Bang Pood.* ☎ *02 583 3748. www.suanthip.com. Meals 500–600 baht. AE, DC, MC, V. Lunch & dinner daily. No metro. Map p 92.*

Somboon Seafood, a warehouse of piscine delights, serves these yam cakes.

Bangkok street food is tasty, cheap, hot and eaten by people of all demographics and social classes.

Tang Jai Yuu CHINATOWN
CHINESE My Chinese-Thai friends love this place for the seafood and, in particular, the barbecue-grilled fresh fish (chosen from a fish tank). *85–89 Yaowaphanit Rd.* ☎ *02 224 2167. Meals 500–600 baht. No credit cards. Lunch & dinner daily. Metro: Hua Lamphong. Map p 92.*

★ **Tapas Cafe** SUKHUMVIT
SPANISH Every time I walk in here there's a fiesta atmosphere. Maybe it's the open-plan design, the fruity sangria or the salsa and Latino tunes. All your Spanish favourites—Serrano ham, Manchego cheese and chorizo sausage—are available on the extensive menu. *1/25 Soi 11, Sukhumvit Rd.* ☎ *02 651 2947. Meals 600–900 baht. AE, MC, V. Lunch & dinner daily. Metro: Nana. Map p 91.*

Street Stalls?

Travellers love to scare each other with ghastly tales of exotic street food that crawled off the plate or that left a customer in a hotel toilet for two weeks. The truth is there's not much wrong with Bangkok's street fare. It's nearly always hygienic, cheap and pretty darn tasty. You don't have to walk far in this city before your senses get hit by sizzling spices, garlic, ginger, barbecued pork and noodles. All Bangkokians eat fried rice or noodle soup in the street at least once or twice a week. You should pull up a plastic stool and give it a go!

Follow this sign for delectable home-style Thai food and panoramic views of the city and Chao Phraya River.

Thip Samai PHRA NAKORN *THAI*
I have no idea why, but visitors to Thailand seem to go nuts for *pat thai* (fried egg noodles and peanuts). If you suffer from a similar disposition, you will be drawn to Thip Samai. *313 Maha Chai Rd, opp. Golden Mount.* ☎ *02 221 6280. Meals 50 baht. No credit cards. Dinner daily. No metro. Map p 92.*

This tasty-looking meal is a typical Thai curry, known as panaeng gai.

★ **Thiptara** THONBURI *THAI* This is Thai home-style cooking at its finest, served delightfully in open-air teak pavilions by candlelight with a panoramic view of the city and the Chao Phraya River by night. Don't miss the *polamai nam pung*, a feast of Thai fruits roasted in honey, chilli and vanilla. *Peninsula Hotel, 333 Charoen Nakhon Rd.* ☎ *02 861 2888. Meals 1400–1600 baht. AE, DC, MC, V. Dinner daily. Metro: Saphan Taksin. Map p 92.* ●

Nightlife Best Bets

Best Aussie Pub
The Office Bar & Grill,
Soi 33, Sukhumvit Rd (p 116)

Best Blues Bar
★★★ Ad Here the 13th,
13 Samsen Rd (p 119)

Best British Pub
Black Swan, *326/8–9 Sukhumvit Rd
(p 115)*

Best Champagne at Sunset
★★★ Moon Bar at Vertigo,
21/100 South Sathorn Rd (p 116)

Best Chance to Bump
into Supermodels
★★★ Bed Supperclub, *26 Soi 11,
Sukhumvit Rd (p 121)*

Best Hip-Hop Club
★★★ Tuesdays at Bed Supperclub,
26 Soi 11, Sukhumvit Rd (p 121)

Best Jam Sessions
★★ Overtone Music Cave,
29/70–72 Royal City Ave (p 120)

Best Jazz Club
★ Brown Sugar,
231/20 Sarasin Rd (p 119)

Best Margaritas
Coyote on Convent,
1/2 Convent Rd (p 115)

Best Party Atmosphere
★★★ Q Bar, *34 Soi 11,
Sukhumvit Rd (p 122)*

Best Smoking Lounge
Bamboo Bar, *Mandarin Oriental
Hotel, 48 Oriental Ave (p 119)*

Best Trance/Techno Club
★ Club Ibiza, *Hotel Intercontinental,
973 Ploenchit Rd (p 121)*

Best Views of Bangkok by
Night
★★★ Sky Bar at Sirocco,
*63rd floor, lebua at State Tower,
1055 Silom Rd (p 117)*

Best Wine Bar
★ Bacchus, *20/6–7 Soi Ruam Rudi
(p 122)*

*Previous page: The night lights
of Chinatown.*

*You can't beat the views from Moon Bar
at Vertigo—and the drinks aren't bad,
either.*

Greater Bangkok Nightlife

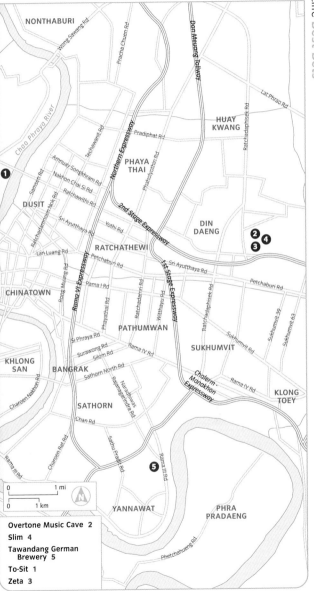

Overtone Music Cave **2**

Slim **4**

Tawandang German
  Brewery **5**

To-Sit **1**

Zeta **3**

Central Bangkok Nightlife

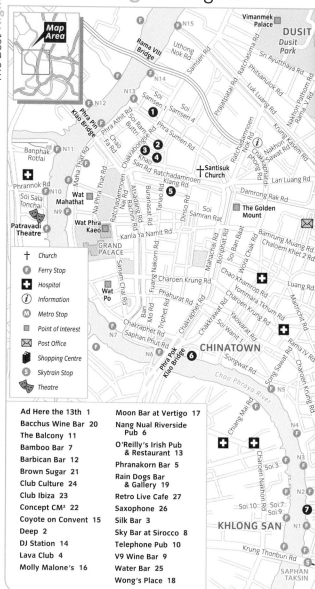

Map Legend

†	Church
	Ferry Stop
	Hospital
(i)	Information
(M)	Metro Stop
	Point of Interest
✉	Post Office
	Shopping Centre
(S)	Skytrain Stop
	Theatre

Ad Here the 13th 1
Bacchus Wine Bar 20
The Balcony 11
Bamboo Bar 7
Barbican Bar 12
Brown Sugar 21
Club Culture 24
Club Ibiza 23
Concept CM² 22
Coyote on Convent 15
Deep 2
DJ Station 14
Lava Club 4
Molly Malone's 16

Moon Bar at Vertigo 17
Nang Nual Riverside Pub 6
O'Reilly's Irish Pub & Restaurant 13
Phranakorn Bar 5
Rain Dogs Bar & Gallery 19
Retro Live Cafe 27
Saxophone 26
Silk Bar 3
Sky Bar at Sirocco 8
Telephone Pub 10
V9 Wine Bar 9
Water Bar 25
Wong's Place 18

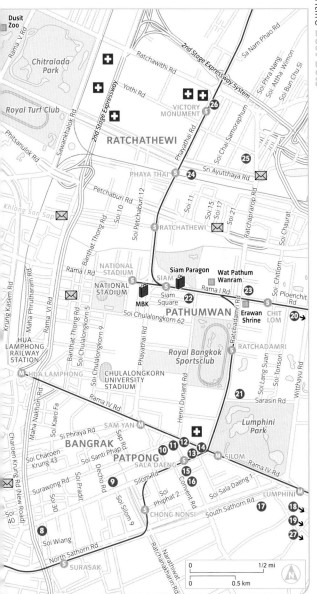

Sukhumvit Road Nightlife

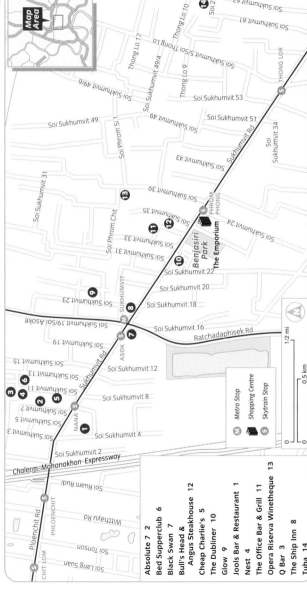

Absolute 7 **2**
Bed Supperclub **6**
Black Swan **7**
Bull's Head &
  Angus Steakhouse **12**
Cheap Charlie's **5**
The Dubliner **10**
Glow **9**
Jools Bar & Restaurant **1**
Nest **4**
The Office Bar & Grill **11**
Opera Riserva Winetheque **13**
Q Bar **3**
The Ship Inn **8**
Tuba **14**

Bangkok Nightlife A to Z

Bars & Pubs

★ **Barbican Bar** SILOM This atmospheric split-level bar is decked out smartly in blonde wood. Known for its great pub grub, Barbican Bar is very popular with expats, tourists and English-speaking locals. I recommend kicking off a night out here with tapas and jugs of draft beer. *9/4–5 Soi Thaniya, Silom Rd.* ☎ *02 234 3590. www. greatbritishpub.com. Metro: Sala Daeng or Silom. Map p 112.*

Black Swan SUKHUMVIT As authentic a British pub as you can get, this is your place if you're homesick for fish and chips, Guinness and John Smith bitter. The fish is flown in from Scotland. The Black Swan is especially popular for live sports on the plasma. *326/8–9 Sukhumvit Rd.* ☎ *02 229 4542 or 02 626 0257. www.blackswanbkk. com. Metro: Asok or Sukhumvit. Map p 114.*

Bull's Head & Angus Steakhouse SUKHUMVIT This is a boisterous British pub with comedy nights, quizzes, club meetings and raucous behaviour by Bangkok expats. The Bull's Head & Angus Steakhouse offers a selection of British and Irish ales and steak pies with chips. *595/10–11 Sukhumvit Rd, Soi 33.* ☎ *02 259 4444/02 261 7747. www.greatbritishpub.com. Metro: Phrom Phong. Map p 114.*

Cheap Charlie's SUKHUMVIT As the name suggests, Cheap Charlie's is an unpretentious watering hole— nay, wooden shack—where young travellers come to drink the night away. Oh, and it's cheap. *Soi 11, Sukhumvit Rd. Closed Sunday. Metro: Nana. Map p 114.*

Coyote on Convent BANGRAK I would describe Coyote on Convent as a Miami-style bar set in a Mexican restaurant. What it does attract, with its frosted fruity margaritas, is an army of young ladies. Wednesday is Ladies' Night and can be a lot of fun. *1/2 Convent Rd (behind Silom Rd).* ☎ *02 631 2325. www.coyoteon convent.com. Metro: Sala Daeng. Map p 112.*

Coyote on Convent offers Mexican food with icy, fruity margaritas to wash it down.

Deep BANGLAMPHU For the young and reckless, this is a spot to wrap up a good night out. Deep is always busy and, oft times, sweaty. It's dark and seedy, but always full of characters and loud pounding beats. *329/1–2 Rambutri Rd. ☎ 02 629 3360. No metro. Map p 112.*

★ **The Dubliner** SUKHUMVIT Bangkok's best Irish pub has all the usual Guinness and Kilkenny, shamrocks and leprechauns you would expect, but what sets it apart is its playful ambience. It's like a homecoming, even if you're not Irish. *440 Sukhumvit Rd (by Washington Square), Soi 22. ☎ 02 204 1841 2. Metro: Sukhumvit or Asok. Map p 114.*

Molly Malone's BANGRAK For an Irish pub it's a bit brightly lit and

Nestle in for a night with good friends at this elegant rooftop bar.

feels like a franchise. Nonetheless, you get a friendly crowd in night after night and all the accoutrements you would expect—Sunday lunches, happy hour (4 to 7pm daily), pool sharks, live music and, of course, Guinness on tap. *1/5–6 Convent Rd (behind Silom Rd). ☎ 02 266 7160 1. www.mollymalonesbangkok.com. Metro: Sala Daeng. Map p 112.*

★★ **Moon Bar at Vertigo** SATHORN Vertigo is the word! This sophisticated open-air bar/ restaurant sits on the rooftop of the 61-storey Banyan Tree. The views are magnificent, so cocktails or champagne at sunset are a must. Dress smartly; don't go if it's raining. *The Banyan Tree, 21/100 South Sathorn Rd, Silom. ☎ 02 679 1200. www.banyantree.com. Metro: Lumphini. Map p 112.*

Nang Nual Riverside Pub CHINATOWN A Chinese-Thai haunt where you can bop around your table with whisky sets, snacks and loud pop tunes. On hot nights it catches sweet breezes from the river. *Trok Krai, Mahachak Rd. ☎ 02 223 7686. No metro. Map p 112.*

★★ **Nest** SUKHUMVIT For a private group of revellers, this is the perfect rendezvous. An elegant rooftop bar (with cover in case of rain), intriguingly designed with gardens and a labyrinth of rattan beds and colourful sofas. Expect excellent service and a quiet atmosphere. *8th floor, Le Fenix, 33/33 Soi Sukhumvit 11. ☎ 02 255 0638 9. www.nestbangkok.com. Metro: Nana. Map p 114.*

The Office Bar & Grill SUKHUMVIT Fans of rugby and cricket will quickly steer towards this watering hole with its big-screen TV, draft beer, steaks and ribs. *Sukhumvit Rd, Soi 33. ☎ 02 662 1936. www.theofficebkk.com. Metro: Phrom Phong. Map p 114.*

Phranakorn Bar BANGLAMPHU
A funky, chic place to meet arty
characters. It has a rooftop terrace
and often hosts exhibitions.
58/2 Soi Damnoen Klang tai.
☎ *02 282 7507. No metro.*
Map p 112.

★★ Rain Dogs Bar & Gallery
SATHORN This bar is so
clandestine, I'm unsure if I should
even advertise it. The in-crowd
seems pretty happy that they've
discovered this hip bar with funky
tunes and homely ambience. Don't
tell them I sent you! *16 Soi Phraya
Phiren (off Soi Sawan Sawat,
near King Rama IV), Lumphini.*
☎ *081 720 6989. Metro: Klong Toey.*
Map p 112.

The Ship Inn SUKHUMVIT The
Tudor-era decor advises you that
you have entered Little England
immediately. Friendly regulars are
quiet and mature, and enjoy pies
and beans, Sunday roasts, draft beer
and darts. *9/1 Soi 23, Sukhumvit Rd.
Metro: Asok. Map p 114.*

Silk Bar BANGLAMPHU This cozy
open-air cocktail bar is ideal for
people-watching on Khao San Road.
Lots of young expats and Thais turn
up here on Friday and Saturday
nights before heading to nightclubs.
129–131 Khao San Rd. ☎ *02 281
9981. No metro. Map p 112.*

★★★ Sky Bar at Sirocco
BANGRAK At first glance the neon-
lit round bar seems to be slipping
off the edge of the rooftop into the
Chao Phraya River, so precarious is
its situation. But, on a clear night, in
your most stylish attire, with martini
in hand and someone special on
your arm, you'll feel like you're on
top of the world. *63rd floor,
lebua at State Tower, 1055 Silom Rd.*
☎ *02 624 9555. www.thedomebkk.
com. Metro: Saphan Taksin.
Map p 112.*

The Sky Bar at Sirocco.

★ Tuba EKAMAI Only in Thailand:
a second-hand furniture shop that
morphs into a retro '70s bar with
pool tables and flat-screen TVs by
night. Popular with college students
and groovy hipsters, Tuba is a great
place to dip your toe into Thai youth
culture without drowning. Try the
mega cocktails! *30 Soi 21,
Sukhumvit Rd, Soi 63 (Soi Ekamai).*
☎ *02 622 9708. Metro: Ekkamai.
Map p 114.*

Water Bar RATCHATHEWI A whisky bar—Thai style. This is a great place to meet tipsy locals as revellers knock back shots and sing along into the wee hours. *107/3–4 Soi Rang Nam, Phayathai Rd. ☎ 02 642 7699. Metro: Victory Monument. Map p 112.*

★ **Wong's Place** SATHORN If you are having a very late night and want to plant yourself somewhere dark and dingy, Wong's is the place on the east side that pulls in the most eclectic characters. Parties often go on until dawn. *27/3 Soi Sri Bumphen, Rama IV Rd, Yannawa. ☎ 02 286 1558. Metro: Lumphini or Klong Toei. Map p 112.*

Gay & Lesbian Bars & Clubs

The Balcony BANGRAK This big-fun tavern is the centrepiece of Silom Soi 4, the city's most overtly gay street. You'll always find a boy beauty contest, a cabaret show or something sexy and outrageous going on. It has a reasonable wine list, too. *86–88 Soi 4, Silom Rd. ☎ 02 235 5891. www.balconypub. com. No cover. Metro: Silom or Sala Daeng. Map p 112.*

DJ Station BANGRAK This nightclub has three floors of grinding tunes, sofas and all-night dancing, and is usually packed with Bangkok boys, expats and tourists. *Soi 2, Silom Rd. ☎ 02 266 4029. www.dj-station.com. Cover 200 baht. Metro: Silom or Sala Daeng. Map p 112.*

Telephone Pub BANGRAK Usually more intimate and less flamboyant than its neighbours on Silom Soi 4, this is a tourist-friendly rainbow bar, named for the old telephones at each table that you can use to dial someone sitting across the bar. *114/11–13 Soi 4, Silom Rd. ☎ 02 234 3279. www. telephonepub.com. No cover. Metro: Silom or Sala Daeng. Map p 112.*

Zeta HUAY KWANG This buzzing women-only club is a little far from the centre, but worth the effort. Especially busy at weekends, this is Bangkok's centre of *tom-dee* networking. *29 Royal City Ave (RCA), Rama IX Rd. ☎ 02 203 0994 or 080 211 1060. www.zetabangkok.com. No cover. Metro: Rama IX. Map p 111.*

Live Music

Absolute 7 SUKHUMVIT A thriving roadhouse with pool hall, clubhouse, restaurant and live music. The Thai band 'Exotic' plays easy-listening tunes every night: The Eagles, Neil Diamond,

Stick to Ad Here the 13th blues bar for a nightly fix of soulful blues.

The impossibly classy Bamboo Bar at the Mandarin Oriental.

The Cranberries and such. *Sukhumvit Soi 7/1, Wattana.* ☎ *02 651 3919. www.absolute7bar.com. Metro: Nana. Map p 114.*

★★★ Ad Here the 13th

BANGLAMPHU Another 'in' place I shouldn't even be telling you about. Singer Georgia fills to bursting this hole-in-the-wall tavern with her booming 'blues mamma' voice. She's backed by her blues band playing Monday to Saturday. There's only space inside for a handful of aficionados; make sure you're one of them! *13 Samsen Rd.* ☎ *02 769 4613. No metro. Map p 112.*

Bamboo Bar BANGRAK An exquisite up-market venue, with marvellous international jazz and blues bands and a play-it-again-Sam ambience. Adjoining the bar is a Cuban cigar store that acts as a smoking lounge. *Mandarin Oriental, 48 Oriental Ave.* ☎ *02 659 9000,* *ext 7690. Metro: Saphan Taksin. Map p 112.*

★ Brown Sugar PATHUMWAN

This is a somewhat legendary spot for jazz lovers. I first came across this intimate and casual roadhouse in the mid-1980s and still see the same characters there. Arrive at about 11pm for the best jazz bands and atmosphere. *231/20 Sarasin Rd, opp. Lumphini Park.* ☎ *02 250 1826. Metro: Ratchadamri. Map p 112.*

O'Reilly's Irish Pub & Restaurant BANGRAK This Irish

pub-cum–sports bar is best known for its live music, including '60s nights, a Thai Frank Sinatra and Celtic folk tunes. If you are into The Beatles, come along on Friday night for the cover band—it's great! *62/1–4 Silom Rd.* ☎ *02 632 7515. www.bkkpubs.com/oreilly. Metro: Sala Daeng. Map p 112.*

If you're looking for jazz and blues bands, Saxophone has been hosting the hippest in town since 1987.

★★ Overtone Music Cave HUAY KWANG I heartily recommend this racy international tavern for those who crave seriously raw tunes. Check the program for rock, blues, jazz, ska, reggae, funk or fusion nights, Wednesday to Sunday, as well as impromptu jam sessions. *29/70–72 Royal City Ave (RCA) zone D, Rama IX Rd. ☎ 02 203 0423 5 or 02 641 4283. Metro: Rama IX. Map p 111.*

Retro Live Cafe KLONG TOEY This large venue acts as a concert hall for raunchy local bands— usually playing middle-of-the-road tunes. A state-of-the-art sound and light system encourages a party atmosphere for the young crowd. It also serves very spicy Thai meals. *Lakeside, Queen Sirikit National Convention Centre, 60 New Ratchadaphisek Rd. ☎ 02 203 4000. Metro: Klong Toey or Sirikit. Map p 112.*

★ Saxophone RATCHATHEWI Everyone knows Saxophone. It's been around since 1987 and pulls in all the swingers and hipsters in town for its rocking atmosphere and jazz and blues bands. It also has an excellent dining area. *3/8 Phayathai Rd, Victory Monument. ☎ 02 246 5472. www.saxophonepub.com. Metro: Victory Monument. Map p 112.*

Tawandang German Brewery YANNAWA A big Bavarian beer hall with steins of frothy beer, German food and Thai-style entertainment—a big band banging out Thai-western hits and the odd cabaret number. *462/61 Narathiwat Rd, Rama III. ☎ 02 678 1114 6. www.tawandang.co.th. No metro. Map p 111.*

To-Sit THONBURI In recent years To-Sit bar-restaurants seem to be popping up all over the city. I go to the venue at Pier 92—it's on the west bank of the river, has a beautifully laid-out floor plan and unobtrusive acoustic music every night. It's a university student hangout and has good food, too. *115 Soi Charansantiwongse 92, Charansantiwongse Rd, Bang Phlad. ☎ 02 879 1717. www.tosit.com. No metro. Map p 111.*

When is a Bar Not a Bar?

Bangkok is notorious for its nightlife; but it's not all go-go dancers and sex workers. There's everything from basement jazz clubs to sophisticated wine bars and old-fashioned pubs to high-tech nightclubs.

There's no cover charge or drinks minimum in bars (if they do ask for an entry fee, it's no doubt a girly bar). However, nightclubs usually ask a cover charge, usually with one free drink included. Note that the admission fee can vary considerably and may depend on 'theme nights', supply and demand, or simply how you look!

Police regulations force most bars to close at 1am, though nightclubs and bars in heavy tourist zones stay open until at least 2am. You must be 20 years old to enter a nightclub. Carry ID and note that there's no smoking inside venues.

Nightclubs

★★★ Bed Supperclub

SUKHUMVIT If your Bangkok friend says 'Let's go to Bed!', they're probably talking about this club. Glamorous, exotic, trendy Bed has been the 'in' place in town for beautiful people for several years now—it's a catwalk! *26 Soi 11, Sukhumvit Rd, Wattana. ☎ 02 651 3537. www.bedsupperclub.com. Cover 500–600 baht. Metro: Nana. Map p 114.*

Club Culture RATCHATHEWI A

notorious nightclub in the '60s, this Thai-style house has now reopened and reinvented itself as one of the city's most popular teenage haunts. International DJs spin drum 'n' bass, house, hip-hop and trance as you swing the night away with Thai uni students. *Sri Ayutthaya Rd, opp. Siam City Hotel. ☎ 089 497 8422 or 02 653 7216. www.club-culture-bkk. com. Cover 200–300 baht. Metro: Phaya Thai. Map p 112.*

★ Club Ibiza PATHUMWAN

Bangkok's newest, coolest nightclub is a fantasia of light and sound. Top DJs spin R & B, techno and hip-hop beats. There are lots of theme nights. *Hotel Intercontinental, 973 Ploenchit Rd. ☎ 02 656 0382. Cover 200–300 baht. www.ibizabkk. com. Metro: Chit Lom. Map p 112.*

The spaceship-like exterior of Bed Supperclub.

Concept CM² SIAM SQUARE
If you like dancing to live bands—
especially hip-hop and trip-hop—
you'll find there's a new one every
night at this tightly packed (loud)
venue. *Basement, Novotel, Siam
Square Soi 6, Pathumwan.* ☎ *02 209
8888. www.cm2bkk.com. Cover 200
baht. Metro: Siam. Map p 112.*

★ **Glow** SUKHUMVIT Small,
intimate and sexy, Glow is popular
with the less pretentious, more
earthy clubber. There are lots of
theme nights—check the website.
96/4–5 Soi 23, Sukhumvit Rd.
☎ *02 261 4446. www.glowbkk.com.
Cover 300 baht. Metro: Asok or
Sukhumvit. Map p 114.*

Lava Club BANGLAMPHU
International backpackers and
funky young Thais descend into
the inferno of Lava late at night to
dance to trance, hip-hop and R & B.
*Basement, Bayon Building
(opp. Nana Plaza), Khao San Rd.*
☎ *02 281 6565. No cover. No metro.
Map p 112.*

Slim HUAY KWANG Slim (also
known as Siam Life in Motion)
is an acquired taste, but those
who go always go back. Evenings
start slowly with small groups of
Thais and expats huddled around
tables. As the night unwinds, so
do the young dudes and dudettes.
Alternative rock and hip-hop are the
staple musical diet. *Block B, 29/22–
32 Royal Crown Ave (RCA), Rama IX
Rd.* ☎ *02 203 0226. Cover varies.
Metro: Rama IX. Map p 111.*

★★★ **Q Bar** SUKHUMVIT It's all go
at this hedonistic clubbers' paradise.
International DJs mix the latest hip-
hop, trance and fusion tunes while
revellers drink and dance into the
wee hours. *34 Soi 11, Sukhumvit Rd,
Wattana.* ☎ *02 252 3274.
www.qbarbangkok.com. Cover
400–500 baht. Metro: Nana.
Map p 114.*

*To-Sit (p 120) is a must for unobtrusive
music, good food and great atmosphere.*

Wine Bars

★ **Bacchus Wine Bar**
PATHUMWAN Bacchus has an
up-market wine cellar downstairs,
leather armchairs on the first floor
and a candlelit 'bedroom' ambience
upstairs. It offers a selection of
400 wines, tasty tapas and cool
jazz tunes. *20/6–7 Soi Ruam Rudi,
Ploenchit.* ☎ *02 650 8986. www.
bacchus.tv. Metro: Ploen Chit.
Map p 112.*

Opera Riserva Winetheque
SUKHUMVIT This place has the
gentle ambience of an exquisite
Italian cafe, with gourmet tapas,
VIP rooms and a selection of the
finest Italian wines. *53 Soi 39,
Sukhumvit Rd.* ☎ *02 258 5601.
www.operariserva.com. Metro:
Phrom Phong. Map p 114.*

V9 Wine Bar BANGRAK With
panoramic views from the 37th floor
of the Sofitel, V9 is a mellow spot for
a sophisticated glass of fine wine.
*Sofitel Silom Bangkok Hotel,
188 Silom Rd.* ☎ *02 238 1991.
www.sofitel.com. Metro: Chong
Nonsi. Map p 112.* ●

Arts & Entertainment Best Bets

Best Art Gallery
★ 100 Tonson Gallery, *100 Soi Tonson, Ploenchit Rd (p 128)*

Best Bicycle Tours Around Town
★ Velothailand, *88 Soi 2, Samsen Rd (p 132)*

Best Cinema
House RCA, *31/8 Royal City Ave, New Petchalouri Rd (p 129)*

Best Classical Thai Dance
★★★ Patravadi Theatre, *69/1 Soi Wat Rakhang (p 130)*

Best Dinner Theatre
Sala Rim Nam, *Oriental Hotel, 48 Oriental Ave (p 130)*

Best Puppetry
★ Joe Louis Puppet Theatre, *Suan Lum Night Bazaar (p 131)*

Best Place to Hear 'No Way She's a Boy!'
★ Mambo Cabaret, *Sukhumvit Soi 22 (p 131)*

Best Place to Listen to the Bangkok Symphony Orchestra
Thailand Cultural Centre, *Ratchadaphisek Rd (p 129)*

Best Place to Rub Shoulders with Royalty
Thailand Cultural Centre, *Ratchadaphisek Rd (p 129)*

Best Siamese Masked Theatre Show
Sala Chalermkrung Royal Theatre, *66 Charoen Krung Rd (p 132)*

Most Spectacular Theatre Show
★★★ Siam Niramit, *19 Tiam Ruammit Rd (p 132)*

Best Thai Boxing Venue
★ Ratchadamnoen Boxing Stadium, *1 Ratchadamnoen Nok Rd (p 132)*

Previous page: A performer at the colourful Siam Niramit cultural show.

This performance of The Ramakien at the Thailand Cultural Centre was produced for the king's birthday celebrations.

Greater Bangkok Arts & Enterainment

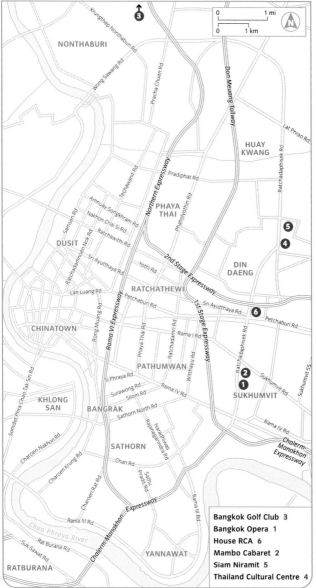

NONTHABURI

Krungthep Nonthaburi Rd

Wong Sawang Rd

Pracha Chuen Rd

Don Meuang Tollway

0   1 mi
0   1 km

HUAY KWANG

Lat Phrao Rd

Northern Expressway

Pradiphat Rd

Phaholyothin Rd

Ratchadaphisek Rd

PHAYA THAI

Amnuay Songkhram Rd
Nakhon Chai Si Rd
Ratchawithi Rd

Techawanit Rd

Samsen Rd

Ratchadamnoen Nok Rd

Sri Ayutthaya Rd

DUSIT

Yothi Rd

2nd Stage Expressway

DIN DAENG

Lan Luang Rd

RATCHATHEWI

Rama VI Expressway

Petchaburi Rd

Sri Ayutthaya Rd

1st Stage Expressway

Petchaburi Rd

CHINATOWN

Rong Muang Rd

Phaya Thai Rd

Ratchadamri Rd

Rama I Rd

Ratchadaphisek Rd

Sukhumvit 55

PATHUMWAN

Si Phraya Rd

Surawong Rd

Silom Rd

Rama IV Rd

Witthayu Rd

SUKHUMVIT

Sukhumvit Rd

KHLONG SAN

Somdet Phra Chao Tak Sin Rd

BANGRAK

Sathorn North Rd

Naradhiwas Rajanagarindra Rd

Rama IV Rd

Chaloem-Manakhon Expressway

Charoen Nakhon Rd

SATHORN

Chan Rd

Charoen Krung Rd

Charoen Rat Rd

Sathu Pradit Rd

Chaloem-Manakhon Expressway

Rama III Rd

Rama III Rd

Rat Burana Rd

Chao Phraya River

Suk Sawat Rd

RATBURANA

YANNAWAT

Bangkok Golf Club	3
Bangkok Opera	1
House RCA	6
Mambo Cabaret	2
Siam Niramit	5
Thailand Cultural Centre	4

Central Bangkok Arts & Entertainment

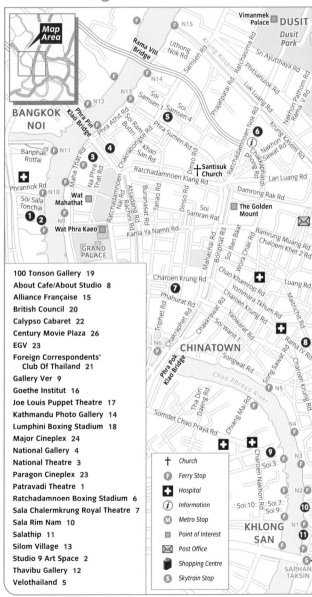

100 Tonson Gallery 19
About Cafe/About Studio 8
Alliance Française 15
British Council 20
Calypso Cabaret 22
Century Movie Plaza 26
EGV 23
Foreign Correspondents'
   Club Of Thailand 21
Gallery Ver 9
Goethe Institut 16
Joe Louis Puppet Theatre 17
Kathmandu Photo Gallery 14
Lumphini Boxing Stadium 18
Major Cineplex 24
National Gallery 4
National Theatre 3
Paragon Cineplex 23
Patravadi Theatre 1
Ratchadamnoen Boxing Stadium 6
Sala Chalermkrung Royal Theatre 7
Sala Rim Nam 10
Salathip 11
Silom Village 13
Studio 9 Art Space 2
Thavibu Gallery 12
Velothailand 5

✝	Church
🅕	Ferry Stop
✚	Hospital
ⓘ	Information
Ⓜ	Metro Stop
▪	Point of Interest
✉	Post Office
🏬	Shopping Centre
🆂	Skytrain Stop

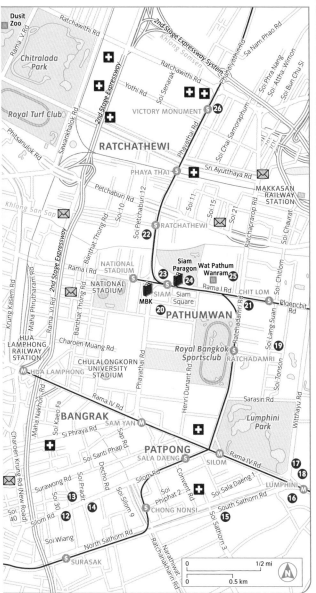

Arts & Entertainment A to Z

Art Galleries

★ 100 Tonson Gallery

PATHUMWAN   This is a cool and modern private gallery. You can discover exhibitions of almost anything here—painting, sculpture, installation, photography, you name it. *100 Soi Tonson, Ploenchit Rd.* ☎ *02 684 1527. www.100tonsongallery.com. Admission free. Thurs–Sun 11am–7pm. Metro: Chit Lom or Ratchadamri. Map p 126.*

★ About Cafe/About Studio

CHINATOWN   If I am ever waiting for a train, I head over to About for a coffee and an amble around the cutting-edge fine art. Call ahead to make sure it's open. *418 Maitrichit Rd.* ☎ *02 639 8057. Admission free. Metro: Hua Lamphong. Map p 126.*

★ Gallery Ver THONBURI

This gallery is owned by Thailand's best-known artist, Rirkrit Tiravanija. You'll probably find Thailand's boldest conceptual art here. *2nd Floor, 71/31–35 Klongsarn Plaza, Charoean Nakhon Rd, Klongsarn.* ☎ *02 861 0933. www.ververinfo. Admission free. Closed Mon & Tues. No metro. Map p 126.*

Kathmandu Photo Gallery

BANGRAK   Housed in a wooden Portuguese colonial house, this is Bangkok's only gallery devoted entirely to photography. (There's also a good Nepalese restaurant opposite.) *87 Pan Rd, off Silom Rd.* ☎ *02 234 6700. www.kathmandu-bkk.com. Admission free. Closed Mon. Metro: Surasak or Chong Nongsi. Map p 126.*

National Gallery RATTANAKOSIN

You'll find contemporary art—including Thai cubism and surrealism—on the ground floor, and traditional Thai art upstairs at

Kathmandu Photo Gallery gives a snapshot of the work of Thailand's photographers.

this gallery. The courtyard hosts a small art market at weekends; entry is free. *Chao Fa Rd.* ☎ *02 282 2639. Admission 30 baht. Closed Mon & Tues. No metro. Map p 126.*

Thavibu Gallery BANGRAK

The gallery's name is a clumsy amalgamation of Thailand, Vietnam and Burma. Visitors will find revolving exhibitions of contemporary art by emerging artists from these three countries. *3rd floor, 919/1 Silom Rd.* ☎ *02 266 5454. www.thavibu.com. Admission free. Closed Mon. Metro: Surasak. Map p 126.*

Cinemas

Century Movie Plaza

RAJATHEWI   Near Victory Monument, this plaza has eight screens featuring the latest movies, plus restaurants, a shopping arcade and a karaoke zone. *15 Phayathai Rd.* ☎ *02 247 1111. www.centurythemovieplaza.com. Tickets 120 baht. Metro: Victory Monument. Map p 126.*

kids EGV SIAM SQUARE
A modern cinema complex with 10 screens that feature all the latest blockbusters and plenty of animated movies. There are four other branches around the city. *6th floor, Siam Discovery Centre, Rama I Rd, Pathumwan. ☎ 02 812 9999. www.egv.com. Tickets 120 baht. Metro: Siam. Map p 126.*

House RCA HUAY KHUANG
The first boutique cinema in town is a refuge for lovers of arthouse/indie films. It also has Thai movies with subtitles and at least three movie festivals a year. *31/8 Royal City Ave, New Petchaburi Rd, Bangkapi. ☎ 02 641 5177 8. www.houserama.com. Tickets 100 baht. Metro: Petchaburi. Map p 125.*

This friendly fellow sits outside the National Gallery.

kids Major Cineplex
PATHUMWAN A six-screen cineplex with Hollywood and Thai movies with subtitles. There are nine branches around the city. *7th floor, World Trade Centre, Ratchadamri Rd. ☎ 02 511 5555. www.majorcineplex.com. Tickets 120 baht. Metro: Chit Lom. Map p.126.*

Paragon Cineplex SIAM
SQUARE This luxurious cinema in Siam Paragon shopping mall shows all the new releases from Hollywood. *5th floor, Siam Paragon, Rama I Rd, Pathumwan. ☎ 02 129 4635 6. www.paragoncineplex.com. Tickets 140 baht. Metro: Siam. Map p 126.*

Classical Music
Thailand Cultural Centre
RATCHADAPHISEK Here's your chance to rub shoulders with the city's cultured high society and listen to the 70 classical musicians of the Bangkok Symphony Orchestra. *Ratchadaphisek Rd, opp. Robinson's. ☎ 02 247 0028 or BSO: 02 255 6617 8. Ticket prices vary. Metro: Thailand Cultural Centre. Map p 125.*

Cultural Institutes
Alliance Française SATHORN
Old French movies, language classes, a French library, a bistro and occasional art exhibitions are available here. *29 South Sathorn Rd. ☎ 02 670 4200. www.alliance-francaise.or.th. Metro: Lumphini, Silom or Chong Nonsi. Map p 126.*

Goethe Institut SATHORN
The German culture centre hosts German movies, language classes, art exhibitions and musical recitals. *18/1 Goethe Gasse, Soi Attakarn Prasit, South Sathorn Rd Soi 1. ☎ 02 287 0942 4. www.goethe.de/bangkok. Metro: Lumphini. Map p 126.*

British Council PATHUMWAN There's not much going on here except English classes and a good library, but the Council does host the British film festival every July. *254 Chulalongkorn Soi 64.* ☎ *02 652 5480 5. www.britishcouncil.or.th. Daily 10am–8pm. Metro: Siam. Map p 126.*

★ Foreign Correspondents' Club Of Thailand PATUNWAN Is it a bar? An art gallery? A restaurant? In fact, the FCCT is an open clubhouse and the favoured watering hole of the city's journalists, photographers and not-so-eminent guidebook writers. It has jazz bands and exhibitions and screens alternative documentaries. See you there! *Maneeya Center, 518/5 Ploenchit Rd.* ☎ *02 652 0580 1. www.fccthai.com. Metro: Chit Lom. Map p 126.*

Dinner Theatre

★★★ Patravadi Theatre THONBURI Take a magical step inside traditional Thai arts with eye-catching dance performances and classical Siamese and Asian epics, often directed by theatre founder

Khon *masks on display at the front of Patravadi Theatre.*

Patravadi Mejudhon. Dinner theatre is only on Friday and Saturday from 7pm. *69/1 Soi Wat Rakhang, Thonburi.* ☎ *02 412 7287 8. www. patravaditheatre.com. Ticket prices vary. No metro. Map p 126.*

★★★ Sala Rim Nam BANGRAK Even though I can't afford to stay at the Oriental, I can always stretch to a superb evening of awe-inspiring traditional Thai music and dance, complemented by a sumptuous meal at this majestic venue. *Mandarin Oriental, 48 Oriental Ave.* ☎ *02 437 3080. www.mandarin-oriental.com. Tickets from 2250 baht (including dinner). Metro: Saphan Taksin. Map p 126.*

★ Salathip BANGRAK Romantic, intimate dining in a teak pavilion can be had here, against a backdrop of Thai classical musicians, dancers, a cultural show and a view of the Chao Phraya River. *89 Soi Wat Suan Plu, Charoen Krung Rd.* ☎ *02 236 7777. Tickets from 2000 baht. AE, DC, MC, V. Daily 11.30am–2.30pm & 6.30–10.30pm. Metro: Saphan Taksin. Map p 126.*

kids Silom Village BANGRAK While many Siamese and Chinese epics may be too longwinded for some, this show caters to those who just want to sample a slice of Thai drama with traditional dance, martial arts performances and an excellent Thai dinner. *286/1 Silom Rd.* ☎ *02 234 4448. Tickets 600 baht. Metro: Surasak. Map p 126.*

Studio 9 Art Space THONBURI If there's no show at the Patravadi Theatre next door, I recommend you take in a Siamese music and dance performance over a riverside dinner at Studio 9. It's run by the same production company. *69/1 Soi Wat Rakhang.* ☎ *02 412 7287 8. www. patravaditheatre.com. Admission free with dinner. No metro. Map p 126.*

Come to the outlandish and colourful Mambo Cabaret for glitz and glamour.

Ladyboy Cabaret

Calypso Cabaret RATCHATHEWI
A lively transvestite cabaret with the emphasis squarely on the ladyboys themselves, from silicone-enhanced Marilyn Monroe to the gay Geisha. Part song and dance, part slapstick—it's inoffensive and good fun. *Asia Hotel, 296 Phayathai Rd.* ☎ *02 653 3960 2. www. calypsocabaret.com. Tickets 600 baht Thais, 1200 baht foreigners. Daily 8.15 & 9.45pm. Metro: Ratchathewi. Map p 126.*

★ **Mambo Cabaret** SUKHUMVIT
A sexier, but nonetheless tourist-friendly, ladyboy show, with glitz, glamour, suggestive humour and lots of scantily clad performers. *Washington Square, Sukhumvit Soi 22.* ☎ *02 259 5715. Tickets 600–800 baht. Daily 8.30 & 10pm. Metro: Phrom Phong. Map p 125.*

Opera

Bangkok Opera SUKHUMVIT
Handel's *Julius Caesar* and Puccini's *La Bohème* have now come to South-East Asia's premier opera house. *232/14–16 Sukhumvit Soi 22.* ☎ *02 663 3236. www. bangkokopera.org. Ticket prices vary. Metro: Sukhumvit, Asok or Sikrit. Map p 125.*

Puppet Shows

★ **kids** **Joe Louis Puppet Theatre** LUMPHINI   There are nightly performances of the Hindu classic *Ramayana* featuring beautifully hand-carved puppets. *Suan Lum Night Bazaar, Rama IV Rd/ Wireless Rd.* ☎ *02 252 9683 4. www.thaipuppet.com. Tickets 400 baht Thais, 900 baht foreigners. Daily 8 & 9.15pm. Metro: Lumphini. Map p 126.*

Sports Venues

Bangkok Golf Club PATHUM THANI   You can rent clubs and a caddy and enjoy a day out on this finely manicured 18-hole course, known for its maze of water hazards. It's 30 minutes north of the city centre by taxi. *99 Tiwanon Rd.* ☎ *02 501 2828. www.golf.th.com. Tickets (non-members) 1600 baht per round. AE, DC, MC, V. No metro. Map p 125.*

Lumphini Boxing Stadium

LUMPHINI A chance to see professional Thai boxing up close and personal. There are bouts on Tuesday, Friday and Saturday evenings. *Sanam Muay Lumphini, Rama IV Rd.* ☎ *02 252 8765. Tickets 230 baht (nosebleed), 920 baht (ringside). Metro: Lumphini. Map p 126.*

★ Ratchadamnoen Boxing Stadium

POM PRAP *Muay Thai* (Thai kickboxing) is the national sport, and this is the country's number-one venue for this fast and brutal bloodsport. The crowd goes crazy and you can eat, drink, gamble and scream throughout. *1 Ratchadamnoen Nok Rd.* ☎ *02 281 4205. Tickets 1000 baht (nosebleed), 2000 baht (ringside). No metro. Map p 126.*

★ kids Velothailand

BANGLAMPHU Explore Bangkok by bicycle? Why not! Every evening at around 6pm, a tour group sets off down backstreets, around temples, along the riverfront, across the bridge to Thonburi and back within four hours. The bikes and equipment are very good quality. *88 Soi 2, Samsen Rd.* ☎ *02 629 1745 or 089 201 7782. Tours 1100 baht. No credit cards. No metro. Map p 126.*

Theatre

National Theatre

RATTANAKOSIN If you are in Bangkok on the last Friday of the month, you can take in a Thai classical drama and masked theatre at this impressive venue. *Note:* closed for renovation until late 2009. *Rachini Rd, Sanam Luang.* ☎ *02 224 1342. No metro. Map p 126.*

Sala Chalermkrung Royal Theatre

PAHURAT Built in 1933, this theatre now hosts *khon* (Siamese masked theatre). It's an acquired taste—the music screeches somewhat—so first have a look at the video clip on the website to see if it's your cup of tea. Shows on Friday and Saturday nights only. *66 Charoen Krung Rd.* ☎ *02 222 0434. www. salachalermkrung.com. Tickets 1000–1200 baht. No metro. Map p 126.*

★★★ Siam Niramit

HUAY KHUANG A colourful and extravagant high-tech production featuring ancient Siamese epics, catering specifically to travellers. *Ratchada Theatre, 19 Tiam Ruammit Rd.* ☎ *02 649 9222. www. siamniramit.com. Tickets 1500 baht. Daily 8pm. Metro: Thailand Cultural Centre. Map p 125.* ●

Muay Thai *(Thai kickboxing) is the national sport of Thailand.*

9 The Best
Accommodation

Accommodation **Best Bets**

Best **Buffet Breakfast**
Grand Hyatt Erawan Bangkok
$$$$$ 494 Ratchadamri Rd
(p 141)

Best **Cocktails by the
Swimming Pool**
★ Marriott Resort & Spa $$$$
257 Charoen Nakorn Rd
(p 143)

Best **Decor**
★★ Conrad Bangkok $$$$
87 Wireless Rd (p 139)

Best **Facilities for Sports
Enthusiasts**
★ Swissôtel Nai Lert Park $$$$$
2 Wireless Rd (p 146)

Best **Flashback to
19th-Century Siam**
★★★ The Eugenia $$$$
267 Sukhumvit Soi 31 (p 140)

Best **Hotel in the World!**
★★★ Mandarin Oriental $$$$$
48 Oriental Ave (p 142)

Best **Riverside Dining**
★★ The Peninsula $$$$
333 Charoen Nakorn Rd (p 144)

Best for a **Romantic
Evening for Two**
★★ Ibrik Resort $$$
372 Rama III Rd (p 141)

Best **Self-Catering**
★ Siri Sathorn $$
27 Soi Sala Daeng, 1 Silom Rd (p 146)

Best for **Shopaholics**
Novotel Bangkok $$$$
Siam Square Soi 6 (p 144)

Best **Stopover Near
Suvarnabhumi Airport**
★ Queen's Garden Resort
at River View $
44 Soi 7, Lad Krabang Rd (p 144)

Best **Views at Sunrise**
★★ Chakrabongse Villas $$$$$
396 Maharaj Rd (p 139)

Best **Views at Sunset**
Shangri-La Hotel $$$$
89 Soi Wat Suan Plu,
Charoen Krung Rd (p 145)

Best **Views of the City**
★ The Banyan Tree $$$$$
21/100 South Sathorn Rd (p 138)

*The Banyan Tree offers a magnificent pool for cooling down in Bangkok's
steamy weather.*

Previous page: The glamorous lobby of the Mandarin Oriental.

Greater Bangkok Accommodation

Bangkok Boutique Hotel **1**
Convenient Resort **8**
The Eugenia **2**
Marriott Resort & Spa **3**
Maruay Garden Hotel **5**
Montien Riverside Hotel **4**
Queen's Garden Resort
  at River View **7**
Refill Now **6**

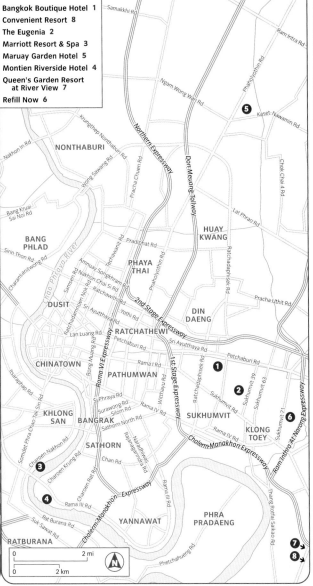

Central Bangkok Accommodation

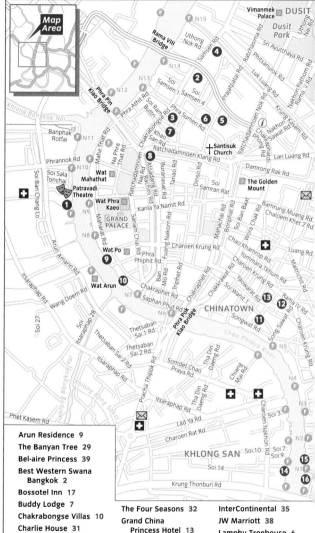

Arun Residence 9
The Banyan Tree 29
Bel-aire Princess 39
Best Western Swana
Bangkok 2
Bossotel Inn 17
Buddy Lodge 7
Chakrabongse Villas 10
Charlie House 31
Conrad Bangkok 37
Diamond House 3
Dusit Thani 26
Federal Hotel 40

The Four Seasons 32
Grand China
Princess Hotel 13
Grand Hyatt
Erawan Bangkok 34
Hotel De' Moc 5
Ibrik Resort 1

InterContinental 35
JW Marriott 38
Lamphu Treehouse 6
lebua at State Tower 18
Lub*D 21
Luxx 20
Mandarin Oriental 15

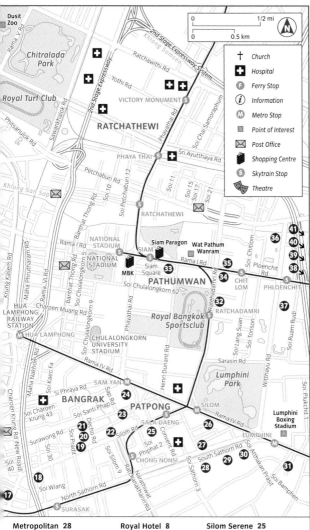

Metropolitan **28**	Royal Hotel **8**	Silom Serene **25**
New Empire Hotel **11**	Shanghai Inn **12**	Siri Sathorn **27**
Novotel Bangkok **33**	Shangri-La Hotel **16**	Sofitel Silom Bangkok **22**
The Peninsula **14**	Sheraton Grande Sukhumvit **41**	The Sukhothai **30**
Phranakorn Nornlen **4**		Swissôtel Nai Lert Park **36**
Rose Hotel **24**	Siam Heritage **23**	Triple Two Silom **19**

Bangkok Accommodation A to Z

★★ Arun Residence

RATTANAKOSIN Opt for this charming boutique hotel if you are spending most of your time visiting the nearby Grand Palace and the historical sites. The romantic suites have an old-world charm and command amazing views of the Temple of Dawn. *36–38 Soi Pratoo Mokyung, Maharaj Rd.* ☎ *02 221 9158. www.arunresidence.com. 7 units. Doubles 3100–5500 baht w/ breakfast. AE, MC, V. No metro. Map p 136.*

Bangkok Boutique Hotel

SUKHUMVIT I like the warm terracotta and beige decor in the rooms at this arty little hotel. This is a good-value mid-range option. *241 Sukhumvit 21, Klong Toey Nue, Wattana.* ☎ *02 261 0850 4. www.bangkokboutiquehotel.com. 50 units. Doubles 2900–4900 baht w/breakfast. AE, DN, MC, V. Metro: Asok. Map p 135.*

★ The Banyan Tree SATHORN

The Banyan Tree is popular with businesspeople, and renowned for

Soak up the sun at the Bel-aire Princess.

its spa (see p 49) and its 61st-storey rooftop restaurant and bar (see p 116). *21/100 South Sathorn Rd.* ☎ *02 679 1200. www. banyantree.com. 216 units. Doubles from 11500 baht. AE, MC, V. Metro: Lumphini. Map p 136.*

★ Bel-aire Princess SUKHUMVIT

This is a lovely hotel set in a quiet side street near Bangkok's business and shopping districts. It has elegant, modern rooms and a restaurant offering a spicy buffet and Thai cooking classes. *16 Sukhumvit Rd, Soi 5.* ☎ *02 255 8850. www.bel-aireprincess.com. 160 units. Doubles 3300–4200 baht w/ breakfast. MC, V, AE. Metro: Nana. Map p 136.*

Best Western Swana Bangkok

PHRA NAKORN The Best Western is a little sterile, but an inexpensive option for those who find comfort in the reliability of a standard chain hotel. *322 Visuttikasat Rd.* ☎ *02 282 8899. www.swanabangkok.com. 55 units. Doubles 1130–1600 baht w/breakfast. AE, MC, V. No metro. Map p 136.*

★ Bossotel Inn BANGRAK

A cozy alternative with all the mod-cons for the budget traveller. And it's not rowdy. *55/8–14 Soi Charoen Krung 42/1.* ☎ *02 630 6120. www.bossotelinn.com. 81 units. Doubles 1800–2200 baht. AE, MC, V. Metro: Saphan Taksin. Map p 136.*

Buddy Lodge BANGLAMPHU

This is the safest and most reputable hotel on Bangkok's most infamous and wild backpacker street. It also has a swimming pool. *365 Khao San Rd.* ☎ *02 629 4477. www.buddy lodge.com. 76 units. Doubles 2000– 2400 baht w/breakfast. MC, V. No metro. Map p 136.*

Sleep like royalty at the Chakrabongse Villas.

★★ Chakrabongse Villas

RATTANAKOSIN If Frommer's paid, I would live here! Formerly a royal residence, these traditional Thai-Chinese-style wooden chalets look over the Chao Phraya River towards the Temple of Dawn. It's an ideal spot for eating breakfast and reading the morning newspapers. Book well in advance. *396 Maharaj Rd, Tha Tien. ☎ 02 622 3356. www.thaivillas.com. 4 units. Doubles 13 000–23 000 baht w/breakfast. MC, V. No metro. Map p 136.*

Charlie House SATHORN Budget travellers rejoice! You don't have to get down and dirty at Khao San Road. Charlie's is cheap, cozy and friendly, and still manages to provide satellite TV, air-conditioning and hot showers. *1034/36–37 Soi Saphan Khu, Lumphini. ☎ 02 679 8330 1. www.charliehousethailand.com. 19 units. Doubles 540 baht. MC, V. Metro: Lumphini. Map p 136.*

★★ Conrad Bangkok

SUKHUMVIT A classic, centrally located hotel in the business district near Lumphini Park. The rooms are luxurious and chic with wooden decor and silk drapes. *87 Wireless Rd. ☎ 02 690 9999. www.conradhotels1hilton.com. 391 units. Doubles 8000–9000 baht w/breakfast. AE, DC, MC, V. Metro: Ploen Chit. Map p 136.*

You won't want to go to sleep with views like this from your room at the Conrad Bangkok.

Convenient Resort LAD
KRABANG Named for its close proximity to Suvarnabhumi Airport; several of the comfortable, modest rooms at this hotel have countryside views. *9–11 Soi 38 On-nuch Rd.* ☎ *02 327 4118 21. www. convenientresort.com. 67 units. Doubles 1100 baht w/breakfast. MC, V. No metro. Map p 135.*

kids Diamond House
BANGLAMPHU You'll be pleasantly surprised by the comfortable, well-fitted rooms at this budget hotel, which is located within walking distance of Khao San Road, the National Museum and Dusit Zoo. *4 Samsen Rd.* ☎ *02 629 4008. www.thaidiamondhouse.com. 22 units. Doubles 1200–1400 baht. AE, MC, V. No metro. Map p 136.*

★★ Dusit Thani SILOM
For me, the amphitheatre-like lobby at the Dusit makes it all happen. The piano bar, the concierge, several lounges and a cocktail bar create an atmosphere that makes this one of Thailand's favourite hotels. *946 Rama IV Rd.* ☎ *02 200 9000. www.dusit.com. 517 units. Doubles from 6000 baht. AE, DC, MC, V. Metro: Silom or Sala Daeng. Map p 136.*

★★★ The Eugenia SUKHUMVIT
This renovated 19th-century colonial

One of Hotel De' Moc's big, comfortable beds.

house is a boutique hotel with a difference and houses an intricate collection of private antiques. My favourite features are the period furnishings, right down to four-poster beds and feather pillows. *267 Sukhumvit Soi 31.* ☎ *02 259 9017 9. www.theeugenia.com. 12 units. Doubles 5800–7200 baht w/ breakfast. AE, MC, V. Metro: Asok, Phrom Phong or Sukhumvit. Map p 135.*

★ Federal Hotel SUKHUMVIT
I consider the Federal a decent, inexpensive option in the busy Nana area, and it has a small swimming pool and a 24-hour coffee shop. *Soi Chaiyos, 27 Sukhumvit Rd, Soi 11.* ☎ *02 253 0175. www.federal-bangkok.com. 93 units. Doubles 1200–1500 baht w/ breakfast. MC, V. Metro: Nana. Map p 136.*

Soak away the day in the deluxe suite at The Four Seasons.

The lobby of the InterContinental is worth visiting even if you're not a paying guest.

★★ The Four Seasons

SUKHUMVIT This tropical paradise in the heart of the city offers spacious deluxe suites decorated with historical Thai murals. I recommend dining here even if you are staying elsewhere. *155 Ratchadamri Rd.* ☎ *02 250 1000. www.fourseasons.com. 353 units. Doubles 10000–16000 baht w/breakfast. AE, DC, MC, V. Metro: Ratchadamri. Map p 136.*

Grand China Princess Hotel

CHINATOWN This Chinese-style hotel offers spacious rooms and a revolving restaurant on the 25th floor. *215 Yaowarat Rd.* ☎ *02 224 9977. www.grandchinacom. 155 units. Doubles 2300–2600 baht. AE, MC, V. Metro: Hua Lamphong. Map p 136.*

Grand Hyatt Erawan

Bangkok PATHUMWAN The palatial entrance of white pillars and marble floors paves the way to stylish executive suites. Don't miss the buffet! *494 Ratchadamri Rd.* ☎ *02 254 1234. www.bangkok. grand.hyatt.com. 380 units. Doubles from 16000 baht w/breakfast. AE, DC, MC, V. Metro: Ploen Chit. Map p 136.*

★ kids Hotel De' Moc PHRA

NAKORN This is a cozy, friendly hotel with surprisingly spacious rooms and all mod-cons. It's located close to vibrant Khao San Road and is next to the expressway, so it's quick to and from Don Muang Airport. *78 Prajatpatai Rd.* ☎ *02 282 2831. www.hoteldemoc. com. 100 units. Doubles 1600–1700 baht w/breakfast. MC, V. No metro. Map p 136.*

★★ Ibrik Resort THONBURI

Calling itself 'The Smallest Resort in the World', the Ibrik has three suites that are romantic, chic and offer lovely views across the river. Going on honeymoon? Book in advance. *372 Rama III Rd, Bangkhlo.* ☎ *02 848 9220. www.ibrikresort.com. 3 units. Doubles 3500–4000 baht w/breakfast. MC, V. No metro. Map p 136.*

InterContinental PATHUMWAN

This hotel is located in the heart of the business district. The rooms have high-speed internet and the huge soundproof windows offer great views. *973 Ploenchit Rd.* ☎ *02 656 0444. www.intercontinental.com. 381 units. Doubles 6650–9500 baht w/breakfast. AE, DC, MC, V. Metro: Chit Lom. Map p 136.*

In this suite of the lebua at State Tower, you certainly won't want for space.

JW Marriott SUKHUMVIT
Popular with businesspeople, this hotel is a bee hive of activity and is located very close to the city's main business, shopping and entertainment centres. *4 Sukhumvit Rd, Soi 2. ☎ 02 656 7700. www.marriott.com. 442 units. Doubles 10 000–12 000 baht w/breakfast. AE, DC, MC, V. Metro: Asok or Sukhumvit. Map p 136.*

★ **Lamphu Treehouse** PHRA NAKORN Come here for traditional Thai-style rooms, all made from and outfitted in 100-year-old golden teak. *Soi Bann Pan Thom, 155 Wanchat Bridge, Prajatpatai Rd. ☎ 02 282 0991 2. www.lamphutreehotel.com. 40 units. Doubles 1200–1800 baht w/breakfast. MC, V. No metro. Map p 136.*

★★ kids **lebua at State Tower** BANGRAK The lebua is easily recognisable by the gilded dome on the 64-storey tower. All suites come with kitchenettes, a washing machine and comfortable lounges. The higher floors have spectacular views. *1055 Silom Rd. ☎ 02 624 9999. www.lebua.com. 350 units. 1-bed suites 12 250 baht; 2-bed suites 24 500 baht w/breakfast.*

AE, DC, MC, V. Metro: Saphan Taksin. Map p 136.

★ **Lub*D** BANGRAK I always find this a fun and friendly hostel, especially popular with young international travellers. It's located close to Silom Road. *4 Decho Rd, Suriyawong. ☎ 02 634 7999. www.lubd.com. 36 units. Doubles 1800 baht. MC, V. Metro: Silom or Chong Nonsi. Map p 136.*

★★ **Luxx** BANGRAK I thoroughly recommend this trendy boutique hotel with minimalist retro '70s decor. If you are here for the nightlife, it's located close to, but out of earshot of, Silom Road and Patpong. *6–11 Soi Decho, Silom Rd. ☎ 02 635 8800. www.bangkok.com/luxxbangkok. 13 units. Doubles 2800–5000 baht w/breakfast. AE, DC, MC, V. Metro: Chong Nonsi. Map p 136.*

★★★ **Mandarin Oriental** BANGRAK Like Joseph Conrad, W Somerset Maugham, Noel Coward and many other writers of old, I would love to lay my hat at the Oriental for months at a time. It's timeless. Founded in 1876, the Oriental has long been regarded as one of the greatest hotels in the world—a testament to Thai history and a tribute to the Thai sense of personal service and harmony. *48 Oriental Ave. ☎ 02 659 9000. www.mandarinoriental.com. 393 units. Doubles 13000–31500 baht w/breakfast. AE, DC, MC, V. Metro: Saphan Taksin. Map p 136.*

★ Marriott Resort & Spa

THONBURI Located on the west bank of the Chao Phraya River, the Marriott is like a tropical beach resort with its exotic pool, outdoor jacuzzi and open-air spa. It's for those who prefer to avoid the big city. *257 Charoen Nakorn Rd. ☎ 02 476 0022. www.marriott.com/ hotels/travel/bkkth-bangkok-marriott-resort-and-spa. 413 units. Doubles 7600–9900 baht w/breakfast. AE, DC, MC, V. No metro. Map p 135.*

Maruay Garden Hotel

CHATUCHAK This Asian-style hotel is a pleasant option if you want to stay in the north of the city, near Don Mueang Airport and Chatuchak Market, or simply want to avoid Western tourists. *1 Phaholyothin Rd, Ladyao. ☎ 02 561 0510 47. www.maruaygardenhotel.com. 315 units. Doubles 1800 baht. AE, DC, MC, V. Metro: Mo Chit. Map p 135.*

★ Metropolitan SATHORN

A stylish, minimalist hotel that prides itself on health and holism with a menu of accessories and activities—such as spas, yoga and meditation—designed to protect your body and soul. *27 South Sathorn Rd. ☎ 02 625 3333. www.metropolitan.como.bz. 171 units. Doubles 10850 baht. AE, DC, MC, V. Metro: Lumphini or Sala Daeng. Map p 136.*

Montien Riverside Hotel

BANG KHOLAEM Located south of the city centre, this towering hotel overlooks the Chao Phraya River and has excellent facilities and graceful service. *372 Rama III Rd. ☎ 02 292 2962 3. www.montien.com. 462 units. Doubles 5500 baht. AE, DC, MC, V. Metro: Saphan Taksin. Map p 135.*

New Empire Hotel CHINATOWN

This inexpensive but impressive hotel is at the heart of Chinatown and close to the main railway station. *572 Yaowarat Rd. ☎ 02 234 6990 6. www.newempirehotel.com. 130 units. Doubles 720 baht w/breakfast. No credit cards. Metro: Hua Lamphong. Map p 136.*

The minimalist retro suites at the boutique Luxx cater to all guests' needs.

Novotel Bangkok SIAM SQUARE Smack in the centre of Bangkok's most popular shopping district, the Novotel offers a relaxing lobby and rooms with wonderfully soft beds. Intriguingly, it hosts a raunchy nightclub in the basement. *Siam Square Soi 6.* ☎ *02 254 1328. www. novotel.com. 429 units. Doubles 6500–8500 baht w/breakfast. AE, DC, MC, V. Metro: Siam. Map p 136.*

★★ **The Peninsula** THONBURI This award-winning east-meets-west hotel is five-star in every way. The marble lobby is exquisite, the service is subtle and refined and the Asian cuisine is sumptuous. *333 Charoen Nakorn Rd.* ☎ *02 861 2888. www.peninsula. com. 370 units. Doubles 8400–10 500 baht w/breakfast. AE, DC, MC, V. Metro: Saphan Taksin. Map p 136.*

Phranakorn Nornlen POM PRAP This cozy and friendly boutique hotel is set around a relaxing garden. *46 Thewet Soi 1, Pharnakorn, Bang Khunprom, Krung Kasem.* ☎ *02 628 8188 90. www.phranakorn-nornlen. com. 23 units. Doubles 2200–2400 baht w/breakfast. MC, V. No Metro. Map p 136.*

★ **Queen's Garden Resort at River View** BANG NA You'll enjoy good value at this clean and friendly hotel, located opposite Suvarnabhumi Airport. It's ideal for an overnight stopover and a relaxing Thai massage. *44 Soi 7, Lad Krabang Rd.* ☎ *02 734 4540 2. www.queensgardenhotel.net. 76 units. Doubles 1200 baht. AE, DC, MC, V. No metro. Map p 135.*

Refill Now KLONG TOEY This friendly budget travellers' tavern is located near the Ekamai Bus Terminal, handy for those catching morning buses to eastern beaches. *191 Soi Predi Bhanomyong 42 Yak 5, Sukhumvit 71.* ☎ *02 713 2044 6. www.refillnow.co.th. 16 units.*

Doubles 1330 baht. MC, V. Metro: Phra Khanong. Map p 135.

Rose Hotel BANGRAK This is a relaxing Asian-style hotel close to Silom's main shopping area. *118 Surawong Rd, Silom.* ☎ *02 266 8268 72. www.rosehotelbkk.com. 72 units. Doubles 2000–2500 baht w/breakfast. AE, DC, MC, V. Metro: Silom. Map p 136.*

★ **Royal Hotel** BANGLAMPHU Close to the Grand Palace and Khao San Road, this shabby old hotel is full of character, inexpensive and always popular. *2 Ratchadamnoen Ave.* ☎ *02 222 9111. www.bangkok. com/royal-hotel-bangkok. 300 units. Doubles from 1180 baht. MC, V. No metro. Map p 136.*

The Peninsula, a renowned five-star resort, is refined and elegant.

Step back to 1930s Shanghai at the Shanghai Inn.

Shanghai Inn CHINATOWN

Enjoy an ambience of 1930s Shanghai at this bustling boutique hotel. *479 Yaowarat Rd. ☎ 02 221 2121. www.shanghai-inn.com. 55 units. Doubles from 2250 baht w/ breakfast. AE, MC, V. Metro: Hua Lamphong. Map p 136.*

Shangri-La Hotel BANGRAK

Book a room on a higher floor to take in the spectacular views across the river. The elegant rooms are outfitted in teak with marble bathrooms. *89 Soi Wat Suan Plu, Charoen Krung Rd. ☎ 02 236 7777. www.shangri-la.com. 799 units. Doubles 7600–9900 baht w/breakfast. AE, DC, MC, V. Metro: Saphan Taksin. Map p 136.*

★★ Sheraton Grande Sukhumvit SUKHUMVIT

The Sheraton is popular with international businesspeople and is renowned for its excellent service and top-notch facilities. *250 Sukhumvit Rd. ☎ 02 649 8888. www. sheratongrandesukhumvit.com. 440 units. Doubles 8000–14 000 baht w/breakfast. AE, DC, MC, V. Metro: Asok. Map p 136.*

★ Siam Heritage BANGRAK

You wouldn't imagine such a delightful boutique resort was just around the corner from the red-light zone, Patpong, but that's Thailand. Suites are furnished in either a central or northern Thai style. For a little extra, the executive suites with living rooms are excellent value. *115/1 Surawong Rd. ☎ 02 353 6101. www.thesiamheritage.com. 73 units. Doubles 2500–3250 baht w/ breakfast. AE, DC, MC, V. Metro: Sam Yan or Sala Daeng. Map p 136.*

For impeccable service and luxurious surroundings, you can't beat the Shangri-La Hotel.

★ **Silom Serene** BANGRAK
At these prices, I don't think you can find many cozier boutique hotels than this one. The garden is lush and shaded and a perfect spot for reading and relaxing. *7 Soi Pipat, Silom Rd Soi 3. ☎ 02 636 6599. www.silom-serene.com. 86 units. Doubles 2900–3300 baht w/ breakfast. MC, V. Metro: Sala Daeng. Map p 136.*

★ **kids Siri Sathorn** BANGRAK
The spacious suites here are like Japanese-style apartments with kitchens, all mod-cons and cozy terraces. This place has good facilities for families and those who prefer self-catering. *27 Soi Sala Daeng 1 Silom Rd. ☎ 02 266 2345. www.sirisathorn.com. 44 units. Doubles 1650–3650 baht. AE, DC, MC, V. Metro: Sala Daeng or Silom. Map p 136.*

Sofitel Silom Bangkok
BANGRAK The bright, modern Thai-style suites here are fitted with dark hardwood and large bathrooms. *188 Silom Rd. ☎ 02 238 1991. www.sofitel.com. 469 units. Doubles from 7200 baht w/breakfast. AE, MC, V. Metro: Chong Nonsi. Map p 136.*

★ **The Sukhothai** SATHORN
If you can weave your way through the labyrinth of pathways, pagodas, shops and archways you'll find a beautiful, tranquil, grassy courtyard in the centre of this eye-catching but pricey hotel. *13/3 South Sathorn Rd. ☎ 02 344 8888. www. sukhothaihotel.com. 210 units. Doubles 12000–19700 baht w/ breakfast. AE, DC, MC, V. Metro: Lumphini. Map p 136.*

★ **kids Swissôtel Nai Lert Park**
SUKHUMVIT Previously the Hilton Bangkok, but now managed by Raffles, this is a family-friendly hotel with excellent sports facilities and a pool. *2 Wireless Rd. ☎ 02 253 0123. www.swissotel.com. 338 units. Doubles 7700–13000 baht w/ breakfast. AE, DC, MC, V. Metro: Ploen Chit. Map p 136.*

★ **Triple Two Silom** BANGRAK
The open-plan suites here are modern yet homely in a chic Japanese way. The hotel runs a free shuttle bus service, which I think is a thoughtful touch. *222 Silom Rd. ☎ 02 627 2222. www.tripletwosilom. com. 75 units. Doubles 4800–5500 baht w/breakfast. Metro: Chong Nonsi. AE, DC, MC, V. Map p 136.* ●

The Alcove Suite at the Swissôtel Nai Lert Park.

Kanchanaburi

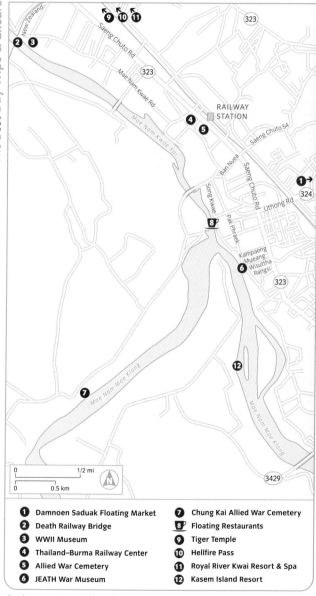

1. Damnoen Saduak Floating Market
2. Death Railway Bridge
3. WWII Museum
4. Thailand–Burma Railway Center
5. Allied War Cemetery
6. JEATH War Museum
7. Chung Kai Allied War Cemetery
8. Floating Restaurants
9. Tiger Temple
10. Hellfire Pass
11. Royal River Kwai Resort & Spa
12. Kasem Island Resort

Previous page: A magical Kanchanaburi scene.

Surrounded by limestone cliffs, rice paddies and fields of sugarcane, Kanchanaburi feels much further than 130km from Bangkok. It's a two-hour drive west towards Burma, though I recommend a stop at the Damnoen Saduak Floating Market on the way. The scenery en route is often breathtaking. Kanchanaburi itself is most famous as the scene of the Death Railway immortalised in the book and film *The Bridge over the River Kwai*. Many foreign visitors to Thailand make the pilgrimage to pay their respects to relatives who died as POWs here. You should rent a bicycle to see the sights and stay overnight and take a trip on one of the floating restaurants, which transform into pulsating discotheques and karaoke cruisers every evening. START: **On Hwy 35 heading southwest, the Southern Bus Terminal or Bangkok Noi Station.**

1 Damnoen Saduak Floating Market. You've seen the images in travel brochures and James Bond films—elderly Siamese women of yesteryear in bamboo hats, rowing their *sampan* boats full of fruit, vegetables and chickens down the busy narrow canals and crying out merrily to customers. Nowadays, I'm afraid, it's all mostly a mock-up for tourists, who arrive in buses every day around 9am or 10am. However, it's colourful and fun and very photogenic. Arrive early to avoid the crowds. ⏱ *1 hr. Bang Phae-Damnoen Saduak Rd. Admission free.*

2 ★ Death Railway Bridge. During World War II, thousands of allied POWs and locals were forced by the Imperial Japanese Army to construct a railway to link Bangkok and Burma. The bridge over the River Kwae (not Kwai) symbolised the sacrifices made. The pleasant surrounding countryside is best visited by bicycle on a nice day. ⏱ *1 hr. 2km north of Kanchanaburi. Admission free.*

The Damnoen Saduak Floating Market is put on mainly for the benefit of tourists, but that doesn't mean you can't get tasty food!

Floating restaurants in Kanchanaburi.

3 WWII Museum. Strictly for war buffs and historians, this modest exhibition has photographs and memorabilia, but little else to spark the imagination. ⏲ *30 min. East bank, Mae Nam Kwae Rd. Admission 40 baht. Daily 9am–6pm.*

4 Thailand–Burma Railway Center. A better museum than **3**, but still only for war buffs. Details the war and politics around the railway. Japanese visitors are advised to avoid it. ⏲ *30 min. Jaokannun Rd.* ☎ *034 512 721. Admission 80 baht adults, 40 baht kids. Daily 9am–5pm.*

5 Allied War Cemetery. This is an immaculately preserved resting place for 7000 allied soldiers who died working on the railway. ⏲ *30 min. Saenchuto Rd. Admission free, donations welcome. Daily 7am–6pm.*

6 ★ JEATH War Museum. Whereas the area's other museums commemorate the deaths of allied soldiers in Kanchanaburi, the JEATH (Japan, England, Australia, Thailand, Holland) Museum depicts the lives of the POWs. Visitors can experience the bamboo huts and bunkers where POWs lived and some personal stories and belongings. It's a moving testimony to the sorrow of war. ⏲ *1 hr. Wat Chaichoompon, Pak Phraek Rd.* ☎ *034 511 263. Admission 30 baht. Daily 8am–6pm.*

7 Chung Kai Allied War Cemetery. This smaller graveyard is located on a scenic plain south of town. ⏲ *15 min. Mae Nam Kwae Noi Rd. Admission free. Daily 7am–6pm.*

8 ★ Floating Restaurants. At night, holidaying Thais love to eat, drink, sing, be merry and bob down the river on a giant raft. The houseboats offer a good variety of spicy Thai dishes and beer. It's a great place to meet Thais, albeit mostly drunk ones. *Song Khwae Rd. Daily 6pm–11pm. $$.*

This fallen soldier is forever remembered at the Allied War Cemetery.

9 kids **Tiger Temple.** A forest sanctuary for wounded animals was founded here about 10 years ago. Now, with 20 or so Bengali tigers, it is essentially a tiger retreat. Can you imagine anything as bizarre as a Buddhist monk escorting an enormous tiger around a garden on a leash? ⏱ *1 hr. Wat Pa Luangta Bua Yannasampanno Forest Monastery, Saiyok District.* ☎ *034 531 557. www.tigertemple.org. Admission 500 baht. Daily noon–3.30pm.*

10 **Hellfire Pass.** A Thai-Australian memorial and walking trail dedicated to the allied POWs who laboured to cut a pass through the mountain; 70 per cent of the POWs died in the process. ⏱ *1 hr. Hwy 323, 75km north of Kanchanaburi. Admission free. Daily 9am–4pm.*

11 **Royal River Kwai Resort & Spa.** This elegant resort boasts a touch of rural luxury in a romantic pastoral setting by the river. Treat yourself to a spa treatment or stay the night. *88 Moo 2, Kanchanaburi-Saiyok Rd.* ☎ *034 653 342. www. royalriverkwairesort.com. Doubles from 2450 baht w/breakfast, spa costs vary.*

12 **Kasem Island Resort.** As far from the big city as you can go in one day. Basic but tranquil cottages

The Tiger Temple offers a home to endangered tigers.

sit on an island on River Kwae. *44–48 Chaichumphol Rd (office on Chukkadon Rd to arrange ferry).* ☎ *034 513 359, or Bangkok 02 255 3604. Doubles from 1300 baht. No credit cards.*

Practical Matters: Kanchanaburi

The easiest way to get to Kanchanaburi is by car (see p 169 for car rental agencies). When you're on Hwy 35, drive 65km to Samut Songkam. Turn right onto Hwy 325 and drive 16km to Damnoen Saduak Floating Market **1**. After visiting the market, continue along Hwy 325, then turn left onto Hwy 323 for 56km.

Catch a bus from the Southern Bus Terminal in Bangkok. Buses leave every 30 minutes and the trip takes 2½ hours; tickets are 106 baht.

Trains run from Bangkok Noi Station at 7.45am and 1.55pm. The trip takes four hours and tickets are 25 baht.

Khao Yai National Park

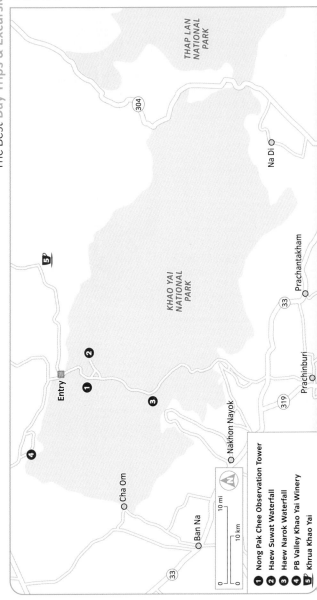

THAP LAN NATIONAL PARK

304

Na Di

Prachantakham

33

KHAO YAI NATIONAL PARK

5

Prachinburi

319

Entry

1

2

3

Nakhon Nayok

4

Cha Om

10 mi

10 km

Ban Na

0

0

33

1 Nong Pak Chee Observation Tower
2 Haew Suwat Waterfall
3 Haew Narok Waterfall
4 PB Valley Khao Yai Winery
5 Khrua Khao Yai

A trip to Thailand's oldest and second-largest national park is a delight. In a city such as Bangkok, where humidity and crowds can be relentless, a venture to the jungle is a breath of fresh air. Much of the 2170-sq-km UNESCO World Heritage Site is located 400m above sea level, making it a haven for varying ecosystems, including monsoon, evergreen and rainforest. From the top of a misty mountain, you can look over a cliff across waterfalls, grasslands, palm groves and bamboo forests to the never-ending tropical jungle beyond. Apart from 3000 species of plants and more than 300 species of birds, you might be lucky enough to spot some rather large mammals. Walk quietly and keep your eyes peeled— they are hiding behind every tree. In the cool season (November to February) nights are sometimes very cold and you'll need warm clothes. In the rainy season (May to September) the entire forest is swathed in a mist and cascading waterfalls seem to descend from the heavens. Waterproof clothes are essential. I recommend renting a car if you feel comfortable driving in Thailand (see p 168).

START: **Mo Chit Bus Terminal or Hwy 1.**

---

❶ Nong Pak Chee Observation Tower. As you pass through the entrance, head to the visitor centre and book your place for this round trip. Climb the wooden ladder up into the observation tower. If you linger here, your patience might indeed be rewarded with some animal sightings—you might spot elephants and deer in the mornings. ⏱ *1 hr.*

❷ Haew Suwat Waterfall. This beautiful 25m teeming waterfall is particularly impressive in the rainy season. If you walk to the bottom of the falls you can enjoy a refreshing swim. Haew Suwat Waterfall has a 'claim to fame' in that it is the location of the famous 'jump' scene in the movie *The Beach*. ⏱ *45 min.*

Gaur, similar to buffalo, live in the tropical woodlands of South-East Asia. You might spot some at the Khao Yai National Park if you're beady-eyed.

Flora and Fauna

National parks cover 13 per cent of Thailand's 514 000 sq km, protecting much of the country's flora and fauna. As a humid tropical country with mountains, rainforest and an abundant coastline, Thailand has great diversity in its plant and animal life.

The mountainous north has mixed deciduous and dry dipterocarp forests and is rich in pines and bamboo. The teak forests, unfortunately, have all but disappeared. Nestled in the canopies of the southern rainforests, you'll find mangroves, rattan, ferns, banana plantations and coconut palms. Exotic flowers can be found everywhere, with orchids and birds of paradise being favourite exports.

Human migration and hunting have killed off many species of mammal, but once upon a time tigers, leopards, elephants, gaurs, tapirs, wild cattle, one-horned rhinoceroses, otters, deer, civet cats, tapirs, gibbons, macaques, bears, wild hogs and various types of monkeys were abundant in Thailand. Today there is little in the way of wild fauna.

There are plenty of reptiles, though—from the harmless mosquito-eating geckoes to crocodiles, monitor lizards and snakes. Venomous snakes include the banded krait, the cobra and the viper. Nowadays, all hospitals in Thailand keep stocks of snake antivenom, which is produced at Bangkok's snake farm (see p 44).

Excluding migratory birds, more than 600 species are indigenous to Thailand, such as hornbills, flycatchers, warblers, pitta, pheasants, egrets, herons, storks and the supreme white-bellied sea eagle.

The seas around Thailand are home to corals, sharks, rays, barracuda, moray eels, reef fish, parrot fish, angel fish, sturgeons and big squelchy sea cucumbers, making them some of the world's most popular diving spots.

The great pied hornbill is one of 600 birds indigenous to Thailand.

3 **Haew Narok Waterfall.** Take a picturesque 30km journey to this lesser-visited waterfall, which is higher and has pools for bathing. At 150m, these are the tallest and most spectacular falls in Khao Yai National Park. ⏱ *1 hr.*

4 **PB Valley Khao Yai Winery.** The temperate climes of the park have, in recent years, sparked an interest in planting grapes. Connoisseurs will surely cringe at the taste, but the wines are getting better every year. Harvest is February to March. ⏱ *45 min.* ☎ *036 226 415 6. www.khaoyaiwinery.com. Admission 200 baht adults, 10 baht kids. Daily 7.30am–4.30pm.*

5 **Khrua Khao Yai.** The park does have some wholesome restaurants and cafes, but for me the pick of the bunch is this one for great homemade Thai and western dishes. Try the ham. *Thanarat Rd. 27 Moo 7, Tambon Moo See, Pak Chong, Nakorn Ratchasima.* ☎ *044 297 138. Sun–Thurs 9am–8pm, Fri & Sat 9am–10pm.*

Khao Yai National Park is known for its lovely waterfalls.

Practical Matters: Khao Yai National Park

Outside Bangkok, of course, the driving is much easier and it is the best way to get around the park. Head out of Bangkok past Don Mueang Airport to Hwy 1. Drive north about 130km to Saraburi, then take Hwy 2 heading east. Drive 30km and turn right at Muak Lek and continue 20km to the national park entrance.

Catch a bus from Mo Chit (North and Northeastern) Bus Terminal in Bangkok to Pak Chong. Buses leave every 30 minutes from 5am to 10pm. The trip takes three hours, and tickets are 139 baht. Then take a red pick-up from Pak Chong train station to the park entrance (about 25 baht).

The other alternative is to book a tour (☎ 081 877 3127; www.dnp.go.th; admission 400 baht plus 50 baht per car; daily 8.30am–4.30pm).

Pattaya

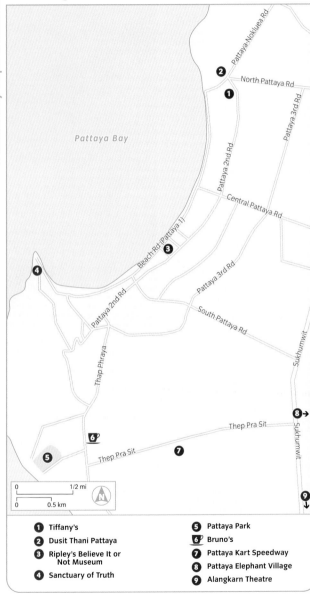

Pattaya Bay

Pattaya-Nokluea Rd

North Pattaya Rd

Pattaya 3rd Rd

Pattaya 2nd Rd

Central Pattaya Rd

Beach Rd (Pattaya 1)

Pattaya 3rd Rd

South Pattaya Rd

Pattaya 2nd Rd

Thap Phraya

Sukhumwit

Thep Pra Sit

Thep Pra Sit

0   1/2 mi
0   0.5 km

1. Tiffany's
2. Dusit Thani Pattaya
3. Ripley's Believe It or Not Museum
4. Sanctuary of Truth
5. Pattaya Park
6. Bruno's
7. Pattaya Kart Speedway
8. Pattaya Elephant Village
9. Alangkarn Theatre

Just 150km south-east of Bangkok, Pattaya is the nearest resort to the big city and is Thailand's most visited beach. It is easily accessible—many tourists jump straight off the plane, grab the next bus to Pattaya and are on the beach in no time. It has hotels, restaurants, bars, nightlife, theme parks and everything else you could imagine of a tropical resort. However, there's no hiding from the fact that Pattaya is perhaps the most notorious resort in the world for sex tourism. Go-go bars, prostitutes, massage services and the like are unavoidable. Those who feel uncomfortable with this should avoid Pattaya completely. Also be aware that visiting sex workers is a crime, and doing so perpetuates abuse. That said, Pattaya does have a lot to offer. In recent years a concerted effort has been made to attract families and non–sex tourists. Kite-surfers and windsurfers flock here to catch the waves, kids are kept amused by theme parks and there are first-class entertainment venues, golf courses, restaurants, scuba diving courses, shopping malls and much more. Or, of course, you can just laze out on the white sandy beach on a lounger, eat seafood from passing vendors, get your hair plaited and swim in the sea. START: **Eastern Bus Terminal, Hua Lamphong Station or Sukhumvit Road.**

1 Tiffany's. Tiffany's is a spectacular transvestite cabaret show in a palatial 1000-seat setting. The show is tasteful and very popular with tour groups. It also hosts the number-one ladyboy beauty pageant in the country. There are four shows nightly from 6.30pm. *464 Moo 9, Pattaya II Rd.* ☎ *03 842 1700. www.tiffany-show.co.th. Admission 500–700 baht.*

A performer in Tiffany's renowned beauty pageant.

Lovely Ladies and Ladyboys

Transvestites are accepted and ubiquitous in Thai society. No party is complete without a few of these colourful characters (known as *khatoeys* or ladyboys). While most Thais may be shy, ladyboys are usually extroverts. Many Thai celebrities and TV stars are ladyboys. In Pattaya, hundreds of *khatoeys* work as prostitutes—often to save money for operations.

2 Dusit Thani Pattaya.
The spacious suites with sea views here are a class above the seedy city below. The Dusit also offers a swimming pool, spa, gymnasium and a Jim Thompson silk outlet. *240/2 Pattaya Beach Rd. ☎ 03 842 5611. www.dusit.com. 457 units. Doubles from 7000 baht. AE, DC, MC, V.*

3 kids Ripley's Believe It or Not Museum. A weird and wacky collection of trivia, a haunted house, a simulator, a walk-through maze and other bizarre activities that are

A close-up view of the Sanctuary of Truth.

great for a rainy day. ⏲ *2 hr. 2nd floor, Royal Garden Plaza, 218 Moo 10, Beach Rd. ☎ 03 871 0294 8. www.ripleysthailand.com. Admission 780 baht adults, 680 baht kids. Daily 11am–11pm.*

4 Sanctuary of Truth. This 105m wooden temple stands out on the Pattaya skyline. It's quite magnificent with Hindu-inspired carvings, Buddha heads, three-headed elephants and a thousand other carved figurines that dance in the sunset. ⏲ *1 hr. 206/2 Moo 5, Naklua Soi 12, Pattaya-Naklua Rd, Banglamung. ☎ 03 836 7815 or 03 838 7229. www.sanctuaryoftruth. com. Admission 500 baht adults, 250 baht kids. Daily 8am–6pm.*

5 kids Pattaya Park. Fun for all the family—a hotel, restaurant and entertainment complex in one. On offer is a water park with slides, tubes and a swimming pool area—excellent for kids. There is a carousel, a rollercoaster, kids' rides and a 'tower shot' plunge, all inside the so-called 'Funny Land'. On the top floor of the tower there's a nice revolving restaurant and, after lunch, you can slide back down to earth on mini ski lifts. ⏲ *4 hr. 345 Jomtien Beach. ☎ 03 825 1201 8. www.pattayapark.com.*

6 Bruno's. Pattaya is wall-to-wall with fast-food joints, so let me suggest you take a taxi to Bruno's for a fantastic French meal instead. The set lunch is always excellent value for money. *306/63 Chateau Dale Plaza, Thappraya Rd, Pattaya Beach. ☎ 03 836 4600. www.brunospattaya.com. AE, MC, V. Daily noon–2.30pm, 6pm– midnight. $$.*

7 kids Pattaya Kart Speedway. A 1km go-kart track with good safety standards. There's also a beginner's track. Prices from

Pattaya, Thailand's most visited beach, can provide you with as much or as little activity as you desire.

200 baht. 🕐 *1 hr.248/2 Thep Prasit Rd, Soi 9.* ☎ *03 842 2044. Daily 9am–6pm.*

8 **kids** **Pattaya Elephant Village.** Here's your chance to ride an elephant and watch the beautiful beasts painting, playing sports and bathing. Tickets include lunch, an elephant ride, rafting and a show. 🕐 *3 hr. 48/120 Moo 7, Tambon Nong Prue, Pattaya City.* ☎ *03 824 9818. www.elephant-village-pattaya. com. Tickets 2000 baht. Daily 8.30am–7pm.*

9 **kids** **Alangkarn Theatre.** Calling itself 'The Extravaganza Show', this late-afternoon dinner theatre and show is part circus, part cabaret. A Thai meal is served at 5pm and the show begins at 6pm. It features elephants, fireworks, traditional dancing, music, theatrical renditions of Thai mythology and much colour and razzamatazz. 🕐 *3 hr. Sukhumvit Rd Km 155.* ☎ *03 825 6000 or 02 216 1869. www.alangkarnthailand. com. Tickets 1000 baht adults, 700 baht kids.*

Practical Matters: Pattaya

Buses leave Eastern Bus Terminal in Bangkok every 30 minutes from 4.30am to 7.30pm and the trip takes two hours; tickets are 84 baht. Alternatively, Suvarnabhumi Airport (☎ 02 134 4099) operates a minibus service direct to Pattaya leaving the airport bus terminal at 9am, noon and 7pm daily. The trip takes two hours and costs 106 baht. Book via ☎ 02 246 0973, hotline 184 or www. bmta.co.th.

Another option is to catch a train from Hua Lamphong Station at 7am (but check first). The trip takes three hours. Book via ☎ 02 621 8701, 24-hour hotline 1690 or www.railway.co.th.

If you have a car, head to Ekkamai from Sukhumvit Road and keep driving east. The road eventually turns into Hwy 34. Follow signs for Chonburi and Pattaya. The trip should take two hours (traffic should ease a bit after Chonburi).

Ayutthaya

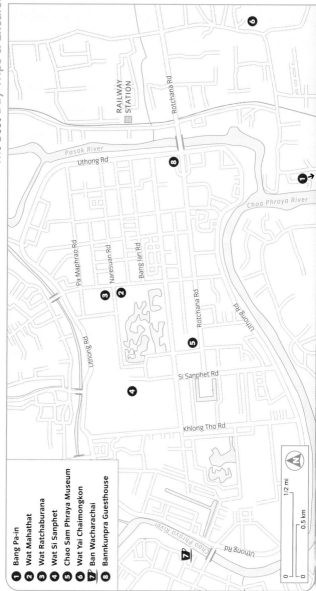

1 Bang Pa-in
2 Wat Mahathat
3 Wat Ratchaburana
4 Wat Si Sanphet
5 Chao Sam Phraya Museum
6 Wat Yai Chaimongkon
7 Ban Wacharachai
8 Bannkunpra Guesthouse

Once the capital of Siam and regarded as the greatest city in Asia, Ayutthaya is now a UNESCO World Heritage Site, and offers visitors the chance to reminisce back to the days when Bangkok was no more than a fort guarding the river to this divine city of 1 million people. The city was founded in 1350, and Ayutthayans were advanced and powerful, their influence felt around the region. They tidily conquered the almighty Khmer at Angkor and extended their kingdom to Burma, Laos and southern China. The glory of Ayutthaya was destroyed in 1767 by rampaging Burmese armies, who looted the Siamese capital and destroyed many of its great buildings. Most visitors arrive by train or tour bus. The best way to see the ruins of Ayutthaya, in my opinion, is to rent a bicycle and meander around at your own speed. You can rent bicycles just outside the train station for about 50 baht a day, or at any one of several stores in town. START: **Mo Chit Bus Terminal, Hua Lamphong Station or Hwy 1.**

❶ **Bang Pa-in.** About 53km north of Bangkok lies the former royal palace of Bang Pa-in. It sits on an island in the Chao Phraya River and is very picturesque. It was built in the 17th century, but fell into disrepair before King Mongkut revived the palace in 1872. The architecture is a real clash of Chinese, Thai and Gothic styles. You can reach Bang Pa-in by boat from Ayutthaya (45 minutes). A dress code applies: long sleeves, no shorts or short skirts. Bang Pa-in makes for a beautiful journey on a nice day.

This Buddha head trapped in tree roots can be found at Wat Mahathat.

🕐 *2 hr.* ☎ *03 526 1044/03 526 1549. www.palaces.thai.net. Admission 100 baht. Daily 8am–4pm.*

❷ **Wat Mahathat.** Like a scene from *The Jungle Book*, these ancient red temples are littered with overgrown pathways and staircases that speak of the decadent times of yore. Built in 1374, the main *pang* (stupa) is Khmer in architectural style, perhaps resembling a melting candle. The most photographed image in Ayutthaya must be the Buddha head at Wat Mahathat which is set within the intertwining roots of a fig tree. 🕐 *30 min.*

❸ **Wat Ratchaburana.** Erected by King Boromracha II in the 15th century, this hulking great temple once housed much of the city's treasure, some of which is now on display at the Chao Sam Phraya Museum ❺. Around the main stupa you can see fine carved figures of the mythical *naga* serpent and the bird-god Garuda. 🕐 *15 min.*

❹ **Wat Si Sanphet.** This beautiful row of *chedis* was built in 1492 to house the ashes of some of the relatives of King Rama

The colourful Buddha figures at Wat Yai Chaimongkon.

Thibodi II. This is probably the most photogenic area in Ayutthaya and a great chance to wander around stone Buddha images and temples in a neat grass park. ⏲ *15 min.*

⑤ Chao Sam Phraya Museum.
Opened in 1961, this is where much of Ayutthaya's wealth is on display—that which wasn't pillaged or melted down by the Burmese. There are bronze and stone sculptures, terracotta pieces, wood carvings, gold jewellery and precious stones. There is also the sculpture of a seated Buddha, which dates to the 11th or 12th century. ⏲ *45 min. 108 Moo 4 Rotchana Rd.* ☎ *03 524 1587. Admission 150 baht. Wed–Sun 9am–4pm.*

⑥ Wat Yai Chaimongkon.
Even if you have cycled around enough temples and Buddhas to last a lifetime, you still have to take in the towering 60m *chedi* here. Built in 1357 by King U Thong, the site boasts a reclining Buddha and a shrine of toys. A small community of white-robed Buddhist nuns live here, mostly practicing meditation. ⏲ *30 min.*

⑦ Ban Wacharachai.
Situated next to Wat Kasat and overlooking the river, this splendid, lush restaurant is a must. It's popular day and night, and is best known for its smoked snakehead fish. It offers a few western dishes, but I highly recommend trying an assortment of central Thai specialties. *9 Moo 7 Baan Pom.* ☎ *03 532 1333. Daily 10am–9pm. $$.*

⑧ Bannkunpra Guesthouse.
This is not luxury accommodation, but rooms in this 100-year-old teak building overlooking the river are authentic and exotic. Staff are friendly and the location is good, but there are only a few ensuite rooms, so book in advance. *48 Moo 3, U Thong Rd.* ☎ *03 524 1978. www.bannkunpra.com. 15 units. Doubles 600 baht.* ●

Practical Matters: Ayutthaya

Buses leave from Mo Chit Bus Terminal (North and Northeastern Terminal) every 20 minutes and the trip takes one hour; tickets start at 60 baht.

Trains to Ayutthaya leave Hua Lamphong Station roughly every 30 minutes and the trip takes 1½ hours; tickets start at 30 baht. Then walk five minutes to the river and take a small ferry ride across.

If you have a car, leave Bangkok via the expressway north of Don Mueang Airport, where the road becomes Hwy 1. Drive 65km to Wang Noi, then turn northwest on the 309 and drive 18km into Ayutthaya. It's a fairly boring drive—the only plus being that you can stop at Bang Pa-in (❶).

The **Savvy Traveller**

Before You Go

Government Tourist Offices

Australia: 111 Empire Circuit, Yarralumla, Canberra ACT 2600 (☎ 02 6273 1149 or 02 6273 2937). **Canada**: 180 Island Park Dr, Ottawa, Ontario K1Y QA2 (☎ 613 7224444). **France**: 8 Rue Greuze, 75116 Paris (☎ 1 4704 3222 or 1 4704 6892). **Germany**: Ubierstrasse 65, 53173 Bonn (☎ 0228 355065). **Japan**: 3/146, Kami Osaki, Shinagawa-ku, Tokyo 141 (☎ 03 3441 1386). **The Netherlands**: 1 Buitenrustweg, 2517 KD. The Hague (☎ 070 345 2088 or 070 345 9703). **New Zealand**: 2 Cook Street, PO Box 17–226, Karori, Wellington (☎ 476 8618 or 476 8619). **Spain**: Calle del Segre, 29–2A, 28002 Madrid (☎ 563 2903 or 563 7959). **UK**: 29–30 Queen's Gate, London SW7 5JB (☎ 071 589 0173 or 071 589 2944). **US**: 2300 Kalorama Rd NW Washington DC (☎ 202 483 7200).

The Best Time to Go

The best time to visit Bangkok is during the cool season, from November to February. This is when most tourists arrive. March to May is the hot season. The rainy season generally runs from May to October. A city of over 10 million people, Bangkok is always busy and the humidity is very high.

Festivals & Special Events

Thailand is a land of many ceremonies and festivals. Many visitors plan their trips especially to take in one or more of the annual festivals. Thais simply love their culture, their religion and their royal family, and any festival is somehow turned into a carnival of fun with lots of eating, drinking, music, fireworks, beauty pageants and millions of smiles.

SUMMER. The **Bangkok Jazz Festival** (☎ 02 203 1240 7, www.bangkokjazzfestival.com) is held on Friday, Saturday and Sunday nights in the middle of December. International jazz bands play at various clubs in the city.

The **River of Kings Festival** in January is a colourful sound and light show. Set on the Chao Phraya River with the Grand Palace as a backdrop, the 10-night spectacle (daily, 7pm and 9.30pm) depicts tales of ancient Siamese kings and warriors, complimented by dancers, fireworks and fountains. You can catch a glimpse of the show free from the riverside or buy tickets to enjoy the performance from the luxury of a river cruiser or a floating stadium (☎ 02 250 5500).

Chinese New Year is a week-long explosion of fireworks and Chinese dragons when Chinatown all but closes down in January. It's a good time to visit Chinatown and Chinese temples.

Makha Bucha is held at the first full moon of the third lunar month (which can be either February or March), and marks the Buddha's first sermon to his followers. It's celebrated with candlelit ceremonies in the evening at all Buddhist temples. I recommend Wat Benchamabophit (the Marble Temple; see p 38, bullet **10**)—it's very photogenic.

AUTUMN. The windy season is between February and April in Bangkok and every Sunday you can see children (and adults) flying—or fighting—kites at Sanam Luang. In March there are contests during the **Kite-Flying Festival.** Call the Tourism Authority of Thailand (TAT) for details on ☎ 02 250 5500.

Previous page: Tuktuks are a great way to zip around Bangkok.

Bangkok International Fashion Week is usually in March and is held at Siam Paragon (see p 26). The event showcases the work of Thai designers (www.thaicatwalk.com).

If Carnival in Rio was ever held in a giant water park, it might be like the **Songkran Festival** (Thai New Year), a week-long extravaganza marking the Thai New Year on April 13 to 14. The country celebrates with the 'Water Festival', a free-for-all frenzy of soaking and splashing. Religious activities also take place among the chaos, notably at Sanam Luang, where the image of the Phra Buddha Sihing is carried out and ritually bathed. Ratchadamnoen Avenue and Khao San Road (see p 54, bullet ⑤) are also popular drenching spots. Visitors beware—you will not be spared! Arm yourself with water guns and prepare for a bath! Carry nothing that cannot survive underwater.

The **Royal Ploughing Ceremony** is reenacted every year in May at Sanam Luang in front of the Grand Palace. This ancient event is performed to gain an auspicious start to the planting season. Sacred white oxen symbolically plough the field, which is then sown with seeds blessed by the king. After that farmers rush in to collect the hallowed seeds to replant in their own fields.

Visakha Bucha commemorates the date of the Buddha's birth, enlightenment and transcendence to Nirvana; candlelit processions and sermons are held at all temples. There's a larger festival at Sanam Luang. For more information, contact TAT (☎ 02 250 5500).

Miss Tiffany Universe (www.misstiffanyuniverse.com), held in May or June, is the Thai version of Oscar Night. This televised pageant in Pattaya selects the country's most beautiful ladyboy.

WINTER. Devotees flock to temples to pray on **Asanha Bucha**, the day commemorating Buddha's first sermon after his enlightenment. The following morning, **Khao Pansa**, you can often watch young men being ordained as monks at temples as Buddhist Lent begins.

Bangkok International Film Festival (☎ 02 203 0624 or 02 641 5917, www.bangkokfilm.org) screens more than 150 movies in 10 days at various locations around the city centre, showcasing Thai, Asian and international indie films. Dates vary every year.

SPRING. The **International Festival of Music & Dance** is a month-long festival of opera, jazz, ballet, symphony and more, usually held at the Thailand Cultural Center on Ratchadaphisek Rd (☎ 02 661 6835 7).

My favourite festival, **Loy Kratong**, is a time for reflection. Similar to making New Year's resolutions, you have the opportunity to atone for your sins of the previous year and promise to make amends and pray for good luck in the year ahead. The cleansing ritual itself involves making *kratong*—tiny banana-leaf boats with masts of incense and candles with sails made from 50-baht notes—then going down to the banks of the river, closing your eyes, making a wish and letting your *kratong* (and your worries) go away with the current. With 60 million Thai people doing likewise that night, the effect of thousands of candles floating downstream together is amazing. You can also light a Chinese lantern (a *kom*) and send it floating up to the heavens. The festival usually takes place under the first full moon in November, and is best enjoyed somewhere along the Chao Phraya River.

The **Savvy** Traveller

BANGKOK'S AVERAGE TEMPERATURE & RAINFALL						
	JAN	FEB	MAR	APR	MAY	JUN
Daily temp (°F)	92	94	92	98	92	92
Daily temp (°C)	33	34	33	36	33	33
Avg. Rainfall (mm)	11	9	175	28	257	102
	JUL	AUG	SEP	OCT	NOV	DEC
Daily temp (°F)	92	92	94	92	90	90
Daily temp (°C)	33	33	34	33	32	32
Avg. Rainfall (mm)	62	149	450	480	37	4

Gay Pride Week (www.pride festival.org) involves parties, contests, parades and more feather boas than you can shake a stick at. It's held at Silom Rd Soi 4 and various locations around the city

Golden Mount Fair runs over eight days and seven nights—from the 11th day of the waxing moon of the 12th lunar month to the 3rd day of the waning moon of the same month. Bangkokians worship the Buddha's relics, which are said to be enshrined in the Golden Mount (see p 53, bullet ❶). There are folk plays, art shows, market stalls and lots of food. The photographic highlight of the evening is a candlelit circumambulation of the mount.

Useful Websites

• **www.1stopbangkok.com:** General information plus suggestive tips on Bangkok's notoriously sexy nightlife.

• **www.bangkok.com:** Lots of tourist information, including hotel deals, rental car discounts and entertainment.

• **www.bangkokpost.com:** The Thai capital's top English-language daily is good for local and international news, weather and sports.

• **www.bkkmaps.com:** You can pinpoint streets, districts, entertainment venues and restaurants, and even get directions between two points on this website.

• **www.teakdoor.com:** A trendy site for forums. Post your comments and opinions, and get others' feedback on places, venues and Bangkok life.

Cell Phones (Mobiles)

You should be able to use your own mobile phone in Thailand if you arrange for international roaming before you leave home. The phone charges are usually calculated from your home country to the destination number and can be expensive, so regular users should buy a SIM card in Bangkok. Service providers include True Move (Orange), AIS and DTAC.

Getting **There**

By Plane

Bangkok has one international airport, **Suvarnabhumi International Airport**, situated 35km east of the city centre. **Getting to and from the airport**: Although many independent **taxi** drivers operate freely at the airport, there is a

24-hour taxi rank on level 2, outside arrivals. Metered taxis are arranged quickly and efficiently with a 50-baht charge added to the taxi fare. The average cost of a taxi to downtown Bangkok is around 300 baht. There is also a limousine service at the airport.

Free **shuttle buses** escort passengers to the car rental centre and local bus terminal.

Public **buses** run 24 hours from the terminal to various parts of the city. The fare is 35 baht.

Avis, Hertz, Budget and several other **car rental agencies** operate 24 hours at the airport.

By Train

Trains to Bangkok arrive at **Hua Lamphong Station** from Singapore and Malaysia.

By Bus

Buses from Malaysia terminate at the **Southern Bus Terminal** (24/6 Moo 8, Bamrung Ratchachonnanee Rd, Chimpli Taling Chun; ☎ 02 894 6122 ext 5). There's no shortage of taxis and local buses heading to the city centre from the front door of the terminal, but there's no metro station nearby. Buses from Cambodia and Laos pull up at the **Northern Bus Terminal** (also known as Mor Chit Terminal; Kampaengphet 2 Rd, Chatuchak; ☎ 02 537 8055). Hordes of taxis wait outside the terminal 24 hours, and there are dozens of local buses to the city centre. The best option for transport is the metro; it's five minutes to Chatuchak Park MRT line or Mo Chit BST line (Skytrain).

Getting **Around**

By Metro

Getting around Bangkok is easier and quicker now than it was 20 years ago, mainly due to expressways and the twin metropolitan rail lines, known collectively as the **metro**—the Bangkok Transit System (BTS) or Skytrain, and the Mass Rapid Transit (MRT) network.

The metro covers the main shopping, business and nightlife centres of the city. For the Old City, you should take taxis and express boats on the river.

The **BTS** is the fastest way to get around; it's clean, efficient, air-conditioned, cheap and runs daily 6.30am to midnight. There are two lines: the **Silom line** runs between National Stadium at the Siam shopping area to Saphan Taksin at the riverside, while the **Sukhumvit line** runs from Mo Chit to On Nut. The two lines meet at Siam station, and also interconnect at two points

with the underground (MRT)—at Sala Daeng and Asok stations. Easy-to-read BTS city maps are free from any station. Fares are 15 to 40 baht. A one-day unlimited **Skytrain Pass** costs 120 baht (ideal for tourists). For more information call ☎ 02 617 7300, BTS Hotline 02 617 6000, BTS Tourist Information Center 02 617 7340 2; www.bts.co.th.

Opened in 2004, the **MRT** is as fast, efficient and modern as the Skytrain. There are currently 18 MRT stations with more in the pipeline. It stretches 20km in a horseshoe shape from **Hua Lamphong** (the main train station) near Chinatown to Bang Sue in the north. Fares are 15 to 40 baht. An unlimited **one-day MRT pass** costs 120 baht; a **three-day pass** costs 230 baht; and a **30-day pass** costs 800 baht. For more information call ☎ 02 612 2444.

By Express Boat

My favourite way of travelling in Bangkok is by boat. It's the best way to get to famous historical attractions such as the Grand Palace. It also affords you the opportunity to visit the canals around the city. While the **express boat** service runs south to north, ferries can be used to cross the river at various points. You can buy tickets as you get on at each port and fares are 10 to 34 baht, or invest in a **day pass** for 150 baht (can only be used outside peak hours). For more information call ☎ 02 222 5330 or 02 225 3003, hotline: 02 623 6143; www.chaophrayaboat.co.th.

By Public Bus (BMTA)

Buses are a very cheap but slow way to get around Bangkok. Since destinations on most **buses** are written in Thai, the best way for visitors to figure out which bus goes where is by the bus number and its colours, which is where the BMTA bus map comes in very handy. Be aware that buses with the same number but different colours don't necessarily share the same route. Fares are collected by the bus conductor, not the driver; use coins and small notes only. Keep the small receipt because sometimes it will be checked. Fares are 7 to 10 baht. For more information call ☎ 02 246 0973, hotline 184; www.bmta.co.th.

By Taxi

Most **taxis** are new, comfortable, air-conditioned and come in an array of bright colours. Taxis will usually find you, especially at hotels, shopping malls and tourist attractions. As almost anywhere in the world, there are taxi drivers who will try to overcharge tourists. However, if you insist on paying by the meter you should be fine. Fares start at 35 baht for 2km, then go up by roughly 2 baht per kilometre.

Therefore a typical journey, say from Silom Road to the Grand Palace, costs 70 baht. Bangkok Taxi Radio Center can be reached on ☎ 02 880 0888 (24 hours).

By Tuktuk

No visit to Bangkok is complete without a bouncing, screeching, heart-thumping ride around town in a **tuktuk**. Designed like mini-discotheques and driven by Formula 1 drivers, these tiny terrors are always popular with visitors. Fares start from 30 baht for a 10-minute journey, but must be agreed with the driver before setting off. Avoid taking a tuktuk during rush hour, because the traffic is very slow and the air is thick with fumes.

By Motorbike Taxi

Bangkok's most frightening experience is zigzagging along Sukhumvit Road at high speed on the back of a 100cc bike, but it is fast and cheap. Easily recognised by their orange vests, motorcycle chauffeurs gather at metro stations, busy junctions, tourist areas, shopping malls and the like. Fares start from 10 baht, but must be negotiated prior to take-off.

By Car

No foreign visitor in their right mind rents a car to drive around Bangkok. It's slow, expensive, irritating, there's nowhere to park and it's dangerous. However, if you are heading out of the city, it can be a good option if you're confident driving in reckless traffic. You will need an international driving license and your passport to rent a car. Prices start at about 1500 baht per day.

By Plane

Domestic flights are relatively cheap in Thailand. In Bangkok there are two domestic airports: Suvarnabhumi and Don Mueang.

By Train

The main station is **Hua Lamphong**, situated in central Bangkok near Chinatown (Rama IV Road; ☎ 02 621 8701, 24-hour hotline 1690; www.railway.co.th). It is on the MRT metro line. Trains run daily north to Ayutthaya, Chiang Mai, Phitsanulok, Nakorn Ratchasima, Ubon Ratchathani and Udon Thani. A line also runs south to Hua Hin, Chumpon, Suratthani, Trang and Songkhla. Another runs southeast to Pattaya.

From **Bangkok Noi** train station in Thonburi (Rod Fai Rd/Train Rd Sirirach, Bangkok Noi; ☎ 02 411 3102; www.railway.co.th), trains run daily to Kanchanaburi.

Fast **Facts**

ATMS ATMs are plentiful in Bangkok and accept most western debit cards. You can use your PIN from home. You'll find 24-hour ATMs in shopping malls, at 7-Elevens, at petrol stations and on busy streets. Or just ask your taxi driver to stop at an ATM en route.

BABYSITTING Asking a stranger to babysit for you is not common in Thai culture and there are no recommended agencies. The best option would be to ask your hotel staff.

BIKE RENTALS Velothailand (see p 132) rents quality bicycles and organises cycling tours of Bangkok. There is also a list of bike rental stores at: www.yellow.co.th/YellowPages/Bangkok/bicycle-rental.

BUSINESS HOURS Banks: 8.30am to 3.30pm Monday to Friday. Government offices: 8.30am to 4.30pm Monday to Friday. Temples: usually 8am to 6pm daily. Bars: usually 6pm to 1am daily. Pharmacies: usually 9am to 7pm Monday to Saturday.

CLIMATE See The Best Time to Go, earlier in this chapter.

CONSULATES & EMBASSIES
Australia: 37 Sathorn Tai Rd, Sathorn (☎ 02 344 6300). **Canada**: 15th Floor, Abdulrahim Place, 990 Rama IV Rd, Bangrak (☎ 02 636 0540). **China**: 57 Ratchadaphisek Rd, Din Daeng (☎ 02 245 7043 4). **France**: 35 Soi Rong Phasi Kao (Soi 36), Charoenkrung Rd, Bangrak (☎ 02 657 5100). **Germany**: 9 Sathorn Tai Rd, Sathorn (☎ 02 287 9000). **India**: 46 Soi Prasanmit, Sukhumvit Soi 23 (☎ 02 258 0300 5). **Japan**: 177 Witthayu Road, Lumphini, Pathumwan (☎ 02 207 8500 or 02 696 3000). **The Netherlands**: 15 Soi Tonson, Ploenchit Rd, Lumphini, Phatumwan (☎ 02 309 5200). **New Zealand**: M Thai Tower, 14th floor, All Seasons Place, 87 Witthayu Rd, Lumphini (☎ 02 254 2530). **Spain**: Lake Ratchada Office Complex Building, 23rd floor, 193/98–99 Ratchdaphisek Rd, Klong Toey (☎ 02 661 8284 5). **UK**: 1031 Wireless Rd, Lumphini, Pathumwan (☎ 02 305 8333). **US**: 120–122 Witthayu Rd, Pathumwan (☎ 02 251 7202 or 02 251 3552).

CURRENCY EXCHANGE Several banks and bureaus de change operate at the airport, though seldom from midnight to 6am. They accept foreign currencies, major credit cards (American Express, Diners Club, MasterCard and Visa) and travellers' cheques. Rates are comparable to regular bank rates.

CUSTOMS REGULATIONS The duty-free allowance for all passengers arriving in Thailand is 200 cigarettes or 250g of cigars or smoking tobacco, and 1 litre of alcoholic spirits or wine.

DOCTORS Private hospitals (see Hospitals) offer a full range of medical, health and cosmetic treatments in Bangkok. Visitors are recommended to use their facilities rather than seek out private clinics, which generally cater for regular patients. Private hospitals have English-speaking staff, are open 24 hours, have doctors specialising in various fields and have on-site pharmacies.

DENTISTS In general, dentists in Bangkok are modern, of high quality and good value for money. Teeth cleaning, whitening, crowns and extractions can all be taken care of with little fuss. **Silom area**: Silomdental (439/4–5 Naratiwatrajnakarin Rd; ☎ 02 636 9091 7; www.silomdental.com; Monday to Saturday 10am to 8pm, Sunday 10am to 5pm). **Sukhumvit area**: Dental Design Clinic & Lab (10 Dental Design Bldg, Sukhumvit Soi 21; ☎ 02 261 9119 20; www.dentaldesignclinic-lab.com; Monday to Friday 9am to 6pm, Saturday and public holidays 9am to 5pm). **Ratchasapisek area**: International Dental Center (BIDC); 157 Ratchadapesik Rd; ☎ 02 692 4433; www.bangkokdentalcenter.com; Monday to Friday 10am to 8pm, Saturday 10am to 8pm, Sunday and public holidays 10am to 5pm.

DRINKING, SMOKING & DRUG LAWS There are no official age restrictions on buying alcohol; however, you must be 20 years of age to enter a nightclub. You must be 18 to buy cigarettes. There is no smoking allowed inside public places. Most bars and restaurants provide outdoor smoking areas.

Buying, using or selling any narcotic drug is strictly prohibited in Thailand. Penalties are severe. Bangkok was once a hippy haven and in the 1970s and '80s many foreigners found they could smoke dope openly in certain bars and resorts. Those days are gone, and Thailand's prisons are full of foreigners who thought otherwise. Remember that foreign tourists are a natural target for police informers, con artists and even sometimes off-duty policemen. A charming, English-speaking person may offer you marijuana or opium, but remember that they can make much more money by turning you in to the police than by selling drugs to you.

ELECTRICITY The voltage is 220 volt AC with flat two-pin plugs. You can buy an adapter for shavers, laptops, mobile phone chargers and so on on arrival at the airport, or at most department stores.

EMBASSIES See Consulates and Embassies.

EMERGENCIES Dial ☎ 191 for the **police**, ☎ 1669 for **ambulance and rescue**, ☎ 199 for the **fire brigade** and ☎ 1554 for a **medical emergency**.

GAY & LESBIAN TRAVELLERS Thailand is one of the most gay-friendly countries in the world. Few Thais will give a second thought to your sexuality, such is the openness of gay culture in the country. The only matter generally frowned upon is displays of physical affection—homosexual or otherwise—in public.

HOSPITALS Bumrungrad International: 33 Sukhumvit 3 (Soi Nana Nua), Wattana; ☎ 02 667 1000; www.bumrungrad.com. **Samitivej**: 133 Sukhumvit 49, Klongtan Nua Wattana; ☎ 02 711 8000; www.samitivejhospitals.com. **Bangkok Hospital**: 2 Soi Soonvijai

7, New Petchaburi Rd, Bangkapi, Huay Khwang; ☎ 02 310 3000 or 1719, heart hotline 02 375 2222; www.bangkokhospital.com.

INSURANCE Check your health insurance policy before leaving home to ensure that Thailand is covered. As a tropical country there may be some restrictions. In the unfortunate event of an accident, medical staff in Thailand will always ask if you have insurance and will call your insurance company—whether it is in Thailand or abroad—to confirm your cover.

INTERNET CAFES You can find internet cafes all over the city, especially at tourist areas and shopping malls. The average rate is about 1 baht per minute. Most guesthouses and hotels also offer internet access. Some good ones are: **Welcome Internet**: 84 Jakkapong Rd, Chanasongkram, Pranakorn; ☎ 02 629 0140 1; daily 7.30am to 9pm; 1 baht per minute; 40 baht per hour. **Planet Earth**: Soi Patpong 1, Surawong Rd; ☎ 02 632 6870; daily noon to 5am; 1 baht per minute. **Cyber cafe**: 2nd floor, Ploenchit Center, Sukhumvit Soi 2; ☎ 02 656 8473; daily 10am to 9.30pm; 5 baht per minute.

LOST PROPERTY There are no lost property offices in Bangkok. If you are lucky, someone will hand your lost item to the police, but don't hold your breath on it. Items left behind in taxis can be traced through the main taxi depot. Ask your hotel staff to help you.

MAIL & POSTAGE Post offices are open 8.30am to 4.30pm Monday to Friday and 9am to midday Saturday. Letters to/from Europe, Australia, the US and Canada usually take a week to arrive. For important documents use Express Mail Service (EMS) or registered post. You can mail postcards, letters and packages at any post office.

Stamp costs are as follows: postcards 2 baht (within Thailand), 9 to 12 baht (international); letters up to 100 grams 3 baht (within Thailand), 24 to 80 baht to the UK, 28 to 100 baht to the US, 24 to 80 baht to Australia. Registered post, DHL, EMS and other international carriers also operate out of public post offices and private outlets. Many tourist-friendly shops and boutiques will arrange postage directly for you for a small commission. **Thailand Post**: 111 M3, Changwattana Rd, Laksi; ☎ 02 831 3131; www.thailandpost.com. **Bangrak**: Bangrak Post Office Building, Charoen Krung Rd; ☎ 02 236 9848. **Silom**: 333 Bangkok Bank head office building, Silom Rd, Bangrak; ☎ 02 231 4813 or 02 231 4888. **Ratchadamnoen**: 81 Ratchadamnoen Klang Rd, Soi Ratcha Damnoen Nua, Boworn Niwet, Pranakorn; ☎ 02 282 1811 ext 35 or 02 2825791 ext 49. **Rattanakosin**: 15–17 Na Pra Lan Rd, Grand Palace, Pra Nakorn; ☎ 02 222 3862 or 02 224 4705. **Pom Prab**: 77–79 Ratchawong Rd, Jakkawad, Sampanthawong; ☎ 02 222 1705. **Chulalongkorn University**: Pathumwan; ☎ 02 252 7404.

PASSPORTS & VISAS Visitors to Thailand receive an automatic 30-day tourist visa on arrival if they are a passport holder from most western countries, including Australia, Canada, France, Germany, the Netherlands, New Zealand, Spain, the UK and the US. Passports must be valid at least six months ahead of arrival. However, visitors who enter Thailand with a visa on arrival generally cannot apply for an extension. Visitors from countries such as China and India receive a 15-day tourist visa on arrival. Visitors who intend to stay longer than 30 days should organise a visa before arriving in Thailand. For more information: www.immigration.go.th.

PHARMACIES Most chemists will serve you if you have a prescription from home in English. Even if you don't, you should still be able to buy medicine and drugs—as long as you don't look like a hippy having a party.

POLICE Dial 191 for the police.

PUBLIC HOLIDAYS

1 Jan	New Year's Day
9 Feb	Makha Bucha Day
6 Apr	Chakri Day
13–15 Apr	Songkran (Thai New Year)
1 May	Labour Day
5 May	Coronation Day
8 May	Visakha Bucha Day
11 May	Royal Ploughing Ceremony
1 Jul	Mid-year Bank Holiday
9 Jul	Khao Phansa Day (Buddhist Lent)
12 Aug	HM The Queen's Birthday
23 Oct	Chulalongkorn Day
5 Dec	HM The King's Birthday
10 Dec	Constitution Day
31 Dec	New Year's Eve

SAFETY There are no 'unsafe areas' as such in central Bangkok. However, there are certainly 'unsafe activities'. Con men currently target tourists to sell fake gems or invite home for whisky and a game of cards. The most unsafe activity in Bangkok, by far, involves spending a drunken night with a sex worker (especially ladyboy sex workers). A spiked drink can result in 30 hours of sleep, a severe headache and the loss of everything but your socks!

SENIOR TRAVELLERS Elderly people are treated with great respect in Thailand and will find themselves bowed to and 'wai-ed' often. Many hotels and venues in popular tourist spots have wheelchair access, but it is uncommon elsewhere. The Skytrain, for example, requires good legs for the stairways. Unfortunately, despite the high status you receive as a senior, you won't get discounts on transport or at entertainment venues.

STAYING HEALTHY Thailand is generally a hygienic and healthy country. Of course, its tropical climate lends itself to diseases such as malaria and dengue fever, but these are 99.9 per cent confined to jungle environments and not in urban Bangkok. The most dangerous aspect in this city is the heat. Beware of sunstroke and sunburn. Drink LOTS of water, but not tap water—even the locals don't drink tap water. Street food is generally safe, although many visitors to Thailand will catch a quick dose of diarrhoea. If you do, stay out the heat, drink bottled water and eat bananas.

TAXES There is no departure tax when leaving the country. It is included in the ticket price.

TAXIS See Getting Around, earlier in the chapter.

TELEPHONES To make **international calls**, dial code ☎ 001, then the country code (Australia: 61, Britain: 44, France: 33, US and Canada: 1, and so on). When phoning the UK, the US and much of Europe, the alternative prefix 008 offers a reduced rate and the code 009 accesses Voice-Over-Internet Protocol (VOIP). It is cheaper to call 9pm to 7am, when rates are reduced by 20 to 30 per cent. For Bangkok **directory enquiries**, dial ☎ 13; for provincial directory enquiries, dial ☎ 1133.

For public telephone booths you can use phone cards or 1, 5 and 10 baht coins. Calls within Bangkok cost just 1 baht per minute. Area code 02 is used for all Bangkok numbers. Calls around Thailand cost 3 baht per minute.

There are always promotions and new services are constantly competing. At the time of writing there is a 50 per cent discount if you dial ☎ 1234 before any national number.

For international calls, the rates are usually 7 to 15 baht per minute. Dial ☎ 007, 008 or 009, before adding your country code (Australia: 61; UK: 44; US: 1), then the number.

To avoid using handfuls of coins, you can of course buy a phone card. They are available at shopping malls, 7-Elevens and convenience stores. Many do not have instructions in English, so you should ask the assistant to dial in your code to get connected.

TIPPING Tipping is seldom expected in local restaurants. In up-market establishments, a 10 per cent service fee may be added to bills. Knowing that westerners like to tip, staff in international restaurants will be grateful for, say, a 100 baht tip for a dinner for two. Taxi fares should be rounded up to the nearest 5 or 10 baht, especially for meter-taxis.

TOURIST INFORMATION The **Tourism Authority of Thailand (TAT)** can be found at 1600 New Phetchaburi Rd, Makkasan, Ratchathewi. Call ☎ 02 250 5500, Monday to Friday 8am to 4.30pm; hotline ☎ 1672 daily 8am to 8pm; or visit www. tourismthailand.org.

TRAVEL AGENCIES **Window Tour Service**: 41/181 Family Town, Soi Intamara 29, Suthisarn Rd, Samsennai, Phayathai; ☎ 02 616 0964 6; www.thailandvoyage. com. **LSH Travel**: Two offices: 3/3 Thedsaban-Nimit-Nua Rd, Chatuchak; ☎ 02 630 6640 1; and inside Saphan Taksin BTS station; ☎ 02 630 6663 or 02 630 6640 1; www.journeyasia.com. **Express International Travel**: 10/12–13 Convent Rd, Silom, Bangrak; ☎ 02 235 0557 8; www.expressinter.com.

TOURIST TRAPS It goes without saying that tourists are often targets for con men, pickpockets and thieves, so beware! Crafty taxi drivers, tricky jewel salespeople and other dodgy characters hang out around the main tourist spots, especially the Grand Palace, Patpong, Silom Road, Khao San Road and Sukhumvit Road, not to mention the major hotels. Overcharging is common and is rarely considered a crime. In cases of theft, assault or danger call the tourist police (☎1155).

VACCINATIONS Visitors do not require any vaccinations to enter Thailand. Only those intending to go to remote areas should consider taking malaria pills.

Local Customs, Traditions & Taboos

There are a number of hints that will help you have a happy stay in Bangkok. Firstly, the Thai royal family is deeply revered and disrespect toward the monarchy is not tolerated. Remember to stand for the Thai national anthem in cinemas, theatres, ceremonies and at certain events. Showing anger or shouting is regarded as crude and will not get you what you want; remain calm, smile and doors will open. You should dress appropriately when visiting temples—don't go shirtless or in shorts, short skirts or spaghetti-strap garments. Remove your shoes when entering a Thai home or a Buddhist temple. Do not point your foot at a person or an object, or touch a person's head with your hand.

Useful Phrases & Menu Terms

Thai language is usually very difficult for foreigners. There are 44 letters in the Thai alphabet, 26 of which are vowels. Each vowel is subject to a tone: rising, falling, high, low or flat. There are short vowel sounds and long vowel sounds. For example, a word with a short 'a' vowel may sound like 'bat' with the 't' clipped. The long vowel sounds more like 'baa', the noise a sheep makes. Listen to your Thai friends and imitate the words rather than concentrate on their spelling. Thais are usually very happy if you try to speak their language. *Chok dee!* (Good luck!)

Greetings & Common Phrases

Note: Using the following expressions, males should add the polite word '*khrup*' at the end, while females should say '*ka*'.

Hello	(m) Sawadee khrup/(f) Sawadee ka
How are you?	Sabai dee mai?
I'm fine, thanks	Sabai dee, khob khun
Excuse me/sorry	Kor tot
What's your name?	Khun cheu arai?
My name is ...	(m) Pom/(f) Chan cheu ...
Nice to meet you	Yin dee tee dai roo juk
Do you speak English?	Khun pood pa-sa angrit dai mai?
I don't understand	Mai khao jai
Can you say that again, please?	Pood eek krang dai mai?
Please speak slowly	Pood cha cha
See you later	Pob kan mai
Goodbye	La gorn
Goodnight	Ratri sawat
Please	Dai prod
What?	Arai?
Where?	Tee nai?
Who?	Krai?
Why?	Tam mai?

Emergencies

Help!	Chuay duai!
Fire!	Fai mai!
Thief	Kha-moy
Call the police	Riak tam-ruat hai noi
Police station	Satani tam-ruat
I need a doctor	Tong-garn mor
I need to go to hospital	Tong pai rong payabarn

Directions

Left	Sai
Right	Kwa
In front of	Khang nar
Behind	Khang lung
Go straight	Trong pai
Turn	Liaw
Stop	Yood
Where are you going?	Khun ja pai nai?
I'm going to ...	Ja pai ...
Where is ...?	... Yoo tee nai?
How do i get to ...?	... Pai yang rai?

Travelling

Bus	Rot mae
Bus station	Satani rot mae
Train	Rot fai
Railway station	Satani rot fai
Ticket	Tua
Airport	Sanarm bin
Ferry	Rua doy sarn
Express boat	Rua duan
Taxi	Taxi
Car	Rot keng
What time does it leave?	Ja ork kee mong?
What time is it arriving?	Ja ma kee mong?
How much is it?	Tao rai?

Places

Temple	Wat
Road	Tanon
Lane	Soi
Shop	Raan kaa
Cinema	Pappayon
Bank	Tanakarn
Embassy	Satan toot
Museum	Pipittapan
Post office	Praisanee
Restaurant	Rarn-a-harn
Hotel	Rong raem
Market	Ta laad

At a Hotel

Do you have a vacant room?	Khun mee hong wang mai?
I'd like a room for one night	Tong garn pak neung keun
What is the charge per night?	Keun la tao rai?
May I see the room first?	Kor doo hong dai mai?
Key	Koon jair
Room	Hong
Single room	Hong diaw

Double room	Hong koo
Soap	Saboo
Towel	Par ched tua
Hot water	Narm ron
Cold water	Narm yen

In a Restaurant

Food	Aharn
Breakfast	Aharn chao
Lunch	Aharn tiang
Dinner	Aharn yen
Dessert	Khong waan
Curry	Kaeng
Rice	Khao
Beer	Beer
Water	Narm plao
Spicy	Ped
Not spicy	Mai ped
Is it spicy?	Ped mai?
Salty	Kem
Sweet	Waan
Sour	Priaw
Can I see the menu please?	Kor menu dai mai?
It is very delicious	Aroi mak mak
Bill/cheque please	Keb ngoen duay

Health

I have a headache	(M)Pom/ (f)Chan puad hua
I have a fever	Pom/chan pen khai
Sore throat	Jeb kor
Cough	Ai
Medicine	Yaa
I'm allergic to ...	Pom pae ...

Numbers

0	Soon
1	Neung
2	Song
3	Sarm
4	See
5	Haa
6	Hok
7	Jed
8	Paed
9	Kao
10	Sib
11	Sib-ed
12	Sib-song
13	Sib-sarm
20	Yee sib
30	Sarm sib
40	See sib

100	Neung roy
1000	Neung pan

Time

Day	Wan
Month	Duean
Year	Pee
Today	Wan-nee
Tomorrow	Prung-nee
Yesterday	Mua wan-nee
Sunday	Wan ar-tit
Monday	Wan jun
Tuesday	Wan ang karn
Wednesday	Wan poot
Thursday	Wan pa-rue-hud
Friday	Wan sook
Saturday	Wan sao
One minute	Neung natee
One hour	Neung chao mong
What time is it?	Kee mong laew?

Phone Numbers & Websites

Airlines

AIR ASIA
☎ 02 515 9999
www.airasia.com

AIR FRANCE
www.airfrance.com

BANGKOK AIRWAYS
☎ 02 265 8777
www.bangkokair.com

BRITISH AIRWAYS
www.britishairways.com

CATHAY PACIFIC AIRWAYS
www.cathaypacific.com

JAPAN AIRLINES
www.jal.co.jp

NOK AIR
☎ 02 627 2000
www.nokair.com

QANTAS
www.qantas.co.au

THAI AIRWAYS
☎ 02 356 1111
www.thaiair.com

UNITED AIRLINES
www.united.com

Car Rental Agencies

AVIS
☎ 02 251 1131 2 or 02 255 5300 4
www.avisthailand.com

BUDGET
☎ 02 203 9222 or 02 203 9294 5
☎ 1 800 283 438
www.budget.co.th

HIGHWAY CAR RENT
☎ 02 266 9393

Credit Card Companies

AMEX
☎ 02 273 5500

AMEX LOST CARDS
☎ 02 273 5100 or 02 273 0022

DINERS CLUB
☎ 02 238 3660

DINERS CLUB LOST CARDS
☎ 02 238 2920 or 02 238 2680

MASTERCARD & VISA (INCLUDING LOST CARDS)
☎ 02 256 7376 7

Index

See also Accommodation and Restaurant indexes, below.

100 Tonson Gallery, 128

A

About Cafe/About Studio, 128
Absolute 7, 118
Absolute Yoga, 50
Accommodation, 133–146. *See also* Accommodation Index
best bets, 134
Ad Here the 13th, 119
Air Asia, 177
Air France, 177
Air travel, 166–168, 177
Alangkarn Theatre (Pattaya), 159
Alliance Française, 129
Allied War Cemetery (Kanchanaburi), 150
Almeta, 79
American Express, 177
Amulet Market, 14, 37, 55, 72
Ananta Samakkorn Throne Hall, 88
Ancient Cloth & Silk Museum, 88
Antiques, exportation of, 73
Arts & entertainment, 123–132
art galleries, 128
best bets, 124
cabaret, 131
cinemas, 128
classical music, 129
cultural Institutes, 129
dinner theatre, 130
opera, 131
puppet shows, 131
sports venues, 131
Asanha Bucha 165
Asia Books, 72
ATMs (automatic teller machines), 169
Avis, 177
Ayurvedic massage, 48, 49
Ayurvedic medicine, 64
Ayutthaya, 19, 160–162
Ayutthaya era, 37, 38, 39, 63, 161

B

Baat, 53
Babysitting, 169
Bacchus Wine Bar, 122
The Balcony, 118
Bamboo Bar, 119
Bang Kwang Chinese temple, 61
Bang Kwang Prison, 61
Bang Pa-in (Ayutthaya), 161
Bangkok Airways, 177
Bangkok Dolls Museum, 42
Bangkok Golf Club, 131
Bangkok International Fashion Week 164–165
Bangkok International Film Festival 165
Bangkok National Museum, 21, 60
Bangkok Opera, 131
Bangkok Planetarium & Science Museum, 45
Bangkok Symphony Orchestra, 84
Bangkok TK Park, 44
Banglamphu, 31
Banglamphu Canal, 60
Banyan Tree Spa, 49
Barbican Bar, 115
Bargaining, 78
The Beach, 153
Bed Supperclub, 6, 121
The Bell Temple, 39, 59
Best bets
accommodation, 134
arts & entertainment, 124
dining, 90
nightlife, 110
shopping, 68
Bicycle rentals, 161, 169
Bicycle tours, 132
Black Swan, 115
BMTA (public bus), 168
Bodhi trees, 19
Bookstores
Asia Books, 72
Elite Used Books, 72
Kinokuniya, 73
Merman Books, 73
Boxing, 28, 132
The Bridge Over the River Kwai, 149

Bridges
Death Railway Bridge (Kanchanaburi), 149
King Rama VIII Bridge, 61
Memorial Bridge, 57, 60, 79
British Airways, 177
British Council, 130
Brown's, 75
Brown Sugar, 119
Buddhism, 14
Budget (car rental), 177
Bull's Head & Angus Steakhouse, 115
Buses, 167–168
Business hours, 169

C

Cabaret, 131
Car rental, 168, 177
Cathay Pacific, 177
Cell phones, 166
Center for the Blind, 50
Central Chidlom, 73
CentralWorld, 74
Century Movie Plaza, 128
Chakri Maha Prasat, 13
Chang Torn, 76
Chao Phraya River, 17, 56–61
Chao Sam Phraya Museum (Ayutthaya), 162
Chatuchak Market, 5, 25, 41
Chaw Rung Reung, 64
Cheap Charlie's, 115
Chen Tai Chi School, 50
Children, families with, 41–45, 85
Children's Discovery Museum, 41
Chinatown, 5, 25, 32, 62–66
Chinese New Year 164
Chitralada Palace, 87
Chung Kai Allied War Cemetery (Kanchanaburi), 150
Cinema, 128–129
Climate, 166
Club Culture, 121
Club Ibiza, 121
Combat Zone Paintball, 45
Concept CM^2, 122

Consulates & embassies, 169
Coyote on Convent, 115
Credit cards, 177
Currency & currency exchange, 169
Customs regulations, 20, 73, 169–170

D

Dallas Pub, 115
The Damage Done, 61
Damnoen Saduak Floating Market, 149
Death Railway Bridge (Kanchanaburi), 149
Deep, 116
Democracy Monument, 54
Dentists, 170
Department stores & shopping malls
    Central Chidlom, 73
    CentralWorld, 74
    Emporium Shopping Centre, 74
    Isetan, 74
    Robinson, 74
    Siam Paragon, 74
    Zen, 74
Diners Club, 177
Dining, 89–108. *See also* Restaurants Index
    best bets, 90
Dinner theatre, 23, 130
Discovery Museum, 25
DJ Station, 118
Doctors, 170
Dragon Flower Temple, 65
Dream World, 42
Dress codes, 13
Drug laws, 170
Drugstores, 172
The Dubliner, 116
Dusit Park, 22, 23, 87–88,
Dusit Thani Pattaya, 158
Dusit Throne Hall, 13, 88
Dusit Zoo, 43, 88

E

EGV, 129
Electricity, 170
Elephants, 88, 159
Elite Used Books, 72
Embassies & consulates, 169
Emerald Buddha, 12
Emergencies, 170

Emporium Shopping Centre, 74
Entertainment, 123–132
    art galleries, 128
    best bets, 124
    cabaret, 131
    cinemas, 128
    classical music, 129
    cultural institutes, 129
    dinner theatre, 130
    opera, 131
    puppet shows, 131
    sports venues, 131
Erawan Shrine, 27,
Etiquette, 101, 173–174
Events, 164–166
Express boat service, 57, 168

F

Families with children, 41–45, 85
Fashion, 75
Fashion Week, 164–165
Festivals & special events, 164–166
Film Festival, 165
Floating markets, 149
Food, 89–108. *See also* Restaurants Index
    best bets, 90
Foreign Correspondents' Club of Thailand, 130

G

Galleries
    100 Tonson, 128
    About Café/About Studio, 128
    Gallery Ver, 128
    Kathmandu Photo Gallery, 128
    The National Gallery, 22, 55, 60, 128
    Thavibu, 128
Gallery Ver, 128
Gardens. *See* Parks & gardens
Gay & lesbian travellers, 170
    bars & clubs, 118
Gay Pride Week, 166
The Giant Swing, 54
Glow, 122
Goethe Institut, 129
Go-go bars, 17
The Golden Buddha, 38, 66
The Golden Mount, 11, 35, 53

Golden Mount Fair 166
The Golden Swing, 36
The Grand Palace, 11, 13, 53, 58–59

H

Haew Narok Waterfall (Khao Yai National Park), 154
Haew Suwat Waterfall (Khao Yai National Park), 153
Haggling, 78
Health tips, 172
Hellfire Pass (Kanchanaburi), 151
Highway Car Rent, 177
Hospitals, 170–171
Hotels, 133–146. *See also* Accommodation Index
    best bets, 134
House of Chao, 72
House RCA, 129

I

Insurance, 171
International Festival of Music & Dance 165
Internet cafes, 171
Isetan, 74

J

Japan Airlines, 177
Jazz Festival 164
JEATH War Museum (Kanchanaburi), 150
Jim Thompson's House, 26
Jim Thompson Thai Silk, 16, 79
Joe Louis Puppet Theatre, 45, 131

K

Kai, 75
Kanchanaburi, 148–151
Kathmandu Photo Gallery, 128
Khao Pansa 165
Khao San Road, 4, 22, 54
    Market, 78
Khao Yai National Park, 152–155
Khlong San Market, 32
Kickboxing, 28, 132
Kids, families with, 41–45, 85
Kim Bowl, 43
The King and I, 23, 36
King Bhumibhol, 88

King Chulalongkorn, 22, 23, 38, 53, 87
  Statue of, 87
King Mongkut, 13, 36, 38, 161
King Rama I, 11, 35, 37, 39, 53, 55, 59, 60
King Rama III, 37, 39, 53
King Rama IV, 13, 36, 38, 161
King Rama V, 22, 23, 38, 53, 87
King Rama VI Statue, 83
King Rama VII, 38
King Rama VIII Bridge, 61
King's Castle, 17
King's Corner, 17
King Taksin, 39, 58
Kinokuniya, 73
Kite-Flying Festival 164
Klong Bangkok Noi, 59
Klong Toey Market, 33
Ko Kret, 61

L

Ladyboys, 131, 157
Lak Muang, 55
Language, 174–177
L'Arcadia, 72
Lava Club, 122
Laws, 170
  drinking, smoking & drug, 170
  exporting antiques, 73
Leng Bai la Shrine, 65
Leng Noi Yee Temple, 65
Lesbian travellers, 170
  bars & clubs, 118
Little India, 64
Local customs, 173–174
  dining etiquette, 101
Lodging, 133–146. *See also* Accommodation Index
Lost property, 171
Lotus Arts de Vivre, 79
Loy Kratong 165
Luangpor Toh, 38
Lumphini Park, 5, 10, 50, 83–86
Lumphini Park Public Library, 84
Lumphini Stadium, 28, 131

M

Mae Toranee, 55
Maharat Road, 20, 80
Mail & postage, 171

Major Cineplex, 129
Makha Bucha 164
Mambo Cabaret, 5, 131
The Marble House, 50
Marble Temple, The. *See* Wat Benchamabophit
Marco Tailors, 77
Markets
  Amulet Market, 14, 37, 55, 72,
  Chatuchak Market, 5, 25, 41, 77
  Damnoen Saduak Floating Market, 149
  Khao San Road Market, 78
  Khlong San Market, 32
  Klong Toey Market, 33
  Or Kor Tor Market, 31
  Pahurat Cloth, 64
  Pak Khlong flower market, 57
  Patpong Night Market, 17, 78
  Phahurat cloth market, 64, 78
  Pratunam Market, 78
  Sampeng Lane, 25, 64
  Saphan Phut Night Bazaar, 79
Massage, 5, 20, 48
  acupressure, 49
  Ayurvedic, 48, 49
MasterCard, 177
Memorial Bridge, 57, 60
Merman Books, 73
Metro (train), 167
Miss Tiffany Universe 165
Mobile phones, 164
Molly Malone's, 116
Mon, 61
Money, 169
Moon Bar at Vertigo, 116
Motorbike taxis, 168
Muay Thai, 28
Museum of Forensic Science, 60
Museums
  Ancient Cloth & Silk Museum, 88
  Bangkok Dolls Museum, 42
  Bangkok National Museum, 21, 60
  Bangkok Planetarium & Science Museum, 45
  Chao Sam Phraya Museum (Ayutthaya), 162

Children's Discovery Museum, 41
Discovery Museum, 25
JEATH War Museum (Kanchanaburi), 150
Jim Thompson's House, 26
Museum of Forensic Science, 60
Photography Museum, 88
Ripley's Believe It or Not Museum, 158
Royal Barges Museum, 15, 60
Royal Elephant Museum, 88
Thailand–Burma Railway Center (Kanchanaburi), 150
War Museum (Kanchanaburi), 150
Wat Phra Kaeo Museum, 13
Music
  classical, 129
  International Festival of Music & Dance 165
  live, 118–120

N

Nakornthon Thai Medical Spa, 49
Nang Nual Riverside Pub, 116
Narai the Great, 58
Narayana Phand, 76
National Gallery, 22, 55, 60, 128
National Museum, 21, 60
National parks, 152–155
National Theatre, 132
Nest, 116
Nightlife, 115–122
  bars & pubs, 115–118
  best bets, 110
  gay & lesbian bars & clubs, 118
  live music, 118–120
  nightclubs, 121–122
  wine bars, 118
Niks/Nava Import Export, 73
Nok Air, 177
Nong Pak Chee Observation Tower (Khao Yai NP), 153
Nonthaburi, 42, 60
Nonthaburi Equestrian Sports Club, 42

O

Oasis Spa, 49
October 14 Monument, 54
The Office Bar & Grill, 116
The Old City, 11, 52–55
Old Maps & Prints, 76
One Tambon, One Product (OTOP), 80
Ong's Tea, 75
Opera Riserva Winetheque, 122
O'Reilly's Irish Pub & Restaurant, 119
The Oriental Spa & Ayurvedic Penthouse, 49
Or Kor Tor Market, 31
Overtone Music Cave, 120

P

Pahurat Cloth Market, 64
Pantip Plaza, 75
Papaya salad, 32
Paragon Cineplex, 129
Parks & gardens
  Dusit Park, 22, 23, 87–88
  Lumphini Park, 5, 10, 50, 83–86
  Pattaya Park (Pattaya), 158
  Queen Sirikit Park, 25, 41
  Siwalai Gardens, 13
  Suan Santichai Prakarn Park, 60
Passports & visas, 171
Patpong, 6, 17
Patpong Road, 17
Patravadi Theatre, 23, 130
Pattaya, 156–159
Pattaya Elephant Village, 159
PB Valley Khao Yai Winery (Khao Yai National Park), 155
Phahurat Market, 78
Pharmacies, 172
Photography Museum, 88
Phra Buddha Sihing, 21
Phra Mondop, 12
Phra Nakorn, 53
Phranakorn Bar, 117
Phra Si Rattana Chedi, 12
Phra Sumen Fort, 60
Police, 172
Post, 171
Pratunam Market, 78
Public holidays, 172

Q

Qantas, 177
Q Bar, 122
Queen Saovabha Memorial Institute, 44
Queen Sirikit Park, 25, 41

R

Rain Dogs Bar & Gallery, 117
The Ramakien, 19, 39, 45, 59
Ramakien Gallery, 12
Rasayana Retreat, 49
Ratchadamnoen Boxing Stadium, 28, 132
Rattankosin, 53, 60
Red Chinese Temple, 63
Restaurants, 89–108. See also Restaurants Index
  best bets, 90
Retro Live Cafe, 120
River City, 79
River Kwae (Kanchanburi), 149
River of Kings Festival 164
Robinson, 74
Royal Barges Museum, 15, 60
Royal Elephant Museum, 88
Royal Kathin Festival, 15, 17
Royal Pantheon, 12
Royal Ploughing Ceremony 165
Royal Project, 80

S

Safari World, 41
Safety, 172
Sala Chalermkrung Royal Theatre, 132
Sala Rim Nam, 23, 130
Salathip, 130
Samma Samadhi, 48
Sampeng Lane, 5, 25, 64, 79
Sanctuary of Truth (Pattaya), 158
Santa Cruz Church, 57, 59
Saphan Phut Night Bazaar, 79
Saxophone, 120
Senior travellers, 172
Sex tourism, 17, 157
The Ship Inn, 117
Shopping, 67–80. See also department stores & shopping malls
  amulets, 72
  antiques, 72, 73
  best bets, 68
  books, 72–73
  cameras, 73
  department stores & shopping malls, 73–75
  electronics, 75
  fashion, 75
  food & drink, 75–76
  handicrafts, 76
  jewellery & gems, 76
  maps, 76
  markets, 77–79
  menswear, 76–77
  objets d'art, 79
  silk, 79
  traditional medicine, 80
Siam Niramit, 132
Siam Ocean World, 27, 43, 74
Siam Paragon, 26, 43, 74
Siam Park City, 42
Silk, 26
Silk Bar, 117
Silom, 33,
Silom Village, 130
Siri Guru Singh Sabha, 64
Siwalai Gardens, 13,
Sky Bar, 5, 28, 117
Slim, 122
Snake farm, 44
Soi Ban Baat, 53
Soi Wanit, 5, 25, 64, 79
Som-tam, 32
Songkran Festival 165
Spas
  Banyan Tree Spa, 49
  Center for the Blind, 50
  The Marble House, 50
  Nakornthon Thai Medical Spa, 49
  Oasis Spa, 49
  The Oriental Spa & Ayurvedic Penthouse, 49
  Rasayana Retreat, 49
Sports, 28, 83, 131, 132
  Horse riding, 42
  Takraw, 85
  Thai boxing, 28, 132
Statue of King Chulalongkorn, 87
Street food, 107
Studio 9 Art Space, 130
Sukhotai, 19, 21
Sukhumvit East, 33
Sukhumvit Road, 69
Surawong, 33

T

Tai Chi, 5, 10
Takraw, 85
Tani Road, 31
Taxes, 77, 172
Taxis, 168
Telephone Pub, 118
Telephones, 172–173
Temperatures, 166
Temple of Dawn, 4, 15, 58, 59
Temples
  dress codes and, 13
  Leng Noi Yee Temple, 65
  Tiger Temple (Kanchanaburi), 151
  Wat Arun, 4, 15, 58, 59
  Wat Benchamabophit, 38
  Wat Bowornniwet, 37, 48
  Wat Chakkrawat, 64
  Wat Chana Songkhram, 37
  Wat Intara Wihan, 38
  Wat Kanlayanamit, 59
  Wat Mahathat, 14, 37, 48
  Wat Mahathat (Ayutthaya), 161
  Wat Mangkol Kamalawat, 65
  Wat Pak Nam, 48
  Wat Phra Kaeo, 11
  Wat Po, 5, 19–20, 48, 58
  Wat Prayurawongsawat, 39, 57
  Wat Rajaburana, 63
  Wat Rakhang, 39, 59
  Wat Ratchabophit, 36
  Wat Ratchaburana (Ayutthaya), 161
  Wat Ratchanatda, 4, 36, 37
  Wat Ratchapradit, 36
  Wat Saket, 11, 35, 53
  Wat Sanjaomaeguanim, 59
  Wat Si Sanphet (Ayutthaya), 161
  Wat Sutat, 36
  Wat Traimit, 38, 66
  Wat Yai Chaimongkon (Ayutthaya), 162
Thai Airways, 177
Thai boxing, 28, 132
Thailand–Burma Railway Center (Kanchanaburi), 150
Thailand Cultural Centre, 129
Thammasat University, 60
Thavibu Gallery, 128

Theatre
  Alangkarn Theatre (Pattaya), 159
  dinner theatre, 23, 130
  Joe Louis Puppet Theatre, 45, 131
  National Theatre, 132
  Patravadi Theatre, 23, 130
  Sala Rim Nam, 130
  Salathip, 130
  Sala Chalermkrung Royal, 132
  Siam Niramit, 132
  Silom Village, 130
  Studio 9 Art Space, 130
Theme Parks
  Dream World, 42
  Safari World, 41
  Siam Park City, 42
Thian Fa Foundation, 66
Tiffany's (Pattaya), 157
Tiger Temple (Kanchanaburi), 151
Tipping, 173
To-Sit, 120
Tourism Authority of Thailand (TAT), 173
Tourist information, 173
Tourist traps, 173
Tours (guided), 22, 59, 88, 132, 155, 169
Tours (self-guided)
  bike, 132, 169
  child-friendly, 141–145
  food, 31–33
  historic, 35–39
  holistic, 48–50
  temples, 35–39
Traditional medicine, 20
Traditions, 173–174
Trains, 167, 169
Transvestites, 131, 157
Travel passes, 137, 168
Tuba, 117
Tuktuks, 6, 168
Twandang German Brewery, 120

U

United Airlines, 177
Uthai's Gems, 76

V

V9 Wine Bar, 122
Vaccinations, 173
VAT, 77
Velothailand, 132
Villa Market, 76

Vimanmek Palace, 13, 22, 23, 87–88,
Vipassana meditation, 37, 48
Visa (credit card), 177
Visakha Bucha 165
Visas, 171
Visitor information, 173

W

Walking tours
  Chinatown, 62
  The Old City, 52
Wang Derm Palace, 58
War Museum (Kanchanaburi), 150
Wat Arun, 4, 15, 58, 59
Wat Benchamabophit, 38
Wat Bowornniwet, 37, 48
Wat Chakkrawat, 64
Wat Chana Songkhram, 37
Water Bar, 118
Waterfalls, 153, 154
Wat Intara Wihan, 38
Wat Kanlayanamit, 59
Wat Mahathat, 14, 37, 48
Wat Mahathat (Ayutthaya), 161
Wat Mangkol Kamalawat, 65
Wat Pak Nam, 48
Wat Phra Kaeo, 11
Wat Phra Kaeo Museum, 13
Wat Po, 5, 19–20, 48, 58
Wat Prayoon, 39, 57
Wat Prayurawongsawat, 39, 57
Wat Rajaburana, 63
Wat Rakhang, 39, 59
Wat Ratchabophit, 36
Wat Ratchaburana (Ayutthaya), 161
Wat Ratchanatda, 4, 36, 37
Wat Ratchapradit, 36
Wat Saket, 11, 35, 53
Wat Sanjaomaeguanim, 59
Wat Si Sanphet (Ayutthaya), 161
Wat Sutat, 36
Wat Traimit, 38, 66
Wat Yai Chaimongkon (Ayutthaya), 162
Weather, 166
Websites, 166, 177
Wichaiprasit Fort, 58
Wine
  Bacchus Wine Bar, 122
  Customs regulations and, 169–170

Opera Riserva Wine
Bar, 122
PB Valley Khao Yai Winery,
155
V9 Wine Bar, 122
Wong's Place, 118
World War II, 150

Y

Yaowarat Road, 32, 66
Yoga, 50

Z

Zen, 75
Zeta, 118
Zoos
Dusit Zoo, 43, 88
Siam Park City, 42

Accommodation

Arun Residence, 138
Bangkok Boutique Hotel, 138
Bannkunpra Guesthouse
(Ayutthaya), 162
The Banyan Tree, 138
Bel-Aire Princess, 138
Best Western Swana
Bangkok, 138
Bossotel Inn, 138
Buddy Lodge, 138
Chakrabongse Villas, 139
Charlie House, 139
Conrad Bangkok, 139
Convenient Resort, 140
Diamond House, 140
Dusit Thani, 140
Dusit Thani Pattaya, 159
The Eugenia, 140
Federal Hotel, 140
The Four Seasons, 141
Grand China Princess Hotel,
64, 141
Grand Hyatt Erawan
Bangkok, 141
Hotel De' Moc, 141
Ibrik Resort, 141
InterContinental, 141
JW Marriott, 142
Kasem Island Resort
(Kanchanaburi), 151
Lamphu Treehouse, 142
Lebua at State Tower,
28, 142
Lub*D, 142
Luxx, 142

Mandarin Oriental, 4, 16,
57, 142
Marriott Resort & Spa, 5, 143
Maruay Garden Hotel, 143
The Metropolitan, 49, 143
Montien Riverside Hotel, 143
New Empire Hotel, 143
Novotel Bangkok, 144
The Peninsula, 144
Phranakorn Nornlen, 144
Queen's Garden Resort at
River View, 144
Refill Now, 144
Rose Hotel, 144
Royal Hotel, 55, 144
Royal Riverkwai Resort &
Hotel (Kanchanaburi),
151
Shanghai Inn, 145
Shangri-La Hotel, 145
Sheraton Grande Sukhumvit,
145
Siam Heritage, 145
Silom Serene, 146
Siri Sathorn, 146
Sofitel Silom Bangkok, 146
The Sukhothai, 146
Swissôtel Nai Lert Park, 146
Triple Two Silom, 146

Restaurants

An An Lao, 94
Author's Lounge, 16
Baan Khanitha, 94
Baan Phra Arthit, 15
Bali, 94
Cafe Primavera, 22
Ban Wacharachai, 162
Banyan Tree Hotel, 49
Bed Supperclub, 94
Bei Otto, 94
Benjarong, 95
Biscotti, 94
Blue Elephant, 95
Bourbon Street, 95
Breeze, 94
Bruno's, 158
Cabbages & Condoms, 96
Cafe Primavera, 22
The Cedar, 96
Chennai Kitchen, 96
The Chinese Restaurant, 96
Cy'an, 49, 97
Deck by the River, 97

Dosa, 97
D'Sens, 97
Eat Me, 97
Floating Restaurants, 150
Glow, 49, 98
Grand China Princess
Hotel, 64
Harmonique, 98
Hemlock, 98
Hua Seng Hong, 98
Indian Hut, 98
In Love, 99
Kaiyang Boran, 99
Khaosarn Center, 55
Khrua Khao Yai, 155
Koi, 99
Kuaytiaw Reua Tha Siam, 99
Kuppa, 100
Lao Li Shark's Fin, 100
La Piola, 100
Le Banyan, 100
Le Bouchon, 100
Le Dalat, 101
Le Normandie, 101
Le Notre, 27
Long Table, 101
Maha Naga, 102
Mango Tree, 102
The Manhora, 6, 102
May Kaidee, 103
Mezzaluna, 103
New York Steakhouse, 103
Oh my Cod!, 103
Patty's Fiesta, 104
Ramentei, 104
Ranee's Guesthouse, 104
Rang Mahal, 104
River View Guesthouse, 66
Roti-Mataba, 105
Rub-ar-roon Cafe, 20
Ruen Mallika, 105
Scoozi, 105
Shangrila Restaurant, 105
Shiro, 106
Sirocco, 106
Somboon Seafood, 106
Suan Thip, 106
Standard Sweets &
Restaurant, 64
Tang Jai Yuu, 107
Tapas Cafe, 107
Thip Samai, 107
Thiptara, 107
Wittayai Nai Wang Ying, 88

Photo **Credits**

All photos by CPA Media/David Henley/© John Wiley & Sons Australia Ltd. except:
p viii: © Photolibrary/Kevin O'Hara; p 5: © Photolibrary.com/Imagestate/Steve Vidler;
p 6: © Marriott Resorts & Spas Thailand Bangkok—Hua Hin—Pattaya; p 10, bottom:
© Photolibrary/Imagestate/Steve Vidler; p 16, bottom: © Photolibrary/Luca Tettoni;
p 17: © Photolibrary/Superstock; p 21, top: © Photolibrary/Luca Invernizzi Tettoni;
p 22: © Photolibrary/Luca Invernizzi Tettoni; p 25: © Photolibrary/Superstock; p 27,
bottom: © Photolibrary/Ingo Jezierski; p 28, top: © Photolibrary/Superstock Inc; p 28,
bottom: © Photolibrary/Ingolf Pompe; p 31: © Getty Images/Travel Ink/Gallo Images;
p 32: © Photolibrary.com/FoodCollection; p 33, top: © Getty Images/Stone/Paul Chesley;
p 33, bottom: © Getty Images/Paula Bronstein; p 36, top: © Photolibrary/Kevin O'Hara;
p 42: © Amy Pascale; p 43: © Photolibrary/Robert Harding Travel/Angelo Cavalli; p 44,
top: © Photolibrary/Animals Animals/Mickey Gibson; p 45: © Photolibrary/Kevin O'Hara;
p 49: © Photolibrary/Delfin Delfin; p 51: © Photolibrary/age fotostock/Angelo Cavalli;
p 61 © Photolibrary/Steve Vidler; p 63, bottom: © Getty Images/Photographer's Choice/
Stephen Studd; p 67: © Photolibrary/Pacific Stock/Larry Dale Gordon; p 68: © Getty
Images/The Image Bank/Tim Graham; p 73: © Photolibrary/Sylvain Grandadam; p 75:
© Photolibrary/Kevin Schafer; p 77: © Photolibrary/age fotostock/Sylvain Grandadam;
p 80: © Photolibrary/Tips Italia/Luca Invernizzi Tettoni; p 83: © Photolibrary/Vidler Vidler;
p 84, bottom: © Tse Seng Goh; p 95: © Louis Allen; p 99: © Photolibrary/EA. Janes; p 100:
© Peter Cuce; p 106: © Ling Chee Chong Adrian; p 107: © Photolibrary/Fresh Food Images;
p 109: © Getty Images/The Image Bank/Shaun Egan; p 110: © Banyan Tree Hotel; p 117:
© Photolibrary/Robert Harding Travel; p 120: © Cody McKibben; p 123: © Vivek Shenoy;
p 124: © Paul Dornau; p 131: © Joseff Indradjaja; p 133: © Photolibrary/Tips Italia/Luca
Invernizzi Tettoni; p 133: © Banyan Tree Hotel; p 138: © Bel-Aire Princess Hotel; p 139, top:
© Chakrabongse Villas; p 139, bottom: © Conrad Bangkok; p 140, top: © Hotel De'Moc;
p 140, bottom: © Four Seasons Hotel Bangkok; p 141: © InterContinental Bangkok; p 142:
© lebua at State Tower; p 143: © Luxx Hotel Bangkok; p 144: © Peninsula Bangkok; p 145,
top: © Shanghai Inn; p 145, bottom: © Shangri-La Hotel Bangkok; p 146: © Swissotel Nai
Lert Park; p 149: © Photolibrary/Bruno Morandi; p 150, top: © Getty Images/Photodisc/
Ingo Jezierski; p 151: Getty Images/AFP/Saeed Khan; p 154: © Getty Images/National
Geographic/Tim Laman; p 155: © Photolibrary/Ingo Schulz; p 157: © AAP/AFP PHOTO/
Saeed Khan; p 159: © Photolibrary/age fotostock/Angelo Cavalli; p 162: Photolibrary/Hemis/
SEUX Paule; p 163: Photolibrary/Bowater Peter.

80025 75540